STATE CAPITAL AND PRIVATE ENTERPRISE

State Capital and Private Enterprise

The case of the UK National Enterprise Board

DANIEL C KRAMER

R

ROUTLEDGE
London and New York

First published 1988
by Routledge
11 New Fetter Lane, London EC4P 4EE
29 West 35th Street, New York, NY 10001

© 1988 Daniel C. Kramer

Printed and bound in Great Britain by
Biddles Ltd, Guildford and King's Lynn

British Library Cataloguing in Publication Data

Kramer, Daniel C., *1934-*
    State capital and private enterprise:
    the case of the UK National Enterprise Board.
    1. Great Britain. Public enterprise.
    Organisations. National Enterprise
    Board, to 1988

    I. Title
    338.6'2

    ISBN 0-415-00915-4

Library of Congress Cataloging-in-Publication Data

Kramer, Daniel C., *1934–*
    State capital and private enterprise: the case of the UK National
    Enterprise Board / Daniel C. Kramer.
        p. cm.
        Bibliography: p.
        Includes index.
        ISBN 0-415-00915-4
        1. Great Britain. National Enterprise Board. I. Title.
    HD4148.K73   1988
    354.410082–dc19   88-23899
                                                                    CIP

This book is lovingly dedicated to:

My Family

CONTENTS

Foreword

1 Introduction: The rise and fall of the NEB 1
   Selective assistance in the UK 1
   The birth of the NEB 4
   The duties and structure of the NEB 9
   The burgeoning of the NEB 15
   The NEB bubble bursts 18

2 The NEB's profit-and-loss record 29
   The data 29
   The data further analysed 32
   The NEB versus other UK venture capitalists 39

3 Obstacles faced by NEB not confronting private venture
   capitalists 44
   The NEB sells at bargain prices 44
   The NEB and the Press 47
   The NEB and the Tory right 54
   Parliament sees the Board's slip showing 58

4 The Board wraps itself in a cloud of mystery: additional
   Parliamentary tribulations of a public venture
   capitalist 64

5 The NEB and the Department of Industry 75

6 Firms aided by the NEB as venture capitalist:
   case studies 81

7 Highlights of the case studies 117

8 Inmos 130

9 The Insac debacle 145

10 The Nexos disaster 152
   Nexos' birth and wares 152
   Nexos' financial woes 154
   The termination of Nexos 158
   Why Nexos failed: the 1985 DOI analysis 160
   Why Nexos failed: other contributing factors 162

11 Alfred Herbert 171

12 Fairey and Ferranti 177

13 Rolls Royce 185

14 British Leyland 194

15 The NEB and the Ministry of Defence 206

16 Is an NEB now needed in the United Kingdom? 211

Contents

17 Does the US need an NEB? 218
18 Government subsidies to specific firms:
    an evaluation of the conservative critique 224
19 Government subsidies to specific firms:
    an evaluation of the radical critique 232
20 The NEB: an example of co-operation 237
Bibliography 244
Index 249

Foreword

This study of the United Kingdom's National Enterprise Board springs from a very strong interest, germinating during my university days studying Politics, in the eternal problem of what is the proper relationship between the state on the one hand and the economic order on the other. For the first 20 years after receiving my PhD and commencing my teaching career, my research interests focused primarily, though not exclusively, upon issues of human rights and US constitutional law. None the less, I kept thinking about questions such as the extent to which the state should own, regulate and/or interact in other ways with the business sector; and I taught courses which had differing labels but which revolved about these problems.

Several years ago, I felt that what I had had to say about rights and liberties matters had come to a temporary dead end. I resolved, therefore, to devote full time to reading about and researching my old topic of state-business relationships. I soon realised that the question I was posing, i.e. what is the most satisfactory way of ordering the inevitable links between polity and economy, was probably too abstract to be meaningful even when limited to advanced capitalist countries alone. That is, I quickly came to the conclusion that there most likely was no one 'correct' answer to it; that the response would have to vary in accordance with national traditions and customs, the health of the economy, the popularity of the administration in power, and even the intelligence, dedication and integrity of the specific individuals involved in a particular collaboraton of the two sectors.

To buttress this conclusion, I decided to carry out a study of programmes of government aid to businesses in the major industrial powers of today (e.g., the US, UK, France, West Germany, Japan, Italy). I speedily ascertained that there was already a considerable literature, both single-country and comparative, analysing these programmes. In the course of my review of these writings, I was perusing the *Financial Times* in the New York Public Library when I came across an article by one of its columnists criticising something-or-other the UK's National Enterprise Board was doing. I forget the content of the article; but was intrigued by its description of the agency's role and activities. It did not take me long to find out (1) that there was not an overwhelming amount of material written about the Board; (2) that much of what was being published was unfavourable; and (3) that there might be another side to the question as most of those who were studying this body adhered strictly to a *laissez-faire* philosophy. I therefore flew to London during my 1983 Easter holidays to interview some NEB and Department of Trade and Industry officials, as well as a Labour MP who had participated actively in Parliamentary Debates on the Board. I had no idea, of course, that the Thatcher Administration was then in the process of deciding that for all practical purposes the NEB had to shut its doors!

After my return to the US my research on the NEB was proceeding at a snail's pace when I was quite unexpectedly granted a Fulbright Fellowship to help the Faculty of Social Sciences at the Open University in Milton Keynes develop their course on *Democratic Government and Politics*. This meant that I was able to spend the entire academic year of 1984-85 in the United Kingdom and to arrange numerous interviews with persons who had had some connection with the Board. A few such meetings convinced me that the most exciting and least publicised aspect of this agency's work was its supplying venture capital to small and medium-sized firms that were finding it tricky to raise money from private sources. I thus resolved to concentrate on this aspect of its agenda; and to treat more briefly the ties between it and its major subsidiaries such as British Leyland and Rolls Royce Aerospace. This book, I feel, is faithful to the spirit of this resolution.

My volume is, as will be seen, not wholly-uncritical of the NEB. Yet it spotlights its successes as well as its failures. As a result, I hope that the men who wholeheartedly devoted several years of their lives to it will obtain the accolades they surely deserve: up to now, they have received only brickbats from the right and deafening silence from the left. On a broader level, I also hope that despite the fever for limiting the role of the political system that rages today in the US, the UK and Western Europe, the work will convince my readers that the

Foreword

UK could benefit from a resuscitation of the NEB and that the US economy, in trouble as I write and likely to slip further in the near future, would be helped by the formation of a counterpart institution. In a different ballpark, this book could make a contribution to the literature dealing with holding company-subsidiary relationships. As will be seen, one of my interviewees emphasised that the interaction between the NEB and his concern was not that different from the dealings between a privately-owned holding company and its investments.

Naturally, writing this book has put me in debt to the many, many people who helped me. (Of course, any errors of fact or logic that plague it are my fault alone.) The US Fulbright Commission, the College of Staten Island of the City University of New York (which granted me a sabbatical) and the Faculty of Social Sciences at the Open University all combined to make it possible for me to live in England in 1984-85. The following Political Scientists (in alphabetical order) lecturing at the Open University went beyond the call of duty to make this stay a pleasant and intellectually stimulating one: Margaret Kiloh, Paul Lewis, office-mate Richard Maidment, Tony McGrew, Josephine Negro, Christopher Pollitt and David Potter. Open University secretaries Mary Dicker and Anne Hunt provided invaluable assistance in typing an infinite number of letters requesting interviews. Mrs Réka Benczédi, President of Innovative Office Concepts in my home community of Staten Island, New York, did a miraculous job of putting this manuscript on the word processor. My wife Richenda Kramer gave up an excellent job to spend my sabbatical year with me in her native England. My mother-in-law, Mrs Marjorie Lee of London, secured us a cosy house in Milton Keynes as well as furniture on which to eat, talk, work and sleep. Professor George Applewhite of the Business Department of the College of Staten Island taught me how to intelligently read an Annual Report; while Professor Steven Warnecke of the same Department introduced me to several books on venture capitalism. Professor Robin Carey, Chair of the Political Science-Economics-Philosophy Department of the College of Staten Island, instructed me in the language of the mysterious discipline of microeconomics. I am also grateful to Professor Carey for her unstintinting support of all my research efforts. However, this book owes most to the dozens of persons in one way or another linked to the NEB whom I interviewed while writing it. Whether Labour or Tory; whether pro or anti-NEB; whether business, labour or civil service, they all took time out from their very busy schedules to speak frankly and at length to me. I deeply appreciate their warmth and kindness!

One more point. Because of the deadline I had to meet for submitting the final copy of the manuscript, I could take little account of events occurring after January 1988. By the time this book appears in print, it may be, e.g., that microchip manufacturer Inmos (see Ch. 8) will be out of business or that the NEB itself will have been legally eradicated. But I cannot assume as of writing this that these events will take place. (In fact, as this book goes to press, Inmos is in the black, but the firm I am calling Ivy is unexpectedly at death's door.)

1
Introduction:
The Rise and Fall of the NEB

Selective Assistance in the UK

I shall in this book describe a controversial British experiment with directing public subsidies to specific companies, the National Enterprise Board (henceforth 'NEB' or 'Board'). The heyday of the Board was 1976 through 1980, though it still exists as a legal entity. The NEB, as will be seen in more detail shortly, was charged with 'bailing out' several major firms that were experiencing economic troubles and with giving assistance to other undertakings for purposes such as increasing jobs and exports and reducing dependence on imports. Its helping hand more often than not involved the taking of equity in the assisted concern, though it made loans as well. A fair amount has been written about the NEB's problems with the larger firms, especially Rolls Royce Aerospace and British Leyland. I shall, therefore, devote relatively little space to the links between the Board and these 'giants' -- though no respectable discussion of the agency can ignore these relationships -- and concentrate upon its successes, failures, agonies and triumphs in acting as angel to less sizeable ventures.

Through depicting its relationship with enterprises of modest size, I shall show that it would make sense for the UK to revive its NEB and for the US to create one. As I shall demonstrate, its profit and loss record was not as poor as it appears on the surface to have been; and was achieved in the teeth of obstacles that its counterparts in the private sector did not have to brave. A couple of its major failures could easily have been avoided. Some flourishing undertakings making fine products would not be in business without its efforts. And

1

it improved the management practices of some of the companies with which it dealt. There are, of course, those from both the right and the left of the political spectrum who argue that public aid accorded to private firms on a case-by-case basis will almost inevitably be harmful or useless. Their contentions are not insubstantial and will be analysed toward the end of this volume.

Before turning to the ins and outs of the NEB, a bit of background is necessary. Government steps to aid business can be general, designed to aid all industries; intermediate, intended to assist all firms in a particular sector (e.g., steel, computers); or selective, designed to support given companies.[1] (The aid awarded by the NEB was really 'selective' assistance, even though firms of all sorts could apply for the funding, since the agency had broad, almost legislative-like discretion to determine whom to bolster.) The United Kingdom (and West Germany) have been described as unlike France in that they favour general over specific aids.[2] Thus Britain has made considerable use of accelerated depreciation and investment allowances, techniques that are 'general' aids to industry because they are available on a non-discretionary basis to all firms that wish to make new investment.[3]

Nevertheless, even before the creation of the NEB, the UK did accord considerable help to specific companies or to specific sectors of the economy. Thus the Conservative Administration of Prime Minister Harold Macmillan enacted a 1959 Cotton Industry Act that gave bounties to the cotton spinning industry to destroy old, unused spindles and looms and replace them with modern equipment.[4] Between 1945 and the end of March 1974 Conservative and Labour governments together contributed £340 million in launching aid for aircraft and £406 million in such subsidies for aeroplane engines. Of the £340 million, £233 million was accorded to build (in conjunction with France) the supersonic Concorde airliner and, of the £406 million, £178 million went to develop the Concorde's Olympus 593 engine.[5] (Launching aid involves assistance for the costs of design, development, tools of production, and the 'extra' manufacturing costs incurred while workers are learning their new jobs.[6]) Shipbuilding in the UK, as in other western countries, has been in trouble for many years. However, most shipbuilding firms are located in 'depressed' areas of the country, e.g., Northern Ireland and Scotland; and form a bulwark of the economy of these regions. Ergo, even before the British industry was nationalised in 1977 under the name of British Shipbuilders, it had received significant chunks of state funding. For example, between 1970 and 1975 the government gave it a total of £69 million, almost 15% of its total revenue.[7]

The Conservative Government under Prime Minister Edward Heath passed the Industry Act of 1972. Under Section 7 of the Act the Department of Trade and Industry (DTI) may offer assistance to firms locating or expanding in regions suffering from severe unemployment. (We shall henceforth call the DTI the Department of Industry (DOI), as it bore this name for most of the period this book covers.) Under Section 8 the Department may assist projects anywhere in the country that promise to benefit the economy and promote the national interest. Section 7 produced £203 million and Section 8 £151.6 million for British industry between 1972/73 and 1977/78. In 1984 alone £189 million went to particular enterprises under these clauses. Recipients of their generosity have included major shipbuilding firms, Ford and Chrysler Motor Corporations, and British Leyland.[8]

The direct institutional antecedent of the NEB was the Industrial Reorganisation Corporation (IRC), set up by the Labour Government in 1966 and abolished by Heath's Tory Administration. The purpose of the IRC was to promote (by, e.g., encouraging mergers of small firms) the reorganisation or development of any industry in order to increase industrial efficiency and profitability. To facilitate a merger it could grant a subsidy to cover the costs. For example, in 1968-69 it supported with a loan of £25 million a marriage between Britain's two largest 'native' automobile makers, British Motor Holdings (Austin-Morris-MG and Jaguar) and Leyland Motors (Leyland and Standard). In 1970 it lent the offspring (British Leyland, later a NEB problem child) £10 million to help it buy tools.[9] And to complete this partial list of UK projects of selective assistance to industry, mention must be made of the birth of the country's main UK-owned computer firm, International Computers Limited (ICL). This arose in 1968 as a result of a government-sponsored blending of various UK computer manufacturers. The state took a 10% shareholding in the new company and over the course of the next several years gave it about £50 million assistance for research and

3

development. As we shall see, the paths of ICL and the NEB were to cross.[10]

The Birth of the NEB

Labour was out of power between June 1970 and February 1974. In opposition, its left wing was more dominant than during the Harold Wilson Prime Ministerial years of 1964-70. And in a UK suffering from economic stagnation and inequality, the idea of a state holding company patterned after Italy's Industrial Reconstruction Institute (IRI) seemed attractive to some on that flank of the Party.[11] Even as far back as 1969 the Party's National Executive Committee statement for the 1969 Conference raised the NEB idea; as did the Party's Programme of 1972.[12] In 1975 there appeared a book entitled *The Socialist Challenge*[13] by the economist (and currently Labour MP for Vauxhall) Stuart Holland. Holland argued that the 'British private sector is now dominated by giant companies who are the leaders in such fields as investment, jobs, pricing and trade'.[14] Were a state holding company to take over about 20 to 25 of the nation's top manufacturing enterprises, the following advantages, among others, would be gleaned. (Holland was a keen though not totally uncritical observer of the IRI experience.)

(1) The state-owned giant company in a particular sector of the economy could pioneer 'a new product or technique on a major scale',[15] thus forcing its privately-owned competitors to imitate it.

(2) The information that the sizable publicly-owned firms would convey to the state about costs and profits would enable it to more precisely identify whether privately-owned multi-nationals were evading UK taxation.[16]

(3) Where a privately-owned multinational was charging excessively high prices, its state-holding-company competitor could compel it to reduce these by lowering its own.[17]

(4) A state holding company controlling about 25 of the country's hundred largest manufacturing companies would be strong enough to absorb any subsidiary in the country abandoned by a private multinational. The very possibility of this would deter a large multinational from blackmailing the UK government by threatening to close the doors of one of its UK subsidiaries.[18]

Holland had close ties to left wing members of the Labour Party's National Executive Committee such as Anthony Wedgwood Benn, Ian Mikardo and Eric Heffer. Though his book was not published until 1975, he had been expounding the theories expressed therein to these individuals since the late 1960s.[19] In April 1973 a Labour Party study group issued a Green Paper based on his ideas and calling for a National Enterprise Board that would take an interest in about 20 to 25 of the UK's top hundred manufacturers. These future NEB subsidiaries would account for one-third of the turnover, half the employment and two-fifths of the profit of these leading enterprises. The purposes of the Board would include the stimulation of investment, the reduction of inflation, and the improvement of the balance of payments situation.[20] These views were incorporated into the National Executive Committee's *Programme for Britain* of June 1973. This document contained other proposals unpopular with British industry such as legislation enabling the government to obtain certain information from private companies and to enter into 'planning agreements' with private firms covering prices, profits and investment programmes.[21] Party Leader Wilson praised these suggestions except for the recommendation about an NEB takeover of the 25 leading firms, a scheme that he thought would lose him votes among the middle classes.[22] Wilson, supported even by left wingers Benn and Michael Foot in his opposition to the 25 undertakings project, convinced the Party Conference to accept his position on this matter.[23]

In February 1974 a plurality (not majority) Labour Government was formed with Wilson as Prime Minister. Wilson's first Secretary of State for Industry was Benn, who was then and is currently a *bête noire* of the British press and industry. In August 1974 Benn issued a White Paper entitled *The Regeneration of British Industry*, which was more moderate than some on the left of the Party had hoped for. It talked about the need for a closer and better relationship between government and industry working together to increase national prosperity. Though the document proposed the establishment of a National Enterprise Board 'to provide the means for direct public initiatives in particular key sections of industry', no mention was made of a Board takeover of 25 leading firms. The Paper made it clear that no concern would be forced to enter into a planning agreement and that the NEB could not buy shares against the wishes of the owners of the equities.[24] (The Government hoped that increased public aid to an enterprise would *induce* it to conclude such an agreement, which would cover subjects such as regional location, export policy, employment, etc.[25])

The Paper did declare that the NEB would be a state holding company owning subsidiary concerns. It would have, among other things, the authority to be a new source of investment capital in providing finance; and when it aided a firm it normally would take an appropriate share of the equity capital. Its 'main strength in manufacturing' would come through the 'extension of public ownership into profitable manufacturing industry by acquisitions of individual firms'.[26] However, it could also aid sound companies facing short-term managerial or financial difficulties and start new ventures, either alone or with private firms. In a prophetic sentence, the White Paper added that 'Although the NEB will be principally concerned with profitable companies, it may on occasion be called on to take over an ailing company which is in danger of collapse but needs to be maintained and restored to a sound economic basis for reasons of regional employment or industrial policy'.[27] The Labour Party's Election Manifesto for autumn 1974 incorporated the White Paper's thoughts about the NEB,[28] even though the President of the Confederation of British Industries had declared that the prospect of the NEB's spreading state control across the private sector would dismay business.[29]

The Wilson Government faced a dilemma after its narrow October 1974 victory. On the one hand, it recognised that it needed the co-operation of private industry, suffering from recession and inflation, to rejuvenate the economy. Also right wing Labour Party figures such as Wilson's wealthy and close friend Harold Lever were not happy with the NEB concept and favoured, rather, the creation of a government investment bank to help with no strings attached companies suffering from a cash flow crisis.[30] On the other hand, the Party had committed itself several times and in detail to the founding of the Board and the Party's left still saw this body as a device, in the words of Anthony Crosland (himself not totally enthusiastic about the NEB proposal), to take over companies 'to compete with private enterprise - to act as highly competitive price leaders and pace-setters, provide a yardstick for efficiency, support the government's investment plans, and above all produce a better product or service'.[31] That is, many in the Party visualised it as the means whereby public enterprise would wake up its private counterpart. (Also some, though not all, on the left probably did hope in their hearts that it would be a device for nationalising the bulk of the private sector and effecting a permanent transfer of power to the working class.) In the event, Wilson did reject Lever's Investment Bank recommendation and, at the end of January 1975, introduced the 1975 Industry Bill providing for the establishment of the National Enterprise Board and permitting the government to enter into planning agreements with private firms.[32]

Organised labour was pleased with the Bill. Len Murray, General Secretary of the Trades Union Congress, thought that the NEB would assist in strengthening Britain's manufacturing industries. However, the Confederation of British Industries speaking for big business attacked the measure as 'damaging and dangerous'. It disliked not only those provisions referring to planning agreements and allowing the state to compel the management of a firm to disclose certain information about it, but also its NEB clauses which, it moaned, gave the government too much power to obtain control over private industry.[33] What seemed to frighten the industrialists most was the possibility that the NEB could take over a concern without the consent of its Board of Directors simply by buying shares from stockholders willing to sell. (The Bill gave the NEB no power to acquire shares by condemnation except in one extremely limited situation; and, actually, it never acquired any shares this way.) Wilson and the Labour MPs handling the Bill emphasised that NEB takeovers were to be done by 'agreement'; but refused to say outright that the NEB would never take over a company without the consent of its directors.[34]

Business breathed a sigh of relief, however, when in June 1975 Benn was sent to the Department of Energy and replaced as Secretary of State for Industry by the more centrist Eric Varley. Also Sir Donald Ryder (now Baron Ryder of Eaton Hastings), a man with long experience in industry and a former director of the papermaking giant Reed International, was selected as the first NEB chairman -- though he could not formally don this mantle until the passage of the Industry Act of 1975 and the creation of the NEB in November 1975. Ryder proclaimed that the NEB staff 'would be selected for their commercial and industrial skills, and would pursue conventional commercial criteria, and that the NEB's main function under his chairmanship would be "the provision of equity funds for private companies which could not obtain enough funds from private sources".[35] Also drafted to soothe business[36] were Guidelines whose content we shall discuss shortly. And yet many in the private arena continued to view the NEB as a spearhead to make public ownership in the UK the norm rather than the exception.

Ominously for the future of the NEB, most members of the Tory Party showed themselves vehemently opposed to it during the Parliamentary Debates on its establishment. Several comments prove clearly the Tory hostility to the Board. Michael Heseltine, the Shadow Industry Secretary and a moderate Conservative, lamented that the Industry Bill could destroy the free enterprise system.[37] On another occasion he declaimed that his Party 'totally and utterly rejects the NEB approach to industrial investment...' and that the proposed Act was 'mischievous and deliberately so. The Conservatives would repeal it.'[38] In the debate on the Third Reading of the measure, he said that he 'regarded the NEB in its doctrinal application as a totally irrelevant act of government'.[39] Mr. Nicholas Ridley complained that

> 'When we put aside the veil of jargon and Socialist ideology we find that the purpose of the National Enterprise Board is to make industry more responsive to the ideas of the trade unions and the workers...The whole purpose of the NEB is that it should not close down factories which should be closed down...Once a business becomes either totally controlled by the State or owned by the State we get in all cases the politicalisation of the decisions that matter.'[40]

And Timothy Renton, adding his mite to the arguments over the Bill, worried that the NEB was a frivolous and expensive experiment that the nation could ill afford.[41]

The far left of the Labour Party also was not that happy about the shape of the agency that was to come into being. Liverpool MP Eric Heffer, who had been part of Benn's team in the Department of Industry, asserted that he had originally envisaged the Industry Bill as ending the power of privilege and the class system by extending public ownership to a much greater extent than the measure provided. However, despite his reservations he supported it as a step in the right direction -- as a small move toward building an egalitarian society where working people through continuity of employment would come into their own and benefit from the labour they put into industry.[42]

The Duties and Structure of the NEB

The 1975 Industry Act came into force on November 12 of that year; and by that moment Donald Ryder had recruited enough staff to enable the Board to begin work immediately. At its apex, the NEB was to consist of a Chairman and not less than eight or more than 16 other members. The Chairman and other members of the Board were to be nominated by the Secretary of State for Industry (henceforth often called Secretary of State). The Secretary of State could make one or more of the Board's members Deputy Chairman(men).[43] Since Section 1.6 of the statute declared that the NEB was not to be regarded as the servant or agent of the Crown, most of its staff could be, and were, hired on short-term contracts.[44] Section 2 of the Act distinguished between the purposes and the functions of the Board. The Board's functions (Sec. 2.2) included:

(a) Establishing or maintaining; or assisting in the establishment or maintenance of; any industrial undertaking.

(b) Promoting or assisting the reorganisation of an industry. (This clause was inserted to enable the NEB to follow in the footsteps of the old Industrial Reorganisation Corporation by urging and facilitating mergers in various industries in order to make their firms more competitive. In fact, the NEB never presided at any mergers; though it once considered taking a stake in a proposed fusion of the turbo-generator interests of General Electric Corporation (UK) and C. A. Parsons.[45]).

(c) '[E]xtending public ownership into profitable areas of manufacturing industry'; and

(d) Promoting industrial democracy in undertakings which it controlled.

The purposes for which the Board was to exercise these functions were (Sec. 2.1):

(a) The development or assistance of the economy of the United Kingdom or any part of the United Kingdom. (In point of fact, the NEB did most of its work in England, as similar agencies already existed for Scotland, Wales and Northern Ireland. A Scottish National Party member, Mr. Douglas Crawford, opposed the NEB because he feared that the London-headquartered body would spread its tentacles to Scotland.[46] One of the NEB's major holdings, Ferranti, had many employees in Scotland, a point that became relevant when the NEB had to sell that company.)

(b) The promotion in the United Kingdom of industrial efficiency and international competitiveness; and

(c) The provision, maintenance or safeguarding of productive employment in any part of the United Kingdom.

Section 2.4 gave the Board the power to acquire securities, form corporations and partnerships, make and guarantee loans, acquire and dispose of property and provide financial, administrative or managerial services for industry. Section 5 allowed the transfer to the Board of publicly owned securities and property. What was dumped in its lap under this clause were several, mostly ailing, 'lame duck' undertakings. The most important were British Leyland; Rolls Royce (the plane engine and not the profitable, privately owned motor car company); Alfred Herbert, a major machine tool manufacturer that had come upon hard days; and Ferranti, a mechanical and electrical engineering enterprise which, like Rolls Royce, did a great deal of work for the Ministry of Defence. These firms, plus smaller outfits Dunford and Elliott (steel manufacturers); Cambridge Instrument Co. (scientific and medical instruments); and Brown Boveri Kent (industrial instruments) were transferred to the NEB from the Department of Industry in early 1976. The government's share in International Computers Limited, the largest UK-owned computer firm, was also handed to the Board.[47]

Though the NEB was and is not a division of the Department of Industry, the Secretary of State for Industry was by Sections 6 and 7 given the power to determine the financial duties of the Board with respect to its various types of assets and activities and to issue guidelines for the exercise of its functions. The Treasury had to approve of the Secretary of State's description of these financial duties; and both Departments had to satisfy themselves that fulfilling them would produce an adequate return on the capital it employed (Sec. 6). As a concession to the Confederation of British Industries, which was much less afraid of Eric Varley than of former Secretary of State Tony Benn,[48] the Secretary had to approve any purchase of company shares by the NEB or any of its subsidiaries if the acquisition would enable the NEB to control more than 30% of the votes at the corporation's general meeting or if the transaction gave it an investment of more than £10 million in a firm (Sec. 10).

Everything in the preceding description of the NEB's powers and functions is consistent with Holland's vision of it as an agency that would take charge of at least one firm in every crucial section of the economy and act as a role-model for competing private firms with respect to product and process development, efficiency, and price reduction. However, the Board under Section 8.2 of the Act was permitted to spend only £700 million. This sum was far from what it needed to take control of a significant number of major undertakings, especially when it is realised that over 80% of the £700 million was invested in British Leyland and Rolls Royce.[49] Section 8.2 did provide that the Board's spending limit could be raised to one billion (i.e. one thousand million) pounds with the approval of the Secretary of State, the Treasury and the House of Commons; and this step was taken in April of 1978. It must be emphasised that these limits were not restraints on annual disbursements; but maxima that the Board could spend over its lifetime until Parliament passed new legislation to up them. Thus it is difficult to disagree with Gabrielle Ganz when she says that the NEB birthed by the 1975 Industry Act was not an 'instrument of nationalisation' (nor, we may add, a Holland-type organisation existing to galvanise private firms by subjecting them to intense competition from a major publicly-owned competitor) but, rather, an 'investment bank...and holding company'.[50] It did function as a holding company for the lame ducks; and, in addition, was an 'investment banker' in the sense that it acted as a *venture capitalist*. How well it performed this latter role will be the main topic of this book.

The Board consisted of two levels: the Board itself and the staff. Formally, decisions to purchase stock, make loans, sell shares, etc. had to be made at the Board level. In practice, however, the resolutions of the paid Chairman of the NEB, himself a member of its Board, were never overturned by it. Moreover, at least during the incumbency of Sir Leslie Murphy, its second Chairman, investments of less than £500,000 were actually approved by an 'investment committee' consisting of

Murphy's Deputy Chairman Richard Morris, the Board's financial director, and the chairmen of the several NEB divisions.

As was evident to the left wing of the British labour movement, the persons who were members of the Board (i.e. who comprised the NEB's Board level) were hardly individuals who would terrify UK industry and finance. (All were part-time except for the Chairman and Deputy Chairman. The staff, however, were full-time.) As noted, the first Chairman was Sir Donald Ryder. His Deputy Chairman was then-Labour Party supporter Sir Leslie Murphy, who was born into a poor family and had a brilliant university career, receiving a First in Maths. Before coming to the NEB he had been Deputy Chairman of respected City merchant bankers Schroder and Wagg. Throughout the Ryder and Murphy eras (i.e. from November 1975 to 21 November 1979, when Murphy and his fellow Board members resigned) there were at any given time after March 1976 eight or nine part-time Board members. Of these, never more than four were trade union representatives: for the bulk of the period only three were. Of these trade unionists, at least one was out of sympathy with the idea of workers' control of industry (which the NEB was supposed to promote) and with the view that undertakings assisted by the NEB should enter into the 'planning agreements' legitimated by the 1975 Industry Act. (The NEB made no move to encourage the spread of industrial democracy and never concluded any planning agreement.)

The Board always had four industry members, five if a woman who was a director of several companies and who listed her profession as 'Economic and Industrial Consultant' is counted as a representative of business. (This person was a *rara avis* on the NEB scene. None of the influential members of the NEB staff was female and none of the thirty-plus officials of NEB-subsidised companies I interviewed was a woman.) Among the business members were Michael Edwardes, Director of the Chloride Group; the former Managing Director of SKF (UK), Ltd; and the Deputy Chairman of huge chemical concern ICI. Richard Morris, Murphy's Deputy Chairman, came from the big firm of Courtaulds; and, don't forget, the Chairman (and Deputy Chairman) were Board members as well as Board officers. All the part-time members were appointed for three years. In 1977 they received £1000 per year; in 1983, £3793. The Chairman and Deputy Chairman were picked for five year

year stints, though none ever served the full period. In 1976 Ryder received £35,400;[51] while Murphy, his successor, was paid about the same in 1978.[52]

The NEB staff, the 'lower' level of the Board, was always rather small. Thus at the end of 1977 it consisted of only 57 persons.[53] By April 1979, just before the Tory victory that ultimately destroyed the NEB, the staff in London and the regions totalled 92.[54] Only three of these were civil servants, who were seconded from other public agencies. The rest were extremely bright men obtained on short-term contracts from industry and banking. Many had a background in finance or accounting: one of their number said to me that on the whole they were not experienced managers. At the time, most were Labour Party supporters with a belief that public and private enterprise can co-operate for the public weal. At present, they retain this view but many (including Murphy) became backers of the late Liberal-Social Democratic Party Alliance. Personality quarrels erupted among them; but all of them I talked with agreed that their cadre contained so many outstanding individuals that, up until the Tory triumph of May 1979, the NEB was an exciting, thrilling place to work -- very much like Washington, D.C. in the early New Deal years.

By spring 1976 Sir Donald Ryder had an outstanding staff, a Board, shares in seven 'lame ducks', and 24.4% of the voting stock of International Computers Limited (henceforth often ICL), an undertaking that, though a bit financially troubled, was perceived to have good profit potential. As seen, these holdings were already owned by the government prior to their transfer to Sir Donald and his subordinates. In March, he also received Guidelines from Secretary of State for Industry Eric Varley. These were viewed by both political right[55] and political left[56] as significantly curtailing the Board's powers. (N.B. For the rest of this volume, 'Board' means the National Enterprise Board as a whole, not just that agency's Board level, unless the contrary is clear from the context.) Guideline 4 mentioned that the NEB had no special powers of compulsory acquisition; but here it was simply following the 1975 Industry Act. Guideline 5 did state that the NEB could buy shares in a company against the wishes of its Board of Directors, the text explaining that without this power the NEB would be 'at a major disadvantage compared with other businesses...' However, when the Board wanted to buy more than 10% of the voting shares of any concern against the will of the Board of Directors, it had, according to Guideline 5, to give the Secretary of State reasonable notice of its intention to acquire these shares and to wait a reasonable time before purchasing them. The Secretary (at this time, remember, the 'moderate' Varley rather than the 'radical' Benn) could nullify the purchase.[57] (In fact, the Board never acquired a company against the wishes of the Board of Directors.) As seen, the Industry Act itself (Sec. 10) required the NEB to get the consent of the Secretary of State where the cost of acquiring the stock exceeded £10 million or where the purchase would give it 30% of the voting rights in the enterprise. Guideline 5 added that his blessing had to be given in the case of any acquisition raising 'new or significant' policy issues. Likewise, under Guideline 9 the NEB was empowered to make loans or provide loan guarantees without the consent of the Secretary of State when the sum involved was £10 million or less, except where the new commitment raised new or significant policy issues or where the credit pushed the total sum allocated for a project over the £25 million mark. In the cases of loans exceeding £10 million or of less than this amount but falling under one of these exceptions, the *imprimatur* of the Secretary of State was necessary. In practice, the curbs on the Board noted in this paragraph were not very meaningful, for the Secretary of State never vetoed a proposed share acquisition or loan. In fact, the Board never made a loan anywhere near the £10 million threshold except to British Leyland and Rolls Royce.

Guideline 16, especially when taken together with Nos. 24-26, reflected what some saw as the contradictions embodied in the Industry Act about the basic purposes of the Board. No. 16 contended that the NEB was designed 'to operate primarily within the profitable sectors of manufacturing industry...' and that 'in taking investment decisions the NEB shall always have regard to the profitability of the investments'. The same Guideline said, however, that 'The NEB's purposes are wider...than those of commercial enterprises. They [the NEB] will be in a position to take a long term view, where appropriate, of their investment opportunities.' Guidelines 24-26 added that the NEB was to create employment in areas of high joblessness and push for the expansion of existing operations or the locating of new undertakings in these regions. Needless to say, it is not self-evident that the most remunerative investments are those in areas of high unemployment, which are often remote sections of the land to which competent managers and researchers do not want to move.

Guidelines 18 and 20 recognised that it would be unfair to expect that the big lame ducks the NEB was holding, especially British Leyland and Rolls Royce, would be consistently profitable. They thus provided in essence that the activities of these firms would be accounted for separately and that separate objectives would be set for them. In accordance with this philosophy, the DOI promulgated a 'Direction' in December 1977[58] requiring that the Board should, with respect to their investments in all concerns except British Leyland and Rolls Royce, aim for a return on capital employed, before interest and taxation, of between 15% and 20% by 1981. Subsequent Directions, issued April 1978 and April 1979, declared that the analogous figures for British Leyland and Rolls Royce were to be 10%.[59]

There are other reasons, in addition to those mentioned three paragraphs ago, why the Guidelines and subsequent Directions did not seriously hobble the Board. There was enough ambiguity in them to justify its buying more failing companies in order to preserve jobs if it had desired to veer in that direction. They clearly permitted and even encouraged it to take shares in profitable or potentially profitable undertakings; and this was exactly the vision of those such as Stuart Holland who conceived of it as a body that, by controlling a significant number of major corporations, would increase the pace of investment in UK industry and see to it that this financing was directed towards economically sensible and socially desirable goals. What, as I hinted earlier, was the major factor keeping the NEB from fulfilling these hopes was not the command that it aim at profitability nor its need to win the approval of Secretary of State Varley for certain actions but, rather, the niggardly £1 billion (most of which had to be used to feed British Leyland and Rolls Royce) that was its spending limit even under the Labour Government that created it.

The Burgeoning of the NEB

First NEB Chairman Donald Ryder wanted the NEB to move quickly right after leaving the starting gate. One of my interviewees said that this was due not only to his energetic personality but to his perception that the Board could never be dismantled once it had its fingers in quite a few corporate pies. (I promised these interviewees that I would keep their names confidential.) In July 1976 he made his first purchase of a firm not given to him by the DOI. This factory manufactured computer peripherals and had 1000 employees. During that year, the Board acquired only a handful of other companies but, by the end of 1977, had interests in 33. These included Sinclair Radionics, a firm set up by the brilliant inventor Sir Clive Sinclair to make calculators and pocket TV sets; Twinlock Ltd., a manufacturer of office filing systems and furniture that in 1977 employed about 2000 individuals; and two promising 'high tech' firms. (The Sinclair Pocket TV with a two-inch screen whose development the Board funded was, alas, less than a smashing commercial success.) It may seem that 33 is not such a massive number; but the NEB had to study the prospects of a company before taking stock in it and the legal formalities of purchase could not always be completed immediately. Ryder resigned on 31 July 1977 and, as mentioned, was succeeded by Deputy Chairman Murphy. Sir Leslie, with his banking background, was possibly a bit more cautious than Ryder; and insisted that the Board should refrain from restructuring industries *à la* the old Industrial Reorganisation Corporation.[60]

However, whether there was a significant difference between the acquisitions policies of Ryder and Murphy cannot definitively be determined. In any event, Murphy felt keenly the need to draft a clear and reasonable Corporate Plan for the NEB. Luckily, his Planning Director and Assistant Planning Director were extremely competent men. They began by looking at the various analyses of the main sectors of UK industry that had been carried out by the Sector Working Parties[61] of the National Economic Development Office (NEDO). (NEDO, a quasi-governmental agency with representatives of government, labor and industry, was established to recommend ways of improving the nation's economic performance, competitive power and efficiency.[62]) The NEB planners then asked themselves various questions about the sectors covered by the NEDO analyses, e.g.,

(1) What was the industry's growth rate?
(2) Was it likely to be commercially viable?
(3) Was it one with export potential?

(4) Would NEB entry into the industry make it more commercially viable and attract additional private investment to it?

The NEB decided in framing its Corporate Plan that it would actively seek to invest in portions of the economy with respect to which the answer to queries two, three and four was 'yes' and which promised to have a good growth rate. These areas included machine tools, biotechnology, electronics, information technology including computers, and service enterprises (e.g., health care providers) that could export 'know-how'. The Board's glossy Annual Report for 1978 specified automotive products, aero-engines, and scientific and medical instruments as among the other areas in which it was currently interested.[63] (A cynic might comment that some of these latter sectors, plus that of machine tools, were listed because they were the fields of operation of the major lame ducks that the Board had inherited.) The Report added that the NEB was also interested in assisting the growth and development of small business and in stimulating development in regions of high unemployment.[64] It will be remembered that the NEB Guidelines commanded the agency to take steps in the last mentioned direction.

Starting with 1978 the NEB concentrated on high technology (i.e. computer hardware and software, information technology, biotechnology) and small business, including many modest-sized firms in the northwest and northeast of England. In January 1978 it acquired the important Fairey Aerospace-Engineering group of companies, then in receivership. During the year it started Inmos, conceived as the first British firm to concentrate on the manufacturing of microchips for computers. (In 1977 it had set up a consortium of several companies called Insac, which was supposed to market British software in the US.) In early 1979 it gave birth to one of its major failures, Nexos, a joint venture that was established to sell 'the office of the future' in the UK and elsewhere. More details about these and other investments will be provided later. (Many more requests for aid came to the NEB than it approved. According to Murphy, by the end of 1977 it had received over 1000 approaches. It investigated thoroughly 350 of these companies and, as seen, took stakes in about 30.[65])

The NEB adopted a divisional structure that to some extent reflected the areas of interest specified in the Corporate Plan. It started out with only two divisions[66] and, under Murphy, expanded to five -- known as A, B, C, D and E. One of these concentrated on small firms, another on electronics and information technology, two on general business, and one on British Leyland and Rolls Royce. In addition to the central Board, located in London, there were Northern (really Northeastern -- Tyneside, Durham, Cleveland) and Northwestern (Manchester-Merseyside) Regional Boards, set up to carry out the Guidelines' mandate that the NEB do something to relieve unemployment in these economically depressed regions. These Regional Boards each had several part-time members who were business people or trade unionists from the regions concerned. They also each had one full-time member, who at times was deemed a Divisional Head of the Central Board,[67] plus a handful of full-time employees. In reality, the full-time members and the miniscule full-time staffs of these Regional Boards had the final say in deciding what small firms under their respective jurisdictions to assist. The Northern Board was located in Newcastle upon Tyne and the Northwestern Board had its office in Liverpool.[68] By 1982 there were also NEB offices in Manchester, Scotland, and as far afield as Plymouth in the Southwest and Leeds in Yorkshire (to cover that county plus Humberside).[69]

By April of 1979 the NEB's commitments against its statutory borrowing limit of £1 billion had been reached. The Industry Act of 4 April 1979 lifted that limit to £3 billion; and the Secretary of State with the consent of the Treasury could hike this to £4.5 billion. However, despite first appearances, the Act did not really make it possible for the Board to take control of the 'commanding heights' of British industry -- an ability that Stuart Holland would have liked it to have. First, and most important, most of the additional funds were destined for British Leyland and Rolls Royce (henceforth often referred to as BL and RR). Second, £800 million in existing borrowings by NEB subsidiaries were to be deemed current NEB commitments. Thus the rise to the £3 billion was, anyway, really one of £1.2 billion rather than of £2 billion![70]

The NEB Bubble Bursts

In May 1979, an unfortunate thing happened to the NEB: the Tories won the national election. Margaret Thatcher became Prime Minister and Sir Keith Joseph Secretary of State for

Industry. These apostles of *laissez-faire* had no love for the agency. Their hostility was a continuation of that manifested by many Conservatives during the 1975 debate on the Industry Act of that year. The intervening years had not mellowed the dislike of certain powerful Tories for the Board (though a liberal Tory such as Heath, had he become Prime Minister in 1979, might have kept it healthy). A 1976 Conservative Strategy Document entitled *The Right Approach* called for closing it down and selling off to private parties as much of its shareholdings as soon as possible.[71] In the 1979 election campaign Mrs Thatcher had promised to strip it of practically all its power to buy companies and to force it to hive off its existing stock.[72] In early 1979, when it had seemed quite possible that the Tories were heading for victory, the NEB Board held long discussions with Conservative leaders explaining that it was not a political organisation. They convinced at least one future member of Mrs Thatcher's Cabinet of the validity of their position, but he was not willing to defend them publicly; and they were unable to shake Mrs Thatcher's antagonism.

On 19 July 1979, a couple of months after the election, Sir Keith made his statement about the future of the NEB. He said that he had 'carefully reviewed the full range of the NEB's activities' and that he paid 'tribute...to the sense of public service and the energy of all concerned with the NEB'. But he reminded the House that the Tories had opposed the 1975 and 1979 Industry Acts and that their election manifesto had promised to reduce the NEB's powers. 'We favour the encouragement of private initiative and enterprise, not the promotion of public ownership.' He added that the NEB would have a continuing role for those companies which had been in difficulties and for which it was now responsible. However there was, he said, no public benefit in enabling the NEB to act as a general merchant bank. Thus its powers to buy shares in businesses would be limited. More specifically, this clipping of the NEB's wings continued, the Board had to dispose of £100 million of its assets during the current financial year. However, the Secretary of State was willing to let the Board operate at half-speed. It was to continue to have the authority to support high tech companies, chiefly in the areas of computer software, microelectronics, and their applications. The cash for new investment in these fields was to come from the receipts from the sale of its other assets; and in all cases it was to invest only in conjunction with private capital. The only other function the Joseph speech envisaged for the NEB was to plough on with its aid to small firms and to concerns in the North and Northwest. He added that a Bill would be introduced to give effect to these recommendations and to reduce sharply the financial limits set forth in the 1979 Industry Act.[73]

Originally, Joseph ordered the NEB to sell the £100 million worth of assets by the end of March 1980; but in February 1980, he gave it additional time.[74] A former high-ranking NEB official mentioned to me that Sir Keith left some scope for the NEB to act because he was intellectually honest and open to logical argument. However, even if he had wanted to do more to preserve the Board's powers he could not have, for Mrs Thatcher was antagonistic both to Murphy and to the NEB concept. To show the extent of her disapproval of Murphy, another person formerly high up in the NEB told me that Murphy and Deputy NEB Chairman Richard Morris lunched before the 1979 election with a leading Tory liberal who was probably sympathetic to the NEB. That gentleman said that he could not commit himself on the fate of the Board but that if he became Secretary of State for Industry, he would have to 'execute' Murphy.

A little later on in this volume, we shall go into more detail in discussing the bad relations between the NEB and its subsidiary Rolls Royce, especially those between Sir Kenneth Keith, the RR Chairman, and Murphy himself. As early as 1978 Murphy felt dissatisfied with RR's performance and sought to have Keith discharged as Chairman. However, Keith successfully lobbied with the Government to keep his job.[75] (Keith achieved his goals with both Labour and Tory administrations -- one ex-NEB official feels that he was listened to by the latter because he was a big contributor to the Conservative Party.) Moreover, he counterattacked by asking that the NEB be deprived of control of RR and that it should be returned to the control of the Department of Industry. As late as October of 1979 it appeared that Murphy was going to win this struggle; but in November a director of British Leyland asked that that lame duck, too, be removed from NEB control and placed under the DOI's aegis.[76] By this time Keith had (whether voluntarily or involuntarily) himself decided to leave RR; but the man designated as his successor said he would not take the job unless the NEB relinquished its grasp on the firm.[77] On 21 November 1979 Joseph announced that he would remove RR from the NEB's auspices. In protest, Murphy and all the other Board members, business representatives included, resigned.[78]

In a sense, these abdications marked the end of the NEB as an important organisation, for many of its bright and talented staff then left for jobs in the private sector. (One resigning Board member told me that the real reason for this mass exodus was that Sir Keith was scrutinising every decision.) In a debate on 26 November 1979, Joseph said that the reason he was returning RR to the DOI was the friction between the NEB and the leadership of RR: he also admitted that most of Kenneth Keith's potential successors were reluctant to work under the NEB.[79] He added that he would listen seriously to BL's plea to be freed from NEB suzerainty.[80] In announcing the transfer of RR, Sir Keith reiterated that the main task of the NEB was to invest in high technology, small firms, and concerns in the regions of high unemployment; and that it was to return the bulk of its assets to the private sector as soon as possible.[81] It was to have a 'catalytic investment role, especially in connection with advanced technology and increasingly in partnership with the private sector, as well as its regional and small firms roles'.[82]

The new Chairman of the NEB was Sir Arthur Knight, the Chairman of Courtaulds and a member of the Council of the Confederation of British Industries.[83] His Deputy Chairman was Sir John King, head of Babcock International Ltd.[84] Of the five other members of the NEB, four were from industry and one was a chairman of a couple of new towns. Knight himself was a part-time rather than a full-time NEB chief.[85] He took the position with the understanding that it would be for a year only and was confronted with a staff whose morale was low and whose members were fleeing. Moreover, as noted, he was under a government-imposed duty to dispose of at least £100 million of the Board's assets. He thus restructured it so that its primary subdivisions were a disinvestment team, a new-initiative group, and a monitoring unit. (He felt that under Murphy the NEB had not done an adequate job of keeping track of the undertakings for which it was responsible.) Of the approximately 90 persons on the staff when he was head, the monitoring team was composed of 25-30 persons, the disinvestment team of two or three.

The Industry Act of 1980, passed on 30 June of that year, embodied some of the ideas about the future of the NEB that Joseph had articulated earlier. Added to the functions of the Board were (Sec. 1.1) 'promoting the private ownership of interests in industrial undertakings by the disposal of securities and other property held by the Board...' Section 2 made it legally possible to order shares in Rolls Royce, British Leyland and other companies owned by the Board to be transferred to the Department of Industry. Section 5 allowed the Secretary of State to lower the NEB's total spending limits to £750 million. And Section 8 abolished his power to direct the NEB to grant selective financial assistance to a company under Sections 7 and 8 of the 1972 Industry Act. (That prerogative, set forth in Section 3 of the 1975 Act, was a device that enabled the NEB to give monetary aid to BL.[86]) Rolls Royce was formally returned to the DOI in August 1980 and British Leyland in March 1981.[87]

Guidelines issued by Sir Keith to the NEB on 1 August 1980 said (No. 3) that before acquiring securities or making loans, the Board had to make sure that the subsidised firm could not get the cash privately. The NEB's investments were to be made only in conjunction with private funds and it was to encourage maximum private sector participation. It was to effect investments only when (No. 4) it saw the prospect of an adequate rate of return within a reasonable time; and (No. 5) it was not to buy voting shares in a company without the consent of the Board of Directors. It had (No. 10) to obtain the approval of the Secretary of State before it contracted to dispose of any voting stock and (No. 12) could not make any financial commitment exceeding £5 million without his consent.

Knight resigned in December 1980 for reasons that are not completely clear. There was speculation that he was annoyed because the Government wanted to force him to sell the £100 million worth of stock by the end of March 1980, though he won this particular battle. The Government may have been irritated because he continued Murphy's struggle to prevent the House of Commons official known as the Comptroller and Auditor General from examining the NEB's books. Another possible cause of his departure will be mentioned in Chapter 5.

Sir Arthur was succeeded as NEB Chairman by his Deputy Sir John King. King left, in turn, in January 1981 and was followed by another businessman, Sir Frederick Wood. Needless to say, these shifts at the top did nothing to rejuvenate already-shaky employee morale. Wood stayed on until November 1983 and was replaced by Mr. Colin Barker, who is Chairman as of this writing. On 21 July 1981, the Secretary of State for Industry announced that the NEB would henceforth operate together with the National Research Development Corporation (NRDC) under the name of British Technology Group (BTG). (The NRDC had been set up in 1948 to develop and exploit inventions resulting from public research. Unlike the NEB, it has been respected by both major parties.[88] Its major financial success has come from its patenting and licensing the therapeutic and life-saving drugs known as Cephalosporins.[89]) As of this moment, the NEB and NRDC still are legally separate entities, but share the same offices, Chairman and Board members.[90] In one of the rare flashes of humour to be struck by individuals on any side of the political spectrum when discussing NEB matters, Sir Frederick Wood proclaimed in the Board's 1982 Report that the 'union of the NEB and NRDC in the British Technology Group is now virtually complete. The union has yet to be legitimised, but, in keeping with a modern tendency, the happy couple already share a common home.'[91]

By 1983 the NEB had more than met its mandate to raise £100 milion from selling its investments. Its first major divestment was that of its entire holding in International Computers Ltd on 17 December 1979.[92] In 1980 it rid itself of its stakes in the flourishing Ferranti and Fairey enterprises -- Ferranti was one of the lame ducks it had inherited from the DOI while, as mentioned, it had purchased Fairey when that group was in receivership.[93] In 1981 the equity in some small NEB concerns was transferred to a new entity called Grosvenor Development Capital.[94] The year 1982 recorded no major disposals;[95] but in 1983 the Board marketed all of its holdings in several large investments as well as more of its Grosvenor Development Capital stock.[96]

The years 1980-83 were not wholly bleak ones for the NEB. It continued to make investments in small companies in the depressed North and Northeast. In 1980 the government approved allocating it a second £25 million for the development of Inmos, its microchip manufacturer.[97] And in February 1981 the Tories gave Nexos, the corporation set up to promote the 'office of the future', £13 million.[98]

As of now, however, the NEB is moribund. In February 1983 the government announced, after a lengthy DOI review of the BTG, that it was giving it as a whole only £10 million, down from £25 million in 1982.[99] The DOI said that too many BTG (read NEB) investments in new technologies had failed. Nexos, it noted, had collapsed with losses of greater than £30 million, while Inmos was still proving to be a burden on the Treasury. (Sir Frederick Wood had urged that the Government hand the BTG a one-shot dowry of £100 million. In fact, the NEB was allowed £15 million extra for Inmos during 1983.)[100]

At the end of September 1983, the Thatcher Administration, further effectuating the disillusion of the DOI's study, told the NEB to dispose of its entire portfolio of investments.[101] Even its role as provider of funds for small firms in the Northwest and Northeast was ordered to come to an end. The Northern and Northwestern Regional Boards have been dismantled and the regional offices closed. (I interviewed someone in one of these offices to the din of the noise accompanying its renovation to accomodate a new tenant.) During the 15 month period ending 31 March 1985 the NEB fully disposed of its interests in 17 companies, including Inmos. In all, its investment portfolio was reduced during this period from a book value of £131.8 million to one of £35.3 million.[102] And in 1985-87 the number of its investments was lowered from 56 to six, the latter having a book value of £3.72 million.[103]

The role that the government now envisages for the BTG was labelled at the end of September 1983 by then Secretary of State for Trade and Industry Cecil Parkinson 'technology transfer' -- i.e. assisting the 'translation into commercial products of new research ideas, particularly those from the public sector where the government is the ultimate owner of the industrial property'.[104] Since that is and has been the duty of the BTG's other constituent, the NRDC, it is apparent that the NEB has, as of this writing, no purpose other than to dispose of its current stocks. As the 1984-85 NEB Report puts the matter, the BTG's 'ongoing technology transfer business' [which is its only task now] will 'be conducted principally within [the]...NRDC'.[105] The handful of remaining NEB employees was transferred to the NRDC in August 1985.[106] Whether the Conservative Government will enact legislation abolishing the NEB totally or legally merging it with the NRDC is unclear at present. In the early 1990s, the voters may abolish the Tory Administration. If the NEB has not been legally erased by then, it will be available to an incoming Labour or Labour-SLDP Government to use for transmitting assistance to the UK economy.

NOTES

1. G. M. Field and P. V. Hills, 'The administration of industrial subsidies' at p. 1 of Alan Whiting (ed.), *The economics of industrial subsidies* (HMSO, London, 1976).

2. Raymond Vernon, 'Enterprise and government in western Europe' at p. 3, 5 of Raymond Vernon (ed.), *Big business and the state* (Harvard U. Press, Cambridge, Mass., 1974).

3. Field and Hills, 'The administration of industrial subsidies' at p. 2.

4. J. Wiseman, 'An economic analysis of the Expenditure Committee reports on public money in the private sector' at p. 77, 83 of Whiting (ed.), *The economics of industrial subsidies;* Peter Maunder, 'Government intervention in the economy of the United Kingdom' at p. 130, 145 of Peter Maunder (ed.), *Government intervention in the developed economy* (Praeger, New York, 1979).

5. N. K. Gardner, 'Economics of launching aid' at p. 141, 153 of Whiting (ed.), *The economics of industrial subsidies.*

6. Field and Hills, 'The administration of industrial subsidies', p. 20.

7. Alan Peacock, *Structural economic policies in West Germany and the United Kingdom* (Anglo-German Foundation for the Study of Industrial Society, London, 1980), p. 97.

8. Ibid., p. 59, 61-2; *New Statesman,* 31 May 1985, pp. 8-10.

9. This paragraph is based upon Ch. 6, 7, 8, 9, 10, 11, pp. 271-72, 299 of Douglas Hague and Geoffrey Wilkinson, *The IRC: an experiment in industrial intervention* (Allen and Unwin, London, 1983); Stephen Young and A. V. Lowe, *Intervention in the mixed economy* (Croom Helm, London, 1974), p. 44, 232-34.

10. Gabrielle Ganz, *Government and industry* (Professional Books, Abingdon, 1977), p. 73; Peacock, *Structural economic policies,* pp. 74-5.

11. David Coates, *Labour in power* (Longmans, London, 1980), pp. 86-7; S. A. Walkland, 'Economic planning and dysfunctional politics' at p. 92, 137 of A. M. Gamble and S. A. Walkland, *The British party system and economic policy 1945-1983* (Clarendon Press, Oxford, 1984).

12. Walkland, 'Economic planning and dysfunctional politics', p. 137; Coates, *Labour in power,* p. 87.

13. Quartet Books, London, 1975.
14. Ibid., p. 178.
15. Ibid., p. 185.
16. Ibid., pp. 201-02.
17. Ibid., p. 202.
18. Ibid., pp. 205-06.
19. Walkland, 'Economic planning and dysfunctional politics', p. 134.
20. See *London Times,* 19 Ap. 1973, p. 1.
21. Document quoted in *London Times,* 8 June 1973, p. 5.
22. See *Economist,* 6 Oct. 1973, pp. 29-30; *London Times,* 8 June 1973, p. 1.
23. *London Times,* 3 Oct. 1973, p. 1.
24. *London Times,* 16 Aug. 1974, p. 4.
25. Coates, *Labour in power,* p. 90.
26. *London Times,* 16 Aug. 1974, p. 4.
27. Ibid.
28. *London Times,* 17 Sept. 1974, p. 1.
29. *London Times,* 16 Aug. 1974, p. 4.
30. John Redwood, *Going for broke...* (Basil Blackwell, Oxford, 1984), p. 61; *London Times,* 18 Oct. 1974, p. 1.
31. *Socialism now* (Jonathan Cape, London, 1974), p. 38.
32. *London Times,* 13 Nov. 1974, p. 1; 1 Feb. 1975, p. 1.
33. *London Times,* 1 Feb. 1975, p. 17.
34. *London Times,* 19 Feb. 1975, p. 6.
35. Coates, *Labour in power,* p. 98.
36. *London Times,* 27 Oct. 1975, p. 15.
37. *London Times,* 1 Feb. 1975, p. 17.
38. *London Times,* 18 Feb. 1975, p. 10.
39. *London Times,* 4 July 1975, p. 8.
40. HC Debates, 22 Oct. 1975, cols. 522-24.
41. See HC Debates, 3 July 1975, col. 1813.
42. HC Debates, 3 July 1975, cols. 1789-91.
43. 1975 Industry Act, Secs. 1.2, 1.3, 1.4.
44. *Tamlin v. Hannaford,* [1950] 1 KB 18, 24 is authority for the proposition that employees of public agencies that are not Crown servants or agents are not civil servants. If NEB staff had been civil servants, it would have been contrary to public policy to hire them for a fixed period of years. See pp. 63-5 (esp. p. 64) of H. W. R. Wade, *Administrative law,* 5th edn (Clarendon Press, Oxford, 1982).
45. See *London Times,* 21 June 1977, p. 17.
46. HC Debates, 3 July 1975, cols. 1794-96.

47. Coventry, Liverpool, Newcastle, N. Tyneside Trades Councils, *State intervention in industry: a workers' inquiry* (Coventry, etc. Trades Councils, Newcastle Upon Tyne, 1980), pp. 169-70. (Author henceforth cited as 'Coventry Trades Councils'.)

48. Redwood, *Going for broke...*, p. 63.

49. See NEB 1977 Annual Report, pp. 38-43. (All NEB Annual Reports published by the National Enterprise Board, London.)

50. Ganz, *Government and industry*, p. 53.

51. NEB 1977 Annual Report, p. 35; 1984 Annual Report, p. 12.

52. NEB 1978 Annual Report, p. 43.

53. Committee to Review the Functioning of Financial Institutions, *Evidence on the financing of industry and trade,* (HMSO, London, 1978), vol. 4, p. 23.

54. NEB 1978 Annual Report, p. 12.

55. *Daily Telegraph,* 2 Mar. 1976, p. 17. These Guidelines can be found at pp. 66ff of the NEB's 1978 Annual Report.

56. Interview by author of a Member of Parliament.

57. *Daily Telegraph,* 2 Mar. 1976, p. 17.

58. NEB 1978 Annual Report, p. 73.

59. Ibid., p. 74.

60. *Daily Telegraph,* 7 Sept. 1977, p. 20.

61. NEB 1978 Annual Report, p. 8.

62. Trevor Smith, 'Britain' at p. 52, 55-6 of Jack Hayward and Michael Watson (eds), *Planning, politics and public policy* (Cambridge U. Press, London, 1975).

63. At p. 13.

64. Ibid.

65. Committee to Review Functioning of Financial Institutions, *Evidence on the financing of industry,* vol. 4, p. 22.

66. Ibid., p. 23.

67. See NEB 1978 Annual Report, p. 4.

68. Ibid., p. 5.

69. NEB 1981 Annual Report, Inside Cover.

70. NEB 1978 Annual Report, pp. 9-10; *Financial Times,* 24 Jan. 1979, p. 9.

71. *Daily Mail,* 4 Oct. 1976, p. 9.

72. *Daily Mail,* 26 Feb. 1979, p. 30.

73. HC Debates, 19 July 1979, cols. 2005-07.

74. *London Times,* 19 Feb. 1980, p. 17.

75. *Guardian,* 22 Nov. 1979, p. 17.

76. *Guardian,* 24 Oct. 1979, p. 17; 10 Nov. 1979, p. 1.

77. *Guardian,* 22 Nov. 1979, p. 17.

78. *Financial Times,* 21 Nov. 1979, p. 1.

79. HC Debates, 26 Nov. 1979, cols. 976-80.

80. HC Debates, 26 Nov. 1979, col. 980.

81. HC Debates, 21 Nov. 1979, cols. 396-97.

82. NEB 1979 Annual Report, p. 3.

83. Coventry Trades Councils, *State intervention in industry,* p. 167.

84. Ibid.

85. NEB 1979 Annual Report, p. 3.

86. See Ganz, *Government and industry,* p. 51; NEB 1977 Annual Report at p. 56; 1978 Annual Report at p. 66.

87. NEB 1980 Annual Report, p. 3.

88. W. Makinson, 'The National Research Development Corporation' at p. 117, 119-21 of David Lethbridge (ed.), *Government and industry relationships* (Pergamon, Oxford, 1976).

89. Ibid., pp. 125-26.

90. NEB 1985-86 Annual Report, p. 2; NRDC 1985-86 Annual Report, p. 2.

91. NEB 1982 Annual Report, p. 4.

92. NEB 1979 Annual Report, p. 13.

93. NEB 1980 Annual Report, p. 29.

94. NEB 1981 Annual Report, p. 4.

95. NEB 1982 Annual Report, p. 5.

96. NEB 1983 Annual Report, p. 12.

97. NEB 1980 Annual Report, p. 3, 5.

98. Transcript of BBC 2 programme of 27 Jan. 1985, 'The money programme', at p. 1.

99. *London Sunday Times,* 27 Feb. 1983, p. 57.

100. Ibid.

101. *London Times,* 1 Oct. 1983, p. 11.

102. NEB 1984-85 Annual Report, p. 3.

103. NEB 1986-87 Annual Report, pp. 20-1.

104. *London Times,* 1 Oct. 1983, p. 11.

105. NEB 1984-85 Annual Report, p. 3.

106. NEB 1985-86 Annual Report, p. 12.

2
The NEB's Profit and Loss Record

The Data

Now that we have given background and history, it is time to discuss in what ways the NEB was a 'success' and in what ways it was a 'dud'. Based solely on the concept of profitability, the NEB's performance was surely far from scintillating, but neither was it always on the verge of bankruptcy.

There are, of course, several ways of measuring 'profitability'. A popular managerial finance textbook asserts that a concept known as the 'return on investment' 'is the key indicator of profitability for a firm'.[1] This is defined as:

$$\frac{\underline{Earnings\ Before\ Interest\ and\ Taxes}}{Assets^2}$$

The NEB's reports show various 'types' of profit. Thus the reports from 1976 through 1983 supply, among other things, a 'consolidated profit and loss account'. Near the top of this table is a figure called 'operating profit before interest', which includes the profits before interest of the Board and its subsidiaries. (A subsidiary of a company is a firm in which it holds more than 50% of the voting stock: British Leyland and Rolls Royce were among the NEB's subsidiaries. The NEB owned 100% of the voting stock of some of its subsidiaries.) The table then reveals the NEB's share of the profits of its 'associated companies', i.e. those in which it held 50% or less of the voting stock. (This share was determined by multiplying the associated companies' profit by the percentage of voting stock held by the NEB.) The 'operating profit before interest' is then

29

added to the 'shares of profits of associated companies'. From this sum is deducted the net interest payable by the Board and its subsidiaries. This subtraction produces a figure called 'consolidated profit before taxation', which is one of the two I shall furnish the reader for the above years. Likewise provided in the consolidated profit and loss account is a number denominated as 'return on capital employed by the NEB and its subsidiaries',[3] a concept analogous to the 'return on investment' described at the start of this paragraph. I shall indicate this result because (1) since it is analogous to the return on investment statistic, it is an important measure of profitability and (2), as we have seen, a Department of Industry Direction placed the NEB under a duty (except for its investment in British Leyland and Rolls Royce) to aim for a return (before interest and taxation) on capital employed of between 15-20% by 1981.

The figures for 1976 cannot be deemed of much significance: most of the NEB's investments were the lame ducks transferred to it by the government and one year is not really enough time to expect a new owner to do much in the way of implementing managerial and production reforms. For the record, however, the consolidated profit of the Board before taxation was £51.3 million and the return on capital employed by the NEB and its subsidiaries was 9.7%. When RR and BL are excluded from the computations, the return on capital employed decreases to 7.3%.[4]

We can look at the 1977 figures in a bit more detail. Here the consolidated profit before taxation was £34.3 million. The return on capital employed by the NEB and its subsidiaries was 7.6% but 11.4% when BL and RR are put to one side.[5] The £34.3 million was, lower down in the balance sheet, reduced by matters such as taxation and £46.5 million for 'extraordinary items', most of which were losses arising from closure by BL of certain of its operations at home and abroad.[6] Subtracting taxation and these extraordinary items means that the NEB actually had a loss of £30.7 million in 1977.

In 1978 the NEB's consolidated profit before taxation declined to £30.7 million. The return on capital employed by the NEB and its subsidiaries was 6.4% but 11.3% when BL and RR were excluded. (Even the 11.3% left much to be desired; as it showed no progress towards meeting the 1981 target of 15-20%.) After scaling down the £30.7 million profit figure by taxation and matters such as £47.3 million in 'extraordinary items' (slightly over 40% of which came from closures by BL), we find the £30.7 metamorphosed into a £41.3 million loss.[7]

In 1979 all the figures in the NEB's Report ignore BL and RR. The Board's consolidated profit before taxation was £6.5 million, which becomes a loss of £16 million after taxation and 'extraordinary items' are subtracted.[8] The biggest chunk in the 'extraordinary item' category was a bundle of £10.6 million arising from the initiation of the winding down of Herbert tool-makers. Most of the remainder of the £17 million in extraordinary items arose from the closure or disposal of other companies.[9] (The investigating arm of the House of Commons known as the Public Accounts Committee remarked that these losses upon closure should not have been deemed extraordinary items.[10]) The return on the capital employed by the NEB and its subsidiaries was only 4.8%.[11]

The consolidated profits for 1980 before taxation were actually a loss of £24.1 million.[12] The major reason for this was a big drubbing on the liquidation of once proud tool-maker Herbert. (In the 1980 Report, this deficit was labelled an 'exceptional item' and was used in determining consolidated pre-tax profit. Had it been sustained in a prior year, it would have been denominated an 'extraordinary item' and deducted only after consolidated pre-tax profit had been computed.) The Board's return on capital employed for 1980 was minus 15.3%.[13]

The 1981 Report shows a consolidated deficit before taxation of £44.1 million, over half of which was due to the disastrous performance of the Inmos and Nexos subsidiaries.[14] Beginning with this year, the Reports do not show return on capital employed by the NEB and its subsidiaries but use an analogous figure: the ratio of the NEB's own (as opposed to the consolidated) operating profit (loss) to the cost of government borrowing, i.e. to the cost to the government of providing the funds invested by the Board.[15] (The NEB's own profits (losses) are calculated by taking into account, primarily, the dividends and interest it receives, its administrative expenses, and its loss or gain on the disposal of its investments.[16]) This Board 'performance against the cost of government borrowing' was minus 30.12% in 1981.[17] For 1982 the consolidated pre-tax profit was a deficit of £14.8 million; while the NEB's performance against the cost of government borrowing was 2.16%, far short of its government-set duty of 13.40%.[18] In 1983 the consolidated accounts reveal a profit of £10.1 million before tax; but the Board's performance against the cost of government borrowing was a puny 0.18%, a far cry from the 13.20% required of it by the government for that year.[19]

The NEB Report for 1984-85 (actually the 15 months from 1 January 1984 through 31 March 1985) does not contain a consolidated account. It shows the NEB itself making a profit before taxation of £51.97 million; £34.39 million of this came from its gain on the disposal of many of its investments, especially a whopping £29.60 million profit on the sale of microchip manufacturer Inmos to Thorn-EMI. Its performance against the cost of government borrowing during that period was 19.70% against a government-imposed duty of 13.12%.[20] (Remember, the numerator used in calculating this percentage took into account the increment coming into the NEB's coffers from its sale of its holdings in Inmos and other enterprises.) In 1985-86 its profit before taxation was £5.18 million, despite a big loss on the disposal of investments. (That year's Report and the 1986-87 Report also do not reveal consolidated profit before tax.) Its performance against the cost of government borrowing was only 8.72% against an ideal of 13.24%.[21] In 1986-87, its profit before taxation was £4.64 million. Its performance against the cost of government borrowing was 12.91%: it should have been 18.96%.[22]

The Data Further Analysed

The 1984-85 figures are particularly important because they make us aware of a crucial point neglected by those critics of the NEB[23] who attacked it bitterly for being a money loser. They assumed that the NEB was to be viewed just like any other business enterprise, i.e. as one that existed merely to make a profit and which was worthless if it did not. However, apart from its job as a holding company for the lame ducks, the NEB's major role was that of *venture capitalist*. Individuals differ among themselves as to who or what a 'venture capitalist' is. I think that the most satisfactory definition is that a venture capitalist is one that invests in companies 'which are unproven in some sense'.[24] The 'senses' referred to in the definition are that the enterprise has had a poor track record in the past; that it is currently in financial difficulty though it has been in the black in previous years; that it is controlled by people in whom ordinary lenders do not have confidence; and/or that it makes a new type of product, especially one that is at the frontiers of technology. It is clear, therefore, that 'the fundamental risk to the venture capital investor is higher than that borne by the marketable securities investor'.[25] It is, accordingly, a mistake to assume that the profit record of the NEB should simply have mirrored that of the ordinary manufacturer or holding company, if in fact it is fair to call it a venture capitalist.

There is, in fact, no doubt that the NEB was a venture capitalist. Its 1975 Industry Act Sec. 2.2(c) mandate to extend 'public ownership into profitable areas of manufacturing industry' only infrequently involved its buying into an established and continually-profitable firm. Just about all the enterprises in which it acquired an interest were 'unproven in some sense'. (Of course, its acquisitions of the lame ducks and ICL from the government were not venture capital transactions since it did not voluntarily acquire them. Thus, when we refer to the NEB as a venture capitalist, we do not have in mind what it did as a shareholder in BL, RR, ICL, Alfred Herbert, etc.) Over 50% of the undertakings in which it took an equity stake were in financial straits or, though solvent, could not get loans from commercial banks. Other concerns it financed were the children of 'management buyouts', considered a few years ago in England a dubious way of starting a company. (A 'management buyout' occurs when the officers and/or workers of a division or subsidiary of a larger company purchase it from the parent in order to keep its doors open.) Most of the rest of the plants it acquired made or sold 'high technology' products. Thus various enterprises in which the NEB invested produced or marketed computer peripherals, computer software systems, submarines to repair offshore oil facilities, computer hardware, computer services, electronic photo-typesetting machines, microchips, word processors, ultrasonic medical equipment, viewdata software, computer-aided-design programs, facsimile equipment and biotechnology products.

The question that we have to answer in the rest of this chapter, then, is how does the NEB's financial record stack up against that of other venture capitalists. (In Chapters 3 and 4 I shall show that it is unfair to the NEB to put this query exactly in this way.) As an introductory matter, though, it should be noted that the activities backed by venture capitalists can provide significant benefits to society above and beyond high returns to their investors. That is, it is desirable that such activities be encouraged whether or not they provide a quick economic or accounting profit for any individuals or group of individuals. These advantages to the nation include increases in productivity and product quality, the creation of jobs, the stimulation of exports, and the growth of the tax base. These in turn, of course, make social programmes more affordable and tend to reduce inflation.[26] In other words, a venture capitalist may be a national blessing even though its balance sheet is negative.

On first glance, the NEB's record as a venture capitalist is quite poor compared to that of American venture capitalists, of whom there are hundreds. Michael Halloran mentions that in the US 'A significant number of venture capital investments have been made which produced returns to the original investors in the range of 20 to 100 times their original capital contributions over a period of years'.[27] The American venture capital firm of Kleiner and Perkins invested $200,005 in bioengineering company Genentech in 1975: on 30 June 1984 its investment was worth $47,289,150,[28] a 23,500% gain over the eight year period. (I computed the percentage gain (loss) on an investment by ascertaining the ratio of the *increase* in value of the investment, i.e. of the potential or actual profit on the investment, to the original value of the investment. Thus the 23,500% gain in Genentech was calculated by subtracting $200,005 from $47,289,150 and dividing the result by $200,005.) The same venture capital outfit invested $1,450,001 in Tandem Computers in 1976; by 30 June 1984 this investment was worth $152,204,847,[29] an increase of 10,400%. John Dizard notes in *Fortune* magazine that during recent years, the average rate of return for the US venture capitalist was somewhere between 20% and 30%.[30] Another writer claims that there is 'substantial evidence that venture investments over the long haul have generated annual rates of return [on investment] of at least 20%'.[31] A study of the performance of 110 private equity investments effected in the US over the 15 year period 1960-75 showed that the annualised rate of return on investment produced by these ventures taken as a whole was 18.9%.[32] Before figures such as these, the NEB's 11.4% rate of return on capital employed in 1977, of 11.3% in 1978, of 4.8% in 1979, and -15.3% in 1980 are not encouraging. Ditto for its 1981, 1982, 1983, 1985-86 and 1986-87 'performance against the cost of government borrowing' statistics of -30.12%, 2.16%, 0.18%, 8.72% and 12.91% respectively. (For reasons noted, all these figures exclude the performance of British Leyland and Rolls Royce. Those after 1980 are for practical purposes not affected by the results of the six other companies transferred to the NEB from the DOI. I did not have the data to calculate what the Board's rate of return on capital employed would have been for 1977 through 1980 ignoring the results of these six non-venture capital holdings (e.g., Herbert, ICL, Ferranti)).

There are respects, however, in which the NEB's record does not stack up so badly against even that of American venture capitalism, the most abundant and prolific of monetary gain in the world. First, American venture capital portfolios contain losers as well as winners. The study of the 110 firms revealed that 18 (16%) were total failures while 29 (another 26%) had a negative rate of return on investment. Twenty-eight showed an annual rate of return of between 0% and 10%, while only eleven (10%) had one of 50% or above.[33] The US General Accounting Office maintains that according to venture capitalists themselves, about 20% of the firms they nurture are successful enough to go public; 40% achieve happiness through being merged into larger outfits; 20% become profitable but continue to operate as small, privately-held firms; and 20% fail.[34] *Business Week* agrees that the last-noted 20% figure is accurate; and adds that only a few venture investments are as dramatically crowned with glory as a Xerox, Intel or Apple.[35] Wilson summarises the portfolio of Kleiner and Perkins, the backers, as seen, of the Genentech and Tandem bonanzas. Of the 17 concerns in that group of holdings four were totally worthless on 30 June 1984 while three others were less valuable on that date than in the year when the initial investment was made. In other words, 24% of the speculations of this well-known venture capital institution were complete failures while another 18% were money-losers.[36]

To continue, between 1976 and 1984-85, inclusive, the NEB made about 150 investments, excluding the eight firms transferred to it by the government in 1976. Of these 150 companies, 37 have as of my writing this gone into bankruptcy or receivership or were sold at a considerable loss. Thirty-seven divided by 150 is 25%, not that far from the figures for utter failures provided by the American studies summarised above. And it must be remembered that the English venture capitalist is stepping into an economy essentially weaker than the American and, furthermore, that the NEB was placing a good proportion of its pounds in the most economically distressed areas of the nation. Also, the NEB faced extraordinary obstacles, which will be recounted in the next chapters.

Moreover, there was a respectable number of NEB stock purchases that ballooned in value from the time they were made to the time that they were disposed of. Thus the 1978 £930,000 investment in Computer and Systems Engineering (CASE) was marketed in 1980 at a profit of £1,220,000,[37] which meant that its worth had been enlarged by 131% (£1,220,000 divided by £930,000) while it had the status of an NEB associated company. The 1977 investment of £550,000 in Computer Analysts and Programmers (CAP Group)[38] was sold in 1984 at a gain of £3,900,000,[39] which meant that its value while under NEB auspices had swollen by 709%. The hiving off of Reed and Smith in 1977 realised a £760,000 increment on a 1976 investment of £790,000, for a growth in value of 96%.[40] Systems Designers, acquired in 1978 for £180,000, was transferred to a buyer at a £1,000,000 profit in 1981,[41] evidencing a gain in worth of 550%. Shares in Automation and Technical Services (ATS), obtained in 1978 for £150,000, were sold in 1981 at a profit of £750,000,[42] for an increase in value of 500%. United Medical Enterprises, which cost £5,770,000 in 1978, was disposed of in 1983 for a profit of £10,720,000,[43] an increase in value of 186%. That in Twinlock, bought in 1979 for £1,000,000, was vended in 1983 for a £2,820,000 million gain,[44] i.e. an expansion of value of 282%. Shares in Focom Systems, obtained in 1983 for £120,000, were unloaded in 1984 for a £680,000 profit, manifesting a rise in worth of 567%.[45] Finally, a 1984 marketing of shares in Britton-Lee costing the NEB £550,000 in 1982 netted the agency a profit of £840,000,[46] an increase in value of 152%.

When the percentage increases in value of these NEB shareholdings are converted into average percentage increases per year, some of the results look even more impressive. The data are summarised in the following table.

Firm	Average % increase in value per year under NEB auspices (total percentage increase in value divided by number of years under NEB auspices)
CASE	65.5%
CAP Group	101%
Reed and Smith	96%
Systems Designers	183%
ATS	167%
Twinlock	70.5%
Focom	567%
Britton Lee	76%

Thus eight (i.e. 5.3%) of the approximately 150 NEB venture capital investments showed a whopping average increase in value per year of more than 50%.

None the less, these genuinely arresting figures must not lead us to wax *too* enthusiastic about the financial success of the NEB's venture capital endeavours. A higher minority (35%) of the firms in the Kleiner and Perkins portfolio mentioned earlier had a 50% or greater average growth in value per year.[47] Moreover, for the years 1977 through 1985-86, the Board's profits on the disposal (i.e. sale or liquidation) of its holdings were as follows.

Year	Profit on Disposal
1977	£920,000[48]
1978	£300,000[49]
1979	-£13,369,000[50]
1980	£4,420,000[51]

1981	-£45,360,000[52]
1982	-£1,680,000[53]
1983	£1,130,000[54]
1984-85	£34,390,000[55]
1985-86	-£12,520,000[56]
1986-87	£6,260,000[57]

The net loss on disposal is thus £25,509,000. However, this figure must be altered by removing from it the losses of £700,000 on Brown-Boveri-Kent, £12,050,000 on Cambridge Instrument Company and (1979 and 1980 total) £57,170,000 on Alfred Herbert -- and also the gains of £24,210,000 on ICL, £160,000 on Dunford and Elliott and £48,230,000 on Ferranti. These modifications give us a net reverse of £28,189,000, a rather dismal tally. (The changes are necessary because we are assessing the record of the NEB as a venture capitalist and the above investments were given to the Board by the government when it was set up.)

However, the analysis of the above paragraph needs to be carried further. The £28,189,000 net deficit includes £34 million in red ink from the disposal of Nexos, the outfit founded to sell the integrated automatic office; and about £7 million in decrement from the winding down of Insac, the firm set up to market British software abroad. (As we shall see in Chapter 10, the Nexos deficit eventually shrank to £24,500,000.) When the setbacks from these two very avoidable disasters -- to be discussed in detail in later chapters, a treatment that shall attempt to demonstrate that these debacles were far from inevitable -- are deducted from the NEB's total venture capital losses, the profit from the NEB's marketing of its venture capital investments becomes about +£12.8 million. The total spent by the Board on its investments of this nature (excluding Insac and Nexos) was approximately £232,810,000. Thus the gain through 1986-87 from the sale of these venture capital investments (again excluding Insac and Nexos) was about 5.5% of the purchase price of these investments. This is not a figure to cheer about; but at the same time it provides no reason to shed torrents of tears.

The NEB Versus Other UK Venture Capitalists

To sum, the NEB's profit record as venture capitalist was in some respects not that weak even when compared to that of American venture capitalists, especially in the sense that it had about the same proportion of real triumphs and dismal failures as did the average US venture capital fund. It is also instructive to set its results alongside those of other venture capitalists operating in the relatively weak UK economy. A company called Investors In Industry (which henceforth will often be referred to as 3i) and formerly known as Finance For Industry (which from now on will often be abbreviated FFI) is frequently pointed to by the advocates of untrammeled private enterprise as the shining example of a UK privately-operated venture capital institution. This company is owned by the Bank of England (itself government-owned, of course, a fact conveniently forgotten by the advocates of *laissez-faire*) and by the major British banks. FFI itself was the issue of a merger of the Industrial and Commercial Finance Corporation (henceforth usually ICFC) and the Finance Corporation for Industry (FCI). Both of these, in turn, were established by the government (another datum that has slipped the mind of the free-marketeers) at the end of World War II, the first to lend to and invest in small and medium-sized companies and the latter to shore up troubled middle-sized and large enterprises.[58] (Despite the merger, ICFC retained its separate identity, becoming a distinct unit of FFI.)

In recent years, it is true, 3i and its predecessor FFI have been in the black. For example, its profits before taxes were £38,500,000 in 1984-85,[59] £38 million in 1983-84,[60] £22,900,000 in 1982-83,[61] and £28,200,000 in 1981-82.[62] However, the NEB was more of a venture capitalist than 3i and its predecessors in the sense of being more willing to invest in companies that in some sense were risks. It is true that about 70% of 3i's new investment occurs in the small business sector.[63] Nevertheless, as will be seen, several of the NEB-aided companies I interviewed said that FFI would not help them at all or would do so only on onerous terms or if the NEB acted as a partner in the investment as well. (Sometimes my interviewees referred to the ICFC unit of FFI rather than to FFI as a whole.) Moreover, despite the overall economic success of 3i, it admits that there is a 'substantial failure rate' among the small concerns that it does fund.[64]

Another private UK venture capitalist is Equity Capital for Industry (from now on, usually ECI), created in 1976 by insurance companies, pension funds, and FFI to raise equity capital for undertakings that could not do so on the market.[65] By May 1981, five years after its founding, it had supported 13 firms, far fewer than the NEB at a comparable stage in its history. Two of these, or 15%, had gone out of business already. By 1983 it had decided to place less than half of its funds in troubled companies.[66] Of 20 venture capital investments ECI made in the three year period ending March 1984, about half have done well but one has failed and eight show 'mixed' results.[67] These figures cannot be said to be significantly more impressive than those racked up by the NEB. Moreover, ECI still operates on a much smaller scale than did the Board before the Government ordered it to stop making new investments. By 1985, eight years after its founding, ECI had invested £48,200,000 in 80 separate businesses.[68] On the other hand, during the period 1976-1984/85 inclusive, the Board, as seen, made about 150 venture capital investments -- and (including Insac and Nexos) spent about £277,000,000 in doing so. Finally Prutec, a company set up in 1980 by the large Prudential Assurance company to finance high technology ventures in the UK, was wound down in the summer of 1985. All but one of its 20 investments were still losing money then; and one of the largest of its gambles was bankrupt.[69] If the government-backed NEB had had such a disastrous average, the beams of Parliament would still be tottering from the roars of angry Tories.

NOTES

1. John Hampton, *Financial decision making: concepts, problems & cases* (Reston Publishing Co., Reston, 1976), p. 102.

2. Ibid.

3. Defined at NEB 1977 Annual Report, p. 37. In its numerator, this figure takes into account the income of the NEB from interest and dividends; the profits of its subsidiaries; and its share of the profits of its associated companies. See also ibid., p. 24.

4. NEB 1977 Annual Report, p. 24.

5. Ibid.

6. Ibid., p. 24, 37.

7. NEB 1978 Annual Report, p. 32.

8. NEB 1979 Annual Report, p. 22.

9. Ibid., p. 38.

10. HC Committee of Public Accounts, *Reports 1979-80, No. 30: Department of Industry, National Enterprise Board, etc.* (HMSO, London, 1980), p. vii.

11. NEB 1980 Annual Report, p. 18.

12. Ibid.

13. Ibid.

14. NEB 1981 Annual Report, p. 27 and 30-1.

15. NEB 1981 Annual Report, p. 25, 58.

16. See ibid., p. 18.

17. Ibid., p. 25.

18. NEB 1982 Annual Report, p. 27, 5.

19. NEB 1983 Annual Report, p. 17, 15.

20. NEB 1984-85 Annual Report, p. 6, 12, 27.

21. NEB 1985-86 Annual Report, p. 8, 29.

22. NEB 1986-87 Annual Report, p. 10, 23.

23. See, e.g., Redwood, *Going for broke...*, p. 72.

24. Michael Halloran, *Venture capital and public offering negotiation* (Harcourt Brace Jovanovich, New York, 1983), p. 138.

25. Ibid., p. 140.

26. US General Accounting Office, *Government-industry cooperation can enhance the venture capital process* (US General Accounting Office, Washington, 1982), pp. 6-10.

27. *Venture capital*, p. 139.

28. John Wilson, *The new venturers* (Addison-Wesley, Reading, Mass., 1985), p. 70.

29. Ibid.

30. 'Do we have too many venture capitalists?', 4 Oct. 1982, p. 106.

31. Wilson, *The new venturers*, p. 25.

32. Blaine Huntsman and James Hoban, 'Investment in new enterprise: some empirical observations on risk return and market structure', *Financial Management*, Summer 1980, p. 44, 46. The annualised rate of return is computed by multiplying the monthly rate of return by twelve or by dividing the rate of return over X number of years by X.

33. Ibid., p. 47.

34. *Government-industry cooperation,* p. 2 of letter of submission.

35. 16 Ap. 1983, p. 78, 80.

36. *The new venturers,* pp. 70-1.

37. See NEB 1980 Annual Report, p. 5.

38. NEB 1977 Annual Report, pp. 40-1.

39. NEB 1984-85 Annual Report, p. 12.

40. NEB 1977 Annual Report, p. 27, 40-1.

41. NEB 1978 Annual Report, pp. 50-1; 1981 Annual Report, p. 22.

42. NEB 1978 Annual Report, pp. 48-9; 1981 Annual Report, p. 22.

43. NEB 1978 Annual Report, pp. 46-7; 1983 Annual Report, p. 12.

44. NEB 1979 Annual Report, pp. 52-3; 1983 Annual Report, p. 12.

45. NEB 1983 Annual Report, pp. 30-1; 1984-85 Annual Report, p. 12.

46. NEB 1984-85 Annual Report, p. 12, 22-3. See also 1982 Annual Report, pp. 44-5.

47. See Wilson, *The new venturers,* pp. 70-1.

48. NEB 1977 Annual Report, p. 27.

49. NEB 1978 Annual Report, p. 35.

50. NEB 1979 Annual Report, p. 25.

51. NEB 1980 Annual Report, p. 29.

52. NEB 1981 Annual Report, p. 22.

53. NEB 1982 Annual Report, p. 22.

54. NEB 1983 Annual Report, p. 12.

55. NEB 1984-85 Annual Report, p. 12.

56. NEB 1985-86 Annual Report, p. 8.

57. NEB 1986-87 Annual Report, p. 8.

58. Committee to Review the Functioning of Financial Institutions, *Evidence on the financing of industry and trade* (HMSO, London, 1977), vol. 1, p. 10; *Economist,* 9 Mar. 1985, p. 85.

59. Investors in Industry Group 1985 Annual Report (Investors in Industry Group, London), p. 4.

60. Investors in Industry Group 1984 Annual Report (Investors in Industry Group, London), p. 6.

61. Ibid.

62. Finance for Industry plc 1981/82 Annual Report (Finance for Industry, London), p. 10.

63. Jon Foulds, *We are searching for hidden entrepreneurs* (Investors in Industry Group, London, 1985), p. 2. Mr Foulds is Chief Executive of 3i.

64. Investors in Industry Group 1985 Annual Report, p. 6.

65. Committee to Review the Functioning of Financial Institutions, *Evidence on financing of industry,* vol. 1, p. 10.

66. See *London Times,* 24 May 1980, p. 19; 21 June 1983, p. 13; *London Sunday Times,* 14 June 1981, p. 54.

67. ECI 1985 Annual Report (Equity Capital for Industry, London), p. 8.

68. Ibid., p. 6.

69. *Economist,* 13 July 1985, pp. 78-9.

3
Obstacles Faced by NEB Not Confronting Private Venture Capitalists

The NEB Sells at Bargain Prices

The NEB faced hurdles that did not stand in the way of private venture capitalists, hurdles that will be depicted in this chapter and the next. Some of these may well have contributed to its demise; some caused its consolidated profit before taxation, return on capital employed and/or profit on disposal of holdings figures to significantly understate its financial achievements both generally and as a venture capitalist.

Clearly falling into the latter category of obstacle were a number of factors that sometimes prevented it from vending its shares at the highest possible price. To put this in another way, it at various times had to take political as opposed to balance-sheet considerations into account when contemplating whether and/or to whom to sell its stock. For example, when the Conservatives came to power in May 1979, they ordered the NEB to rid itself of £100 million of its assets by the end of March 1980.[1] Though, as mentioned, this deadline was relaxed in 1980,[2] the Tories kept pushing it to empty a good portion of its portfolio. Thus Guidelines issued on 1 August 1980 by Secretary of State Sir Keith Joseph commanded (No. 8) that the Board 'shall exercise their powers with a view to disposing to private ownership, as soon as commercially practicable, all of their securities and other property and their subsidiaries' securities and other property'. The carrot accompanying this stick was that 'The Board will be allowed to retain and invest some part of the receipts from the sale of certain investments, to be determined by the Secretary of State from time to time'. Thus during late 1979, 1980 and 1981 the Board was under strong pressure to wave goodbye to its holdings quickly -- by the end of March 1981, 13 had been privatised.[3] Obviously, when an institution is under compulsion to sell, there is a very real danger that it will jump at the first halfway decent offer and not withhold what it is merchandising in the hope of hearing a better bid from someone else. And some of the men at one time or another connected with the NEB whom I interviewed confirmed that it did not get as good a price for some of its venture capital and other holdings as it could have received had it been able to wait a little while longer to clean out its larder. Though it is impossible to put an exact figure on how much more the NEB could have recovered had Joseph not demanded that it proceed swiftly in divesting itself of its equity stakes, it is clear that this sum is in the millions or tens of millions of pounds. A former NEB official told me, for example, that because the Thatcher Administration was demanding that the NEB privatise in a hurry, the receiver in bankruptcy unloaded a segment of machine tool manufacturer Alfred Herbert for £1 million that could have gone for £4 million. Another one of my respondents mentioned that the Board sold the high tech firm we shall call Olga very cheaply. And an investor in a high tech company in the North set up with NEB assistance in the early 1980s purchased the Board's equity at a price that gave it a 25% profit but very shortly resold the shares to other private parties for many times what he received from the NEB.

There were other political grounds besides the Tories' fixation with the rapid divestiture of the NEB's assets that forced it to wash its hands of its stocks at less than the maximum possible figure. One purpose for the creation of the Board, as will be remembered, was job preservation. Ergo where a possible NEB disposal at a high sum would have threatened the closing of the transferred undertaking and thus a reduction in employment, the Board naturally had to think twice about the transaction. Even the Tory Government would not have been too happy with such a sale, for the high UK unemployment rate is the Conservatives' Achilles heel and Tory as well as Labour backbenchers have constituents who would have been forced on to the dole if a firm that left Board control had been wound up soon afterward. Accordingly, the NEB decided not to deed its interest in a subsidiary that makes a technically excellent motor to a party that was willing to pay top value because it feared that the purchaser might shut the concern's doors. Though the factory is located in a constituency represented by a Labour MP, all the surrounding communities are Tory and some of the plant personnel reside in these rural areas. The business was finally sold in 1984 at a loss of two million pounds.

This fear-of-creating-unemployment factor operated to depress the amount at which one successful ex-lame duck was privatised. A considerable portion of Ferranti's operations is located in Scotland, a region of high joblessness. Scottish MPs were terrified that the sale of this group to a competitor would lead to the winding down of the Ferranti plants in Scotland. So they plus the Secretary of State for Scotland lobbied the Thatcher Government to ensure that the NEB's Ferranti holdings were marketed on conditions that would make it highly unlikely that these Scots operations would be phased out. Accordingly, 300 individuals and institutions, as opposed to just one firm, bought these shares. Moreover, each of the new shareholders agreed to hold on to his/her/its stock for at least two years. As a consequence, as the NEB 1980 Annual Report admits, the price received by the Board was less than could have been obtained on the open market.[4] A former NEB staff member told me that that sum (almost £7 million) was about 15% below market price.

Also, the Board was founded, *inter alia,* to increase the strength of the economy of the *United Kingdom*. Thus requests to purchase a company it owned that came from a foreign source were bound to be viewed with suspicion, even though the suggested price was right. For example, many American companies wanted to buy one of the most successful NEB ventures, a concern (that we shall call Zelda) that marketed British technical and management skills in the Third World. The Board turned down these bids and disposed of its interest to a British concern. It did make a good profit on this divestment; but, according to one ex-NEB official I spoke to, quite possibly not as much as it would have had it transferred its shares to a transatlantic buyer. The sales price was, in fact, about £8 million less than the press had estimated that the government would get for it. (On one occasion, the Board did work hard to jack up the price it received for one of its properties. The staff of a dynamic, successful high technology concern located in the London area made an offer to the NEB to buy its holdings in the company. The NEB first accepted this bid but then received a higher tender for these shares from the now-privatised Ferranti. The Board then announced that, despite the previous understanding, it intended to transfer this stock to its former lame duck subsidiary. Despite the high technology firm's lobbying with important figures in the Tory Party and its bringing of a lawsuit, the staff had to increase its offer. After this rise, the NEB let them buy the shares for the higher price.)

The NEB and the Press

Other obstacles above and beyond pressures to sell at less than the best price that faced the NEB, but do not confront private venture capital firms, were vitriolic press and parliamentary criticism. Let us turn first to the Fourth Estate. It could not, of course, be expected that press reaction to the NEB would be uniform in a free country such as the United Kingdom, given the different political orientations of the nation's newspaper proprietors and the different social classes to which they appeal. On the whole, with some exceptions we shall note in this chapter, the quality press (i.e. *The Times*, the *Telegraph*, the *Guardian*, the *Financial Times*, *The Sunday Times*, the *Sunday Observer*, and the *Sunday Telegraph*) was objective in its coverage of the Board. For example, the NEB agreed to finance a management buyout of a small division of a large US corporation. The new company, known as Powerdrive PSR, is located in the midlands town of Leamington Spa and makes air-operated clutches and brakes for packaging, metalworking, textile and other machines. *The Times*, the *Financial Times*, the *Telegraph* and the *Guardian* for 11 September 1978 all have columns describing how much the NEB was investing, what type of shares it was taking, and mentioning the company (Eaton, of Cleveland, Ohio) that was selling out to the division's management.[5] The *Telegraph*, *Guardian* and *Financial Times* noted that the unit had been consistently profitable: a paragraph in the latter is headed 'No "lame duck"'. *The Times* and the *Guardian* mention that the reason Eaton is selling is that the Leamington plant is considered too small to fit in with its corporate plan. They add that Powerdrive hopes to concentrate on the export market.

The next day, 12 September, the *Financial Times* continued describing the deal in a manner that meets the canons of impartial journalism.[6] It stated that the three managers of the Leamington branch could come up with only £30,000 of the asking price of £400,000 but were insistent that they maintain control of the new corporation. They visited the major clearing banks, the merchant banks, and the pension funds: all refused to go along with an arrangement under which the directors would retain a controlling shareholding at a price they could afford. Mr. John Pigott, the eventual Managing Director, singled out private venture capitalist Industrial and Commercial Finance Corporation (ICFC) as the object of his scorn, saying that it was 'completely negative' and that it was hard even to establish contact with it. Pigott is reported criticising the City as 'hidebound by standard rules of business' and asserting that it thought he must be joking when he said that he wanted to retain control. He is then mentioned as turning to the NEB a bit reluctantly but finding its executives 'exceptionally professional' and going to work 'in double quick time'. They eventually developed a plan that he liked. This gave him and his two colleagues a majority of voting shares but the NEB subscribed to £250,000 in preference shares.

On 18 September 1978, the same newspaper pointed out that ICFC had financed 23 management buyouts of small firms, in most of which instances it ended up with less than half the equity of the concern.[7] There is, of course, nothing unjust in reporting accurately the activities of this NEB 'competitor'. But on 12 September it had published an editorial about the NEB's assistance to Powerdrive which was somewhat unfair to the Board.[8] It admitted that some City institutions are not as flexible as they ought to be and that this rescue attempt should stimulate the private sector to improve the marketing and flexibility of its own financial facilities. However, the editorial grumbled that 'Whether the NEB should be in this business [of financing companies that would have preferred to use the private sector] at all is another matter'. It continued that the NEB arguably should steer undertakings like Powerdrive to private sector institutions when they are faced with problems with which the latter can deal, but that this was unlikely to happen as long as the Labour Government was in office. This shaft ignores the fact that Powerdrive had tried private enterprise, found it wanting, and thus for practical purposes was placed in a dilemma that the City could not solve. What use would it have been for the NEB to recommend that Powerdrive contact a private financier when the institutions of this type had already turned it down!!!! The editorial is fascinating, though what it says makes little sense, because it reveals the irrational mindset of the current British right, even its more educated members, to government intervention in the economy.

An extreme anti-statist prejudice is even more evident in the columns devoted to the NEB by the *Daily Mail* and *Daily Express*, both organs of the far Tory right. During the first few years of the Board's existence, they waged an acerbic campaign against it. For example, page 1 of the *Mail* for 14 January 1976 shouts in headlines that NEB's first Chairman Sir Donald Ryder was involved in a £7 million land deal that was the subject of a report to the Director of Public Prosecutions: one has to look to the body of the article to find that he did not benefit personally from the transaction. A page 1 column on the same affair in the *Mail* for 23 March 1976 claims that because of new developments, Ryder's future is in jeopardy. Once again, it is only later in the story that one finds an admission that Sir Donald was not involved in anything illegal. By way of contrast, *The Times* ran a page 2 article on the land deal in its March 24 issue and a page 1 item on this matter in its March 29 edition. Neither headline mentioned Ryder: his name did not crop up until fairly far down in the stories.

Shortly after Rolls Royce was presented to the NEB by the government, Sir Kenneth Keith, its Chairman, and Ryder began squabbling about the extent to which the Board should control RR. The *Mail's* journalism depicted the former as a hero and the latter as a villain. On page 25 of its issue of 5 February 1976 it said that Ryder was trying to bring the NEB subsidiaries 'to heel' and that the agency was accountable to no one. The paper added that Ryder thought he could run things better than anyone else and worried that Keith and the other RR directors would be downgraded to a committee of management. On page 9 of its 10 February 1976 issue it referred to a bitter talk between Ryder and Keith on the subject of the RR-NEB clash. It claimed that Ryder made it plain that RR should form an integral part of his empire. On page 24 of its 17 September 1976 edition it mentions one Major Webb, who though an owner of 10% of Twinlock was being ousted from its board because he opposed the NEB purchase of a stake in the firm. A page 6 column of 17 March 1977 refers to Ryder as the Chairman of the 'seriously misnamed' National Enterprise Board and laments that he is doling out millions to British Leyland without insisting that its excessive labor force be slimmed.

On 19 May 1977 the *Mail* really went to work on him. A page 1 headline and story screamed that BL with his approval was bribing automobile distributors in foreign countries and defrauding the governments of these lands in order to get orders for BL cars. The article referred to a Ryder letter to a BL official that made incriminating statements. Two days later, the *Mail* shamefacedly admitted that that piece of correspondence (which it paid £15,000 to acquire) was a forgery sold to it by a BL executive and apologised to Sir Donald. The Editor offered to resign because of the incident but the owners did not accept this overture. Ultimately the forger went to jail[9] and the NEB chief recovered a libel judgement against the paper; but the affair was one that caused him considerable heartache.[10]

Undaunted by the forgery episode, the *Mail* fired again at Ryder on page 2 of its 12 July 1977 issue in a story headlined 'Lord Ryder repays "gratuity" of £49,500'. On page 1 of its 26 July 1977 edition it had a bold headline saying 'How That £49,000 Went To Ryder'. One who read these headlines might well have assumed that the accompanying articles would reveal that, e.g., the NEB Chairman had been given a packet of pounds by someone connected with organised crime. However, the stories contained the bland disclosure that he believed that it was a gift from a Canadian company for past services, a company that had engaged in a joint venture with the Canadian subsidiary of Reed International, the undertaking with which he had been connected before joining the NEB. The July 26 issue admitted that he returned it as soon as he realised that it was not such a gift. Purchasers who had hoped to be titillated with a juicy scandal must certainly have been disappointed.

The NEB's plans to aid Inmos, the British microchip company, were greeted with derision in a *Mail* article of 9 September 1978 on page 33. The story was inserted under a headline saying 'NEB as big as Texas'. The writer claimed that the entire world need for 64K microchips could be met by a workforce of 10,000 and that Inmos would cost the taxpayer £50 million. Inmos, he mentions, intends to employ 4000 persons. However, if it does so its plant will be extremely inefficient: if it is well-run it will not hire this many. He concludes with a wish that our money were not being bandied about so freely by the NEB.

The *Daily Express* was no more lenient toward the NEB, at least during the initial stages of that body's existence. Its 15 January 1976 issue mentions on page 1 the land deal in which Ryder was involved. The article notes that he was director of a company that made a gain of £3.7 million when it sold 302 acres of land to a local authority for building houses. The company had purchased it a few months earlier for £3.3 million and received £7 million from the authority. An article of 7 October 1976 asserts at page 10 that

'With a staggering contempt for Parliament and the taxpayer the government is quietly pressing ahead with plans to spend hundreds of millions waging Labour's war on private industry. And countless millions more are to be pumped into the corpses of those companies that have already succumbed to state control. The instrument of this policy is the ill-named National Enterprise Board...'

BL was specified as the best example of a hopeless company into which the NEB was about to toss money. A story of 2 December 1977 at page 31 was headlined 'Lack of Enterprise in NEB Targets'. The column began with a lament that 'The expectations of the National Enterprise Board, outlined to Parliament yesterday, should not strain the talents of Leslie Murphy, a former chairman of Merchant Bankers Schroder Wagg'. The writer complained that the NEB's target rate of a 15-20% return, before interest and taxes, on capital employed was too low. He thought that the Board should strive for 30% by 1981. He grudgingly admitted that the Board did not have the same breadth of choice that a private entrepeneur had when deciding where to invest, since the poor and the needy were its clients.

The same paper continued slugging on 13 January 1978 at page 10. The headline read 'Let's destroy this monster before it destroys us'. The 'monster' was, of course, the Board. The article grouched:

'What a strange bureaucratic monster we have in the National Enterprise Board. This body, a creature of the Labour Government, has many different roles assigned to it...Its purposes are self-contradictory, for on the one hand profitability is the criterion and on the other the creation or maintenance of employment.'

The writer asks why and how a bureaucratic body not answerable to any shareholders and with state funds at its disposal should secure more efficient management. He continues by blasting the Board for outbidding a private company in the acquisition of the Fairey group and for setting up its Northeastern Regional Board, a body that duplicated other organisations already in existence and which was responsible to London, not to the people of the region. The Board acquires but hardly ever sells. Therefore it will

'inevitably grow more and more gargantuan, swallowing up companies for the sake of its appetite, getting fatter and fatter, and almost inevitably less and less efficient, and less and less able to oversee the companies it owns or controls. The only thing to be done with a monster such as this...is to kill it.'

It is a tool for 'reducing the private sector bite by monstrous bite'.

Later that year it took another jab at the NEB with a story receiving the headline 'My Share'. The body of the article notes that the daughter of Lord Ryder was fined £40 for fare dodging; and naturally refuses to omit the fact that Ryder was the former Board Chairman.[11] And a couple of months before the fall of the Labour Government in 1979 the *Express* ran a story headlined 'Jim's [Callaghan's] Lavish Legacy'. It complained about the Government's raising the money available for the NEB from £1000 million to a possible £4500 million. The Board, it moaned, will be able to spend the extra £3500 million without anyone's by-your-leave and without Parliament's being able to scrutinise the expenditure. The agency, the paper admitted, had not even asked for this much -- the 'greedy young brat' has not even 'hollered for' this 'magnificent endowment', which will enable it to 'keep British Leyland in the style to which it has become accustomed'.[12]

To be fair, not every article in the *Express* or the *Mail* that mentioned the NEB panned it. On one occasion the former admitted that the rescue of Ferranti (which had become profitable under the auspices of the NEB) was a successful example of government support of private enterprise. Referring to the fact that the NEB was selling off enough shares to reduce its holding from 62% to 50%, it suggested that the Board auction off even more of its equity in this group.[13] The *Mail* confessed that Ferranti was the Board's biggest success;[14] and a 14 December 1978 story in the same journal[15] was entitled 'Systime [a high tech company] Thrive on NEB Cash'. Both *Mail* and *Express* had some columns reporting without comments various steps taken by the Board.[16]

Though its coverage of the NEB was much more objective and comprehensive than that of the *Mail* and the *Express,* even the 'quality' *Daily Telegraph* on occasion lashed out nastily against it. (We have already provided a similar example from the pages of the *Financial Times.*) In its issue of 13 July 1977 at page 19 and of 18 July 1977 at page 3 it implied that there was something improper about the payment of £49,500 from a Canadian company to Ryder, a sum that, it will be remembered, had also exercised the *Mail*. Neither story adduced the slightest evidence to show that his receipt of this money was wrongful: they just hinted that it was. Thus the July 13 column was headlined 'Questions for Lord Ryder to answer' and the July 18 issue declared that the payment was made by a 'circuitous route'.[17] A story noting the purchase of a company making spark erosion machines to remove metal by electrical discharges was introduced by the headline 'NEB Buys a Minnow'.[18] It was especially scathing when the Board opted to support microchip fabricator Inmos. An article on this topic on 31 July 1979 at page 14 was headlined 'ITT Has Two Year Lead on NEB Chips Plan'. It claimed that a UK subsidiary of the US multinational would distribute samples of 64K memory modules on single silicon chips in a few weeks and be in full production in a year, while Inmos would take 24 months to reach the manufacturing stage from the time it got going. And on 7 November 1978[19] another story on the fledgling microchip outfit was headed 'Inmos Will Fail Says Fairchild Chairman'. The *Telegraph* quoted him as contending that Inmos could not survive because it was entering the integrated circuit market too late.

The point of the above discussion of the relationship between the press and the NEB is not that Fleet Street had no right to lambaste it as it did. On the contrary, in a democracy such as the United Kingdom it is not only the right but the duty of the journalistic profession to investigate the doings of government agencies and give the public information about where they are falling down. Certainly some albeit not all of the barbs in the stories about the Board appearing in the papers we have cited hit the mark. Nor am I contending that the acid in some of the stories about the NEB that appeared in the *Express, Mail* and even the *Telegraph* should have been watered down. If a newspaper believes that a public institution is fundamentally useless and even detrimental to the economy, which was doubtlessly the view of the editors of these three sheets, it is their right to attack it bitterly. If these acerbic criticisms are sometimes or frequently unfair, let it be: this is a small price to pay for the benefits of a free press. (The libel laws can take care of the excesses: witness Ryder's judgment against the *Mail* when it falsely charged him with approving BL bribes.) The point I am emphasising, rather, is that while the UK press did not focus the glare of adverse publicity on UK venture capitalists (e.g. ICFC, ECI) in the private sector, it certainly did so (sometimes quite justly, sometimes in an unsportsmanlike manner) with respect to the Board. In other words, several of the nation's newspapers presented an obstacle to the NEB that its counterparts in the private sector did not have to hurdle.

The NEB and the Tory Right

There were certain MPs on the right wing of the Tory Party who were thorns in the flesh to the NEB -- another problem that private venture capitalists did not have to concern themselves about. We have already seen some members of that Party suffering from an apoplectic fit as the Industry Bill of 1975 was moving through Parliament. On various occasions during the remainder of the Labour Government's tenure the NEB came up for discussion in Parliament and favourable Tory remarks about it were hardly ever heard. (All the following comments came from Conservatives.) Thus on 18 March 1976 Michael Marshall complains in debate that the NEB's activities are being foisted on the House without proper scrutiny. Rolls Royce has been in a mess, he avers, since the NEB became its guardian. No thought has been given to the question of how relations between RR, the government and the NEB are to be managed; and the NEB has so much money that it can build empires. Michael Grylls, a determined and pertinacious opponent of the NEB, complains that it has leased a fancy office in a high rent area and has accumulated an unnecessarily large staff. It may, he worries, act as an unfair competitor using the taxpayer's money: he laments that a British Leyland subsidiary is giving huge and unnecessary discounts on its forklifts.[20] On 2 August 1976 he tells Secretary of State for Industry Eric Varley that it is stupid to take money from industry by taxation and then give that money to the Board.[21]

On 21 January 1977 the House of Commons held a debate about the Board and the Guidelines issued to it by the Secretary of State for Industry. Anthony Nelson leading off for the Tories suspected that this agency would fall far short of its goal of reviving British industry. State control of the economy, threatened by the NEB's activities, could well promote inefficiency and nip new ideas in the bud.[22] Norman Lamont worried that the NEB would pressure some of its subsidiaries to trade with other undertakings with which it was connected and added that it was spread too thin: how could 50 persons have responsibility for so many sectors of industry (e.g., aerospace, miniature television sets, advanced scientific instruments). Also, if businesses are not bailed out by the government the resources freed will be used by the private sector to engender new firms and more jobs.[23]

On 10 April 1978 the House held a debate on the Government's plan to raise the Board's financial limits from £700 million to £1000 million. Grylls groaned that

'I think that if a body such as the NEB asks for an extra £300 million borrowing limit, we in the House of Commons are entitled to look with a rather cool eye at what the Board has been doing over the last few years. It is not a cheap Board, with half a dozen people, a man and a dog and a girl secretary. It is a rather extravagant organisation. It has cost £1.7 million this year simply to run and administer. It has pleasant offices in Grosvenor Gardens. They are all beautifully done up.'[24]

There is no real gap in the investment scene, he continued. There are a lot of financial institutions like the banks and FFI that have plenty of money for ventures that are likely to go well.[25] Timothy Renton, another consistent opponent of the Board, noted that it had in recent months gone into tanning, electronics, engineering, medical equipment, hydraulic tube and pipe bending -- and also outbid another company for Fairey Engineering. 'It appears to be setting itself up...as a conglomerate without any industrial logic behind it whatsoever.'[26] Sir Keith Joseph averred that there were already a bundle of agencies according funds to business: we do not need the NEB to do this and punt with the taxpayer's money.[27]

Even after the Tories won in 1979, the hatred of most of the Tory right for the NEB remained undiminished. Sir Keith, Mrs Thatcher's first Secretary of State for Industry, had, as just seen, said uncomplimentary things about the Board while he was in opposition. However, his first speech as Minister about the NEB's future was a rather moderate one. As will be remembered, though he ordered it to dispose of £100 million of investments during the current fiscal year, he envisaged it as continuing to look after the lame ducks as long as they had some prospect of viability and no private sector purchaser was on the horizon; as investing in high technology companies; and as supporting small firms, especially in the industrially-depressed North and Northwest.[28] Grylls commented that he welcomed the Secretary's statement as cutting the spendthrift agency down to size. He asserted that the Secretary should think again about his willingness to support microchip manufacturer Inmos: few people in the electronics industry think it will succeed and there is already plenty of activity in the microprocessor industry through other UK firms.[29] Peter

Hordern remarked that while Sir Keith may believe that the market is not particularly familiar with high technology, 'some of us feel that the NEB could be rather more familiar with high technology...'[30] Antony Marlow asked whether Sir Keith was 'aware that the British electorate will be delighted that this antediluvian engine of back-door nationalisation is about to be cut down to size...'[31]

As will be seen, there were Tories as well as Labourites who, whatever their rhetoric about the glories of pure free enterprise, would have been very happy to see the NEB nourish a project in their own constituencies. To give them credit for consistency, some of the members of the Tory right for whom the Board was a favourite target did not have this reaction. One of the agency's most successful investments was in a south-of-England high technology undertaking. This is located in a community represented by one of the Board's bitterest Parliamentary adversaries. When this MP heard that the firm had received NEB cash he wrote its Chairman a letter. The missive congratulated the Chairman, whom the MP knows and who is a fellow Tory; but added that the NEB should not get involved in aiding companies such as his. This investment, the Member lamented, would make it even harder for the Party to dismantle the Board once it came to power. Grylls's dislike of this body was so passionate that he was moved to become co-author with John Redwood of a 1980 book entitled *National Enterprise Board: a case for euthanasia.*[32] The monograph has just about nothing favourable to say about the Board. Even its rescue of Ferranti, praised, as seen, by the *Mail* and *Express,* came in for nasty comments. Grylls and Redwood complain that a private company could have accomplished the same results and that the Board pushed the group into new engineering activities where it was weak in order to save jobs threatened by a rationalisation of one of its divisions.[33] And the turnaround under NEB auspices of Fairey Engineering is dismissed by bitterly pointing out that one of Fairey's subsidiaries 'took a stand at the 1978 Boat Show selling luxury motor yachts costing £80,000 - no doubt one of socialism's commanding heights'.[34]

Parliament Sees the Board's Slip Showing

The NEB had troubles with Parliament that it brought upon itself, troubles that none the less did not afflict private venture capitalists. First, it made early in its existence a couple of unwise deals that were, among other things, bound to harden the belief of right wing Tories that the NEB idea was a stupid one. Second, a problem that we shall deal with in the next chapter, it withheld certain data from the House that many in that body wanted to become acquainted with. In early 1977 it invested £240,000 in a small clockmaker called Thwaites and Reed (T and R). This made outdoor clocks such as the one on the building of Fortnum and Mason, the world-famous purveyors of gourmet foods. It also repaired and maintained Big Ben. It was admitted that it was a money-loser; but the NEB considered that it had export potential.[35] In fact, the Board had not scrutinised its history carefully enough. If it had, it would have realised just how weak its financial condition was: an ex-Board official admitted to me that T and R sold it a false bill of goods. In name, it was an old, established clockmaker that had been doing business for a century. In reality, however, it was an outfit that had been set up during the 1970s. The scenario was that the old T and R had been floundering: in 1973 it had lost £293,000 on a turnover of only £260,000. The Managing Director, who had been associated with it for many years, then set up a new firm and agreed to pay the former owners for the use of the T and R name. The old T and R then faded out of the picture. The NEB money went to the reborn T and R (which continued, perhaps without justification, to label itself Turret Clockmakers to the Queen); and at least part of these funds were applied not to expand production but to satisfy the fledgling T and R's debt to its predecessor.[36]

The above would have been bad enough; but the head of F. W. Elliott, another clockmaker located in the same town as T and R, complained to then NEB Chairman Ryder and to his MP that the agency, in subsidising T and R, was propping up a competitor of his. He further pointed out that he already was selling clocks to Germany, the US and Japan; and that he himself had turned down the opportunity to buy T and R because it was bankrupt with no assets. Moreover, its management had no record of profitability and technical expertise: its previous activities had all been subcontracted. (It is not clear that this particular accusation was true. Moreover, as an ex-NEB official told me, F. W. Elliott and T and R complemented rather than competed with each other. The former specialised in indoor, the latter in outdoor, timepieces.) An NEB employee answered F. W. Elliott's head in a piece of correspondence that pointed out that if he had come to the Board, it would have considered financing his firm as well. The employee continued that he was aware of the need for technical and marketing strength at T and R, but that he felt that it had good export potential. The letter said accurately but rather tactlessly that

'It is true that we are financing a competitor to you. However, it is a fact of life that any investment we make is in someone's competitor and we cannot accept the argument that we should let companies decline until the survivor has a monopoly, since it is our aim to strengthen manufacturing industry in the UK.'[37]

From the NEB's point of view, the worst thing about the T and R arrangement was that the Tory MP of the constituency in which both clockmakers were located was a member of the House of Commons' Public Accounts Committee, whose function is to ensure that appropriations of public funds are properly spent. This MP complained to Ryder during a Committee session that the Board's backing of T and R was undermining F. W. Elliott though the latter had been improving its export record. Ryder's counterargument was the general and therefore rather weak one that his agency always looked to see the impact of its purchases upon the rivals of the concerns it bought.[38] Earlier in the hearing he had boasted that the Board was convinced of T and R's technical skills and that with a new range of product models it was starting to export more to the US. The loss that it had sustained in its first year was due to exceptional 'setting up charges'.[39]

The first seven months that T and R was under NEB control, i.e. June through December 1977, it lost £230,000 before taxation on a turnover of £100,000.[40] By October 1978 the Board had become convinced that T and R had no future and thus sold its equity to, of all concerns, F. W. Elliott. To help

Elliott pay off T and R's debts, the Board lent it £200,000.[41] Ultimately, the T and R adventure cost it £450,000,[42] a far cry from Ryder's projection that under T and R's five year plan, turnover would increase to £3,400,000.[43]

A former NEB official whom I interviewed felt that Ryder, when he was NEB Chairman, pressured his subordinates into making as many investments as they could as quickly as possible. He also felt that as a result of this insistence on investing rapidly, the NEB staff in its early days did not check the economic situation and prospects of some of its prospective purchases as carefully as they should have. As seen, the T and R fumble sprung from this lack of great prudence; and the same is true of another of its initial ventures that caused the NEB much in the way of criticism,[44] heartache and money. (The man responsible for bringing T and R under the Board's wing soon was eased out of his job.) In late 1976 a large UK concern, Barrow Hepburn (henceforth BH), announced that it would have to close all its tanneries, which were in the red and in debt to it. This shutdown would have cost 2000 jobs.[45] The NEB thus agreed with BH to set up a new undertaking called British Tanners Products (BTP), which would operate the tanneries formerly under the sole control of BH. The Board's initial investment, effected in early 1977, was £3 million. Because BTP suffered big losses during 1977, both BH and NEB had to buy £1.5 million in additional shares in February 1978.[46] Despite the abandonment of BTP's largest plant and the reduction in size of another, which contractions cost about 700 positions, the price of hides continued to rise substantially and it continued to produce red ink in 1978.[47] In July 1979 the company was placed in receivership, causing the Board a loss of about £5.6 million.[48]

This alleged 'bailout' of the BH tanneries infuriated their independent competitors. At that time the entire UK tanning industry was facing a bleak future and the independents felt that the Board's aid to BH would only drive them closer to bankruptcy. So they brought legal action, alleging that the formation of BTP by the NEB violated the agency's Guidelines under which, among other things, it was to make acquisitions only when it saw the prospect of an adequate rate of return within a reasonable period. The plaintiffs said that at the time of the purchase, the Board could not have possibly visualised such a prospect, at least if it had been acting reasonably.[49] No decision ever was reached in the case and the suit was eventually withdrawn; but only after BTP had gone into receivership.[50]

MPs such as Grylls were incensed not only because the NEB was putting money into a shrinking industry and threatening the survival of the unaided tanners, but also because BH supposedly received £10 million as part of the contract under which it and the Board set up BTP. When Mr. Robert Taylor in the Public Accounts Committee asked Sir Leslie Murphy where this sum came from, the NEB Chairman had to admit that he did not know. Taylor retorted that this ignorance was 'astonishing'.[51] To relieve its head's embarrassment, the Board then filed with the Committee a memorandum[52] explaining that for various reasons BTP owed BH £13 million. Of this £13 million, £6.5 million was given to BH in cash, including £3 million from the NEB's payment for BTP's equity and loan stock. The other £3.5 million of the £6.5 million came from a bank overdraft.[53] Unfortunately, the high interest rates it had to pay its bankers turned out to be one of the reasons for BTP's eventual collapse.[54]

NOTES

1. *London Times,* 19 Feb. 1980, p. 17.
2. Ibid.
3. NEB 1980 Annual Report, p. 3. See also *Financial Times,* 12 Dec. 1979, p. 36.
4. NEB 1980 Annual Report, p. 3, 53. On the conditions under which Ferranti was sold, see Redwood, *Going for broke...,* p. 68, 97-8.
5. At p. 18 of the *Daily Telegraph;* p. 34 of the *Financial Times;* p. 18 of the *Guardian;* and p. 15 of *The Times.*
6. At p. 33.
7. At p. 4.
8. At p. 16.
9. *Daily Mail,* 12 Aug. 1978, p. 1.
10. *Daily Telegraph,* 12 July 1977, p. 1.
11. *Daily Express,* 16 Sept. 1978, p. 7.
12. *Daily Express,* 25 Jan. 1979, p. 8.
13. *Daily Express,* 5 Sept. 1978, p. 31.

14. 7 Feb. 1978, p. 29.

15. at p. 39.

16. See, for example, *Daily Express,* 23 Mar. 1978, p. 2; *Daily Mail,* 6 Dec. 1977, p. 31.

17. The *London Sunday Times* (17 July 1977, p. 1) and *London Times* (12 July 1977, p. 1; 18 July 1977, p. 2; 26 July 1977, p. 1) also had articles about the £49,500 (Canadian $100,000). The headlines were more restrained than those appearing in the *Mail. The Sunday Times* article dealt with the situation in the most depth. This and *The Times* stories show that Ryder had been a non-executive director of Canadian Forest Products, the concern engaged in the joint venture with the Canadian subsidiary of Reed. A senior executive of that subsidiary had asked CFP if it would be willing to make a retirement gift of the $100,000 to Ryder. CFP said that it would do so only if the subsidiary agreed to reimburse it. When Ryder got the money he reasonably assumed that it was a donation from CFP in gratitude for his serving many years as one of its unpaid non-executive directors. When Ryder found that the source of the gift was not really CFP but Reed's Canadian subsidiary, he immediately sent it back, as even the *Mail* admitted. The senior executive of the subsidiary who had arranged for the payment by CFP and the subsequent reimbursement by the subsidiary to CFP had never had that reimbursement properly approved; but Ryder had no way of knowing this when he accepted the money. In retrospect, it is hard to see what all the fuss was about except under an assumption that many organs of Fleet Street were searching vigorously for weapons they could use to attack the NEB. At the time the £49,500 story broke, Ryder's resignation from the NEB had already been announced but he had not yet vacated the Chairmanship.

18. *Daily Telegraph,* 16 Sept. 1976, p. 19.

19. at p. 21.

20. HC Debates, 18 Mar. 1976, cols. 1653-56, 1661-62.

21. HC Debates, 2 Aug. 1976, col. 1185.

22. HC Debates, 21 Jan. 1977, cols. 842-43.

23. Ibid., cols. 884-85, 888, 910.

24. HC Debates, 10 Ap. 1978, col. 1080.

25. Ibid., col. 1083.

26. Ibid., col. 1100.

27. Ibid., cols. 1021-22.

28. HC Debates, 19 July 1979, cols. 2005-06.

29. Ibid., col. 2008.

30. Ibid., col. 2010.

31. Ibid., col. 2015.

32. Centre for Policy Studies, London, 1980.

33. Ibid., pp. 32-4.

34. Ibid., p. 4.

35. *Financial Times,* 27 Mar. 1977, p. 9.

36. *Daily Mail,* 26 Mar. 1977, p. 29.

37. Both letters can be found in Grylls and Redwood, *NEB: a case for euthanasia,* pp. 47-8.

38. HC Committee of Public Accounts, *Reports 1976-77, No. 8: Department of Energy, etc.* (HMSO, London, 1977), p. 308.

39. Ibid., p. 304.

40. NEB 1977 Annual Report, pp. 32-3.

41. NEB 1978 Annual Report, p. 29.

42. Ibid.

43. Grylls and Redwood, *NEB: a case for euthanasia,* p. 48.

44. See, e.g., ibid., pp. 43-5.

45. HC Committee of Public Accounts, *Reports 1977-78, No. 8: Atomic Energy Authority, Department of Industry, National Enterprise Board* (HMSO, London, 1978), p. 103. (Murphy's testimony.)

46. NEB 1977 Annual Report, p. 18.

47. Ibid.; also NEB 1978 Annual Report, p. 26.

48. NEB 1979 Annual Report, p. 25.

49. Grylls and Redwood, *NEB: a case for euthanasia,* p. 44.

50. *Daily Telegraph,* 19 Oct. 1979, p. 21.

51. HC Committee of Public Accounts, *Reports 1977-78, No. 8,* pp. 110-11.

52. Appendix xi to the Report noted in the preceding footnote.

53. HC Committee of Public Accounts, *Reports 1977-78, No. 8,* pp. 172-73.

54. *Guardian,* 21 July 1979, p. 17.

4

The Board Wraps Itself in a Cloud of Mystery: Additional Parliamentary Tribulations of a Public Venture Capitalist

The NEB was unduly secretive when it came to transmitting information to the House of Commons about its activities. The Parliamentary Reports from November 1975 to the Labour Government's fall are replete with instances where the Secretary of State for Industry or a junior Minister in the Department refused to answer what seemed to be perfectly reasonable questions about the Board's operations. Let me give several examples. In November 1975 Edward Gardner (a Tory) asked Minister of State for Industry Gerald Kaufman about the cost of decorating the NEB's Grosvenor Square office and John Stanley (also a Tory) inquired about the number of staff it was employing. Kaufman responded that these were matters for the Board.[1] In May 1976 Michael Grylls requested that the Secretary of State publish the total number and cost of the NEB's staff and its expected overhead costs for the next few years. Undersecretary of State Les Huckfield responded that these were matters for the Board.[2] In August 1976 Grylls lamented that the Secretary of State would not indicate how much extra money the Board was to be allocated for 1977-78. Secretary of State Varley answered that the figures for assistance to the NEB for next year 'are necessarily arbitrary and will be kept under review'.[3]

Grylls kept trying to find out about the activities of the Board. In November 1976 he asked whether the Secretary of State would publish lists of firms to which the Board had made loans totalling £5.6 million and indicate the amount and conditions of each loan. Huckfield retorted that these were matters for the Board.[4] On 18 January 1977 Huckfield responded to a whole host of questions put to him by Grylls by telling him that the way that Parliament can monitor the

Board's Corporate Plan is to read its annual report which must, pursuant to the 1975 Industry Act, be submitted to the UK legislature. He added that issues of commercial confidentiality prevented him from indicating whether he had received any requests from the Board to dispose of any of its securities.[5] However, he did furnish Grylls with a list of investments it had already made and informed him rather vaguely that it was satisfactorily discharging its employment responsibilities in areas of high unemployment and that its regional office staff was actively engaged in seeking opportunities for investment.[6] The next day, when Grylls queried whether the Secretary of State intended to conclude any planning agreement with an NEB subsidiary, Huckfield noted that a statement would be laid before the House when an agreement had been consummated.[7] In February 1977 Grylls asked if the Government would publish the conditions under which the NEB lent money to undertakings in which it had an interest. Huckfield rejoined that these conditions were commercially confidential while admitting that it had made loans to BL and RR.[8] In May 1977 Conservative Nicholas Ridley interrogated the Secretary of State about why the NEB's accounts for 1976 showed an annual return on capital employed after interest but before taxation of 11.8% when (according to Ridley) the correct figure was 5.15%. Huckfield claimed that that was a matter for the Board and its auditors.[9]

Even Labour Party members did not always get straight answers about the Board's operations. Robert Kilroy-Silk was then a Labour MP from Liverpool. In November 1977 he asked how many persons would be employed at its Northwest regional headquarters. Huckfield responded that this was a matter for the Board.[10] Returning to the Tories, we find that Grylls a bit later that month asked if the Secretary of State would give details of an NEB investment he refused to allow it to sell and to explain the reason for this veto. Huckfield declined to answer on the ground that the information was commercially confidential.[11] Likewise, he said shortly afterward, the list of the companies the Board had permission to dispose of was also commercially confidential.[12]

In January 1978 Huckfield told Tory Robert Taylor, in response to a query about the number of persons on the NEB payroll, that payments to members of its Northern Regional

Board and all aspects of staffing that body were matters for the central Board. However, he did add that eight members of the central Board were paid by the government and that two Board members were eligible for compensation but not drawing it.[13] In February 1978 he mentioned to Grylls that investments made by the NEB's Northern Region up to 31 January of that year were a matter for the Board.[14] He also informed that same NEB critic that the principal activities of three NEB companies -- Francis Shaw, Systems Designers and Systime -- were matters for the Board since the Secretary's approval was not required for these particular acquisitions.[15] Likewise, the major functions of a firm named Hivent would not be revealed by the Secretary since he did not have to give his *imprimatur* to the Board's purchase of it.[16] In March 1978 Huckfield declared to Grylls that he was under no obligation to reveal any part of the NEB's Corporate Plan but that he would consider the possibility of disclosing to Members the non-commercially-confidential segments of it.[17] He informed Labourite George Grant that it was a matter for the Board how many applications for support it received from a region.[18] Similarly, he indicated to Tory Sir John Rodgers that the costs of printing and distributing the NEB Annual Reports were matters for the Board.[19] In July 1978 Kaufman told Sir Keith Joseph that any information about whether the American partners in Inmos would be paid overseas to avoid UK tax would be made available by the Board if not commercially confidential.[20] In August of that year Secretary of State Varley insisted that the NEB's Corporate Plan, and the discussions about it, were commercially confidential even though the Department of Industry had just endorsed that document. He contended that the Board's 1977 Annual Report provided a full statement of its activities and of its general policy.[21]

In November 1978 Huckfield replied to Labour MP Max Madden that it was a matter for the Board which NEB enterprises traded in South Africa. However, he agreed to make known to the Board and its subsidiaries the Government's policy on investment in that Republic.[22] At the end of the month, he advised Grylls that who the directors of NEB investment United Medical Enterprises were and what their salaries amounted to was a Board matter.[23] In January 1979 he emphasised to Grylls that the details of the borrowings of the Board's subsidiaries were commercially confidential.[24]

I asserted in the first sentence of this chapter that the NEB was being 'unduly secretive' in withholding much of the information that the above pages have indicated that they (via Ministers of the DOI) refused to give the House. Let me indicate why this reticence was excessive. In the first place, some of the data that the Secretary or his deputies refused to make public were soon revealed in the Board's Annual Reports and so there was no reason why they could not have been disclosed as soon as an MP asked for them. They include the investments made by the Northern Regional Board and the products fabricated by certain companies in which the Board had taken a stake. Likewise Murphy himself in November 1977 testimony to the Wilson Committee reviewing the functions of UK financial institutions noted that the Board as of the date of his testimony had approved only 30 of 350 requests for aid.[25] Thus it is hard to see why Huckfield in early 1978 maintained that how many applications the Board had received from a region was a matter for the Board.

Moreover, some of the documents kept from Parliament would have been useful in helping it determine whether the Board was performing its functions efficiently. One does not have to accept the Reagan-Thatcher *laissez-faire* philosophy of government to feel that agencies expending taxpayers' moneys should not be profligate but, rather, use their funds to achieve the goals that the public, acting through its elected representatives, has set for them. Accordingly, information should be given to a legislature when that will enable it to ascertain whether the public body has been employing its assets this way. Thus material about how much the Board was spending to decorate its offices, its total expenditures on staff, and the fees paid members of the Northern Regional Board should have been placed in Parliament's hands as soon as it was available. Similarly, the Board should have let the Secretary of State disclose to the House the conditions of the loans it had made; the names and salaries of the directors of its subsidiary United Medical Enterprises; and the liability to UK tax of the American partners in Inmos. (Were the Board unjustifiably giving windfalls to individuals or firms, it certainly would not have been using its resources in such a way as to best meet its statutory goals!) Moreover, turning over to the House the NEB's Corporate Plan, i.e. the description of the paths it intended to pursue in the near future, would obviously have helped the public's representatives evaluate the Board by revealing its concrete ideas for stimulating the UK economy and fulfilling its other duties. Thus the Plan, to the extent that it did not mention the possible purchase of named firms, should have been made a matter of public knowledge. (The disclosure that the Board was contemplating the purchase of this or that specific undertaking might have been unwise because, *inter alia,* such a briefing might have caused other concerns to join the bidding and thus ultimately raised the cost of the investment to the Treasury.)

As noted in the previous chapter, the Public Accounts Committee is the organ of the House of Commons that is supposed to keep an eye on the functioning of public institutions to insure that they are spending the taxpayers' funds legitimately and wisely. It is aided by the Comptroller and Auditor General (henceforth C and AG), whose function is to carry out audits of Government Departments.[26] The NEB played a game of cat and mouse with the C and AG, refusing him certain information he needed to check up on its activities. For example, he found from the Department of Industry that the NEB in requesting funds said that by an unspecified future date it expected an adequate return on its investment, but that these requests were unaccompanied by concrete information showing why it anticipated such a profit. What the C and AG wanted from the Board was, for a sample of concerns, the details of the forecasted returns from acquiring equity in them and the market research about them that it had undertaken.[27] The Public Accounts Committee admitted that Parliament intended that the NEB should enjoy a considerable amount of entrepreneurial freedom.[28] But the Committee felt that there should be Board accountability to Parliament as well. Unless the Committee and C and AG had access to the Board's records, it maintained, they had no independent way of discovering how it was discharging its statutory functions and thus could not give the legislature a meaningful report on this matter.[29]

In all fairness, the NEB did provide arguments on behalf of its unwillingness to let the C and AG look at the studies it had conducted about the undertakings in which it had been contemplating taking an interest. (These arguments must have converted Tory appointee Sir Arthur Knight, for he, too, opposed C and AG monitoring.) The Board claimed that firms would be reluctant to deal with it if they knew that confidential information they funished would reach the C and AG and/or House Members.[30] Murphy argued, in addition, that the Board would never be successful if it were compelled to defend every judgement it made.[31] Likewise, the Board contended, there was an easy way for Parliament and the public to judge whether it was making sensible investments: peruse its Annual Reports to see whether it was meeting the financial targets set for it by the Department of Industry.[32] There was no real need, it insisted, for it to be audited by the C and AG: professional auditors study its books and those of its subsidiaries.[33] Murphy felt that the NEB was very similar to a private holding company; and such a company has itself and its subsidiaries audited but its own shareholders do not hire an accountant to comb its records.[34] Likewise, a private holding company does not disclose the facts and figures about the companies it controls without those companies' permission; and, therefore, the NEB should be under no obligation to do so either.[35]

Some of the above arguments are weak. It really is not sufficient to grade the NEB using the criterion of whether it was meeting the financial targets set for it by the DOI. In the first place, even if it were, this might have happened through sheer luck and not through intelligent forecasting, a fact that can be discovered only by looking at its records. Second, the financial target criterion gives no indication of whether the Board had considered, only to reject, takeovers that might have proven even more profitable or socially valuable -- a factor the House would surely have liked to have known in judging whether it was well-managed. Third, and the Board should have been aware of this contingency given the high-risk nature of its investments and the gloomy economic outlook facing the country, it was quite conceivable that it would fail to meet its financial targets. In that case, allowing the C and AG to inspect its market research, etc. might well have protected it and increased its stature in the eyes of Parliament; for the minutes might have shown that its investments were, all things considered, prudent and socially beneficial, and thus that it could not be blamed for their not being as lucrative as hoped. A Labour member of the Public Accounts Committee in essence made this point when he said that we have to have some sort of explanation about why the public's money has gone in a certain direction in order to be able to back judgements about expediting Board funding.[36] Similarly, as hinted by another member of the Committee after the NEB had become moribund, information acquired by the C and AG and turned over to the Committee could have been the basis for suggestions to the Board that might well have helped it avert unnecessary difficulties.[37]

The Board's plea that companies might have feared to negotiate with it if there had been a possibility that the information about their prospects it gleaned would be laid before Parliament is not on its face unreasonable. However, it did not adduce any evidence backing it up; and so for this reason and those noted above the Committee *was* justified in telling the NEB that it should give the C and AG the records dealing with its investment decisions. There is little excuse for not divulging agency data when those in custody of that material simply assert rather than establish that the disclosure will hinder them from functioning properly.

What we must now ask ourselves is whether the bitter right wing Tory and press criticism of the NEB and/or its struggles with the House over furnishing it with information actually contributed to its demise or, at least, made it operate less aggressively and effectively. Turning to the refusal to provide data factor first, we see that Edward du Cann, Chairman of the Committee on Public Accounts, was certainly irritated at the NEB's refusal to open its books, as was another Tory, Norman Lamont.[38] The Committee as a whole was not happy with the NEB's continual balking.[39] What is most surprising is that, according to Grylls and Redwood, even its Labour members wanted the C and AG to be given access to the NEB's papers[40] and that since the Board was set up, 'MPs from all parties have been deeply concerned about the Board's lack of accountability to Parliament'.[41] They continue that

'Though the Secretary of State and the Department of Industry's Accounting Officer...have a certain measure of control over the Board's activities, the House of Commons effectively has none. Parliamentary Questions often produce the stone-walling reply "That is a matter for the Board".[42]

Grylls, of course, was strongly against the NEB from its inception and thus his testimony (in conjunction with his co-author) that some Members of Parliament were unhappy with its lack of forthrightness about its operations may be considered suspect, though it surely accords with common sense. (If Institution A withholds important data from Institution B, is it likely that the members of B will be fervent supporters of A?) However, Gabrielle Ganz is an objective observer of the Board and other government attempts to aid industry. She notes that Members of Parliament did regard the NEB as a barrier between themselves and its subsidiaries. What concerned them was the sort of Ministerial answers to questions we detailed a few pages ago, i.e. responses where Varley, Kaufman or Huckfield would claim that such and such is a matter for the Board.[43] It is thus clear that its secretiveness did annoy politicians from all parties. What must remain speculative, unfortunately, is the extent to which this irritation made liberal Tories and members of the Labour Party less willing to fight Mrs Thatcher's efforts to emasculate it. (One person who worked for it for many years told me that he does not believe that its policy of confidentiality hurt it politically for it kept briefing the Conservative Party about its operations. But this flies in the face of the fact that the Committee of Public Accounts and rank and file MPs *were* miffed by its secretiveness about its studies of the companies in which it invested and by the veil the Government drew over its activities.)

Whatever the political impact of the NEB's frequent nondisclosures, there is no doubt at all that the hostility of the Tory right (in the sense of those Tories strongly committed to the belief that the state must not intervene in economic affairs) had a significantly adverse effect on the NEB's life expectancy, authority and ability to achieve its financial and other goals. The main reason why this is the case is a very simple one: Mrs Thatcher, one of its adherents, was the Party's leader and dominant figure during the events that we are describing. Given her hostility, the post-May 1979 misfortunes

71

of the NEB were almost inevitable: its loss of Rolls Royce and British Leyland; its coerced sales of International Computers Limited, Fairey and Ferranti; the whopping reduction in the total amount available to it; provisions in the 1980 Guidelines such as the one preventing it from investing in concerns that could receive finance from other sources; and the speed with which it had to sell its holdings. More subtly, even while Labour remained in power, the Tory right had a negative impact on the operations of the Board because, as one ex-Board official told me, answering the frequent blasts of Grylls and his colleagues took time and effort. This time and effort, of course, could otherwise have been devoted to supervising more closely the Board's various firms, developing ideas for these to pursue, and analysing the prospects of potential investments more thoroughly.

Next, it is true that ex-officials of the NEB to whom I spoke believed that press criticism did not have a negative effect on the NEB. One mentioned that the agency just learned to live with it. Another felt that the Board was not unfairly treated. A third said that Fleet Street became more sympathetic the more it understood that the Board was a commercially-minded organisation. Nonetheless, that same man admitted that it lived very much in a goldfish bowl -- much more so than did private venture capitalists. And this goldfish-bowl atmosphere may have made it somewhat more fearful of consummating certain potentially sensible deals out of a fear of being pilloried by antagonistic journalists. In fact, one MP who followed the NEB's activities rather closely commented to me that both press and Tory attacks on it did deter it from attempting to gain control of various concerns in order to try to make them more dynamic. (Once again, let me emphasise as strongly as possible that the press (and, of course, Parliament) not only had the right but also the duty to criticise the Board. However, it still remains the case that the UK's (then) few private venture capitalists were not subjected to these intense cannonades and the traumas that sprung from them and the hostility that produced them.)

It will be remembered that big business was very hostile to the proposals for establishing the NEB, feeling, among other things, that it was an instrument that the Labour Government would use to take over larger and larger chunks of the private sector. Despite the concessions that Prime Minister Wilson made to the Confederation of British Industries that we discussed earlier, (e.g., the Secretary of State for Industry could veto certain of the Board's proposed acquisitions), this enmity (which, like the Parliamentary and press antipathy, was not directed against a private sector Board 'competitor' such as the ICFC) was slow to dissipate[44] and did limit the scope of the public body's operations. Chapter 9 on Insac will furnish one good example. Moreover, a former high-level NEB official remarked to me that a major financially-troubled British tyre corporation refused to take a Board loan because its Chairman disliked this body. Another such officer told me that one reason that it insisted on keeping its records relating to the circumstances surrounding its investments confidential was a desire not to irritate the large corporate sector even more. Its staff reasoned that if it did reveal to the C and AG its market forecasts and research not only would individual firms refuse to deal with it but, moreover, the dislike many in the business community manifested for it would persist. What these people may not have realised, however, is that this policy of secrecy into which they were pushed by the ill feeling of big business would get under the skin of even basically-sympathetic members of the House of Commons and thus perhaps function as one of the factors making it politically easy for Mrs Thatcher to bury their agency.

NOTES

1. HC Debates, 26 Nov. 1975, cols. 189-90. (Written Answers.)
2. HC Debates, 26 May 1976, cols. 222-23. (Written Answers.)
3. HC Debates, 2 Aug. 1976, col. 1185. (Oral Answers.)
4. HC Debates, 15 Nov. 1976, col. 425. (Written Answers.)
5. HC Debates, 18 Jan. 1977, cols. 185-86. (Written Answers.)
6. Ibid., cols. 185-87.
7. HC Debates, 19 Jan. 1977, col. 233. (Written Answers.)
8. HC Debates, 2 Feb. 1977, col. 216. (Written Answers.)
9. HC Debates, 23 May 1977, cols. 357-58. (Written Answers.)
10. HC Debates, 14 Nov. 1977, col. 39. (Written Answers.)
11. HC Debates, 21 Nov. 1977, col. 551. (Written Answers.)
12. HC Debates, 28 Nov. 1977, cols. 81-2. (Written Answers.)

13. HC Debates, 16 Jan. 1978, cols. 75-6. (Written Answers.)

14. HC Debates, 6 Feb. 1978, col. 377. (Written Answers.)

15. HC Debates. 21 Feb. 1978, col. 569. (Written Answers.)

16. HC Debates, 23 Feb. 1978, col. 794. (Written Answers.)

17. HC Debates, 9 Mar. 1978, cols. 728-29. (Written Answers.)

18. HC Debates, 21 Mar. 1978, col. 535. (Written Answers.)

19. HC Debates, 12 May 1978, col. 656. (Written Answers.)

20. HC Debates, 10 July 1978, cols. 1012-13. (Oral Answers.)

21. HC Debates, 1 Aug. 1978, cols. 185-86. (Written Answers.)

22. HC Debates, 10 Nov. 1978, cols. 369-70. (Written Answers.)

23. HC Debates, 30 Nov. 1978, col. 364. (Written Answers.)

24. HC Debates, 25 Jan. 1979, col. 225. (Written Answers.)

25. Committee to Review the Functioning of Financial Institutions, *Evidence on financing of industry,* vol. 4, p. 22.

26. A. H. Hanson and Malcolm Walles, *Governing Britain* (Fontana/Collins, London, 1970), p. 75.

27. HC Committee of Public Accounts, *Reports 1977-78, No. 8,* p. xxix.

28. Ibid., p. xxxi.

29. Ibid., p. xxxii.

30. Ibid., pp. xxx-xxxi.

31. Ibid., p. 97.

32. Ibid., p. xxx.

33. Ibid., p. xxxi.

34. Ibid., p. 75.

35. Ibid., p. xxix.

36. Ibid., p. 98.

37. HC Committee of Public Accounts, *Nexos: minutes of evidence* (HMSO, London, 1985), p. 108.

38. HC Debates, 21 Jan. 1977, col. 883. (Lamont was not a member of the Committee.)

39. HC Committee of Public Accounts, *Reports 1977-78 No. 8,* p. xxxii.

40. *NEB: a case for euthanasia,* p. 33.

41. Ibid., p. 51.

42. Ibid.

43. *Government and industry,* p. 81.

44. See *Daily Telegraph,* 12 July 1977, p. 1.

5
The NEB and
the Department of Industry

The problem of the Board's accountability to Parliament and the public naturally raises the question of whether its relationship with the Department of Industry was a satisfactory one. The Board could not, of course, ignore the DOI because, as seen, the Industry Act of 1975 creating it placed it to some extent under the control of the Secretary of State (a member of Parliament, of course). Thus he was required to determine the Board's financial duties (Sec. 6) and had the right (Sec. 7) to issue Guidelines for its direction. In fact, as will be remembered, it gave as one reason why the C and AG should not have access to its records the fact that the degree to which it met the financial targets set by the Secretary of State gave outsiders an adequate basis for judging it.[1] More generally, the requirement that it be monitored by the Department was brought forth by it as another consideration buttressing its position that the C and AG should not be allowed to peruse its files.[2]

One would expect that, in practice, the interaction between an agency like the Board, staffed mainly by ambitious, talented non-civil servants and headed by strong-willed ex-businessmen and the civil service-manned DOI would have been filled with mutual suspicion and anger. Though the goals of Board and DOI were in the last analysis similar -- e.g., to increase the growth rate of British industry, to stimulate exports, to reduce import-dependence, to cut unemployment -- the Department was not in the habit of setting out to achieve these ends by what became the Board's major route, i.e. taking stock in potentially promising firms that were having difficulty obtaining financing from conventional sources. In other words, one would naturally have predicted that the 'tradition orientated' Department would have looked askance at its young ward's adopting the role of venture capitalist. One would also have anticipated that Department's losing its 'lame duck' firms and ICL to the NEB would have been another factor stimulating some of its personnel to work behind the scenes to limit the growth of the new kingdom headed by Ryder and Murphy.

In point of fact, however, the relations between the Board and the DOI were fairly good despite some tensions. A former Board official referred to the DOI approach to his agency as 'hands off' and 'sympathetic'. Recall, first, how the Secretary of State for Industry and his deputies frequently refused to answer Parliamentary questions about its operations, contending that they were matters for the agency. Moreover, though the Board did not allow the Department to study its files describing the prospects of the concerns in which it invested,[3] the DOI in testimony before the Public Accounts Committee backed the NEB's right to withhold these dossiers from the C and AG. In the course of this defence, the Department's Permanent Secretary asserted that it was monitoring the Board by satisfying itself that the latter had enough ability to supervise its investments well.[4] He added that since the NEB provided aid to companies on a commercial basis there was less need for his Department to be informed about the Board's investments than about the companies that the Department aided directly under Secs. 7 and 8 of the 1972 Industry Act.[5] He also told the Committee that relations between the Department and the Board were 'close'.[6]

Another example will show how the Department often fought for the Board. Giving evidence before the Committee in 1980 the same DOI official maintained that he was not dissatisfied with the way the Board was performing its regional role; and that it was not a matter of surprise to him that the Board wasn't more successful in performing the 'quite difficult' task of aiding small firms in regions of high unemployment.[7] When a question from the Committee's Chairman implied that the NEB had not been as commercially profitable as it should have been, the Permanent Secretary interjected that when venture capitalists assist small, risky companies in the field of high technology, it sometimes takes a fairly long time before rewards start flowing back to the investor.[8] In response to a question from a Committee member, the DOI executive did admit that the returns on the Board's investments to date had been 'disappointing' though not 'nonexistent'. The MP then pointed out to him that he, the Permanent Secretary, was maintaining now as he had in the past that he approved of the performance of the Board; and then asked him why he was happy with it now when on previous occasions his feeling of satisfaction had proven unjustified. All the Secretary responded to this was that under the new (Conservative) Industry Act of 1980 the agency had a new and more limited series of tasks and that 'I doubt whether the record would show that I have demonstrated satisfaction with the performance of the previous Board. I recall using words...about a somewhat lack-lustre performance'.[9] He quickly added, however, that at some stage there was a good chance that the Insac and Nexos ventures would become very profitable and that this would make the Board more commercially successful.[10]

The Department did have a division responsible for relations with the NEB. This group kept in regular touch with the agency's officials on an informal basis. Its members and the Permanent Secretary conveyed to the Board the views of the Secretary of State but, when doing so, were conscious of the NEB's need for independence. As noted earlier, the Secretary of State never vetoed a proposed Board investment, though he had the power to do so on certain occasions. One way that the Department did exercise control over the Board, however, was through the Secretary's use of his power to appoint its membership.[11]

The DOI and NEB worked together especially well, at least until the resignation of Sir Leslie Murphy in November 1979, in relation to the latter's management of the big lame ducks Rolls Royce, British Leyland and Alfred Herbert. For example, in the bitter feud between the NEB and RR Chairman Sir Kenneth Keith, the DOI shared the Board's feeling (to be described in much more detail in a later chapter) that the aero-engine manufacturer ought to be more efficient. (Keith's referring to the NEB as a 'bureaucratic contraceptive' shows how bad things were between Murphy and himself.) Ultimately, both the NEB and many DOI civil servants became convinced that Keith should leave RR; though Keith feels that Secretary of State for Industry Varley supported him over his adversary. With respect to the other lame ducks, many leading figures in the DOI and the NEB were of the opinion that Alfred Herbert should have been put into receivership rather than transferred to the Board as a candidate for future rescue efforts. The Department backed the NEB's efforts to get BL to achieve staff and other cost reductions. Thus in March 1977 the Board told the strike-plagued auto manufacturer that it had a month to put its house in order; that without a return to work and an increase in productivity government aid would be cut off.[12] This ukase was supported by Varley. In May of that year he, backed by Ryder, developed a plan to change BL's top management.[13]

Not that the waters of the relationship between the DOI and NEB always flowed smoothly. One well-known Labour member of Parliament told me he believed that Varley thought that the 1975 Industry Act potentially gave the agency too much power and that his 1976 Guidelines were intended to significantly weaken it. One Conservative newspaper saw these Guidelines in the same light, topping its story with the banner 'Varley Clips Ryder's Wings'.[14] But, as seen in Chapter 1, some of the limitations set forth in the Guidelines were not much greater than those in the 1975 Industry Act itself, and thus provide no clear indication that the Secretary of State wanted to shackle the NEB. One other Labour MP hinted to me that Varley was much less supportive of the agency than was Anthony Benn. A Labour MP said to me that he felt that the DOI's Permanent Secretary really did not like the Board; and one former NEB staff member remarked that he had the impression that the DOI felt that it had been given too much money to play with. But a person who served with the NEB for many years commented to me that Varley saw it as an instrument that the government could use to bring about changes (e.g., the shutting of an outmoded British Leyland plant; the discharge of some British Leyland staff) that the Cabinet desired but were afraid for political reasons to bring about directly.

The individual mentioned just above asserted that while Labour was in power, there was never a serious clash between the DOI and NEB except over one issue. Just before the 1979 elections the Government for political reasons demanded that in one way or another the two money-losing Scottish plants of BL's refrigerating equipment subsidiary, Prestcold, be kept in operation though the auto-maker wanted to close them. Murphy asserted that these factories were not commercially viable and said that the Cabinet would have to order the Board to keep them open. However, the pressure temporarily proved too strong for the NEB and eventually he recommended that BL accept a state offer of a two month government subsidy to cover the loss at these locations (which made compressors for domestic refrigerators). Very soon thereafter, at a meeting between Varley, Murphy and Michael Edwardes, Murphy's handpicked Chairman of BL, the Secretary of State proposed that the Board instruct the auto concern to put off abandoning the plants until Ministers had had a chance to review the wider issues. Here the NEB Chairman turned against the Government again and said that such an instruction would be *ultra vires* since the Board was not supposed to undertake the day-to-day management of BL. Varley then asked him whether the Board would take over all of Prestcold. Murphy retorted in essence that he was not prepared to pay the price the motor car concern would expect to receive. Later that day Varley did decide to order the Board to buy Prestcold at a fair price agreeing, however, that during the negotiations the Scottish plants' deficits would be borne by the government. They were thus kept humming past election day but the Tories, after their victory, stopped the Board from going through with the purchase. The installations were closed on 7 June 1979. Edwardes describes the Prestcold episode as one of the few occasions where BL and the NEB fell out while he was BL head; but it is evident that the dispute was really between the auto manufacturer and the Government with the Board caught in the middle and, in fact, tilting to Edwardes' position.[15]

Though, to repeat, the ties between the DOI and NEB were generally good, they were better when Murphy was Chairman than during the tenure of his successor Sir Arthur Knight. (I received conflicting information from former NEB staff about whether its investment policy was too slow or too fast for Varley during the Ryder-Murphy years. One commented that the Government and DOI inveigled them to spend more than was reasonable given the state of the market; while another felt on the other hand that Sir Leslie wanted to go a bit fast for a cautious Varley. But note again that Varley never vetoed any proposed Board purchase.) When Sir Keith Joseph was Secretary of State for Industry in 1980 and Knight was NEB head, the Secretary and the Department attempted to keep a tight rein on the agency. Civil servants often turned up at its headquarters while Joseph made decisions himself that in the Ryder-Murphy-Varley years had been left to it. The DOI also imposed a lot of paperwork on Knight and held up some of his proposals. This loss of autonomy may be another reason why he left the chairmanship after only one year in office though he, like Joseph, was a member of the Conservative Party.

NOTES

1. HC Committee of Public Accounts, *Reports 1977-78 No. 8*, p. xxx.
2. Ibid.
3. Ibid., p. xxxi.
4. Ibid., pp. 73-4.
5. Ibid., p. 76.
6. Ibid., p. 84.
7. HC Committee of Public Accounts, *Reports 1979-80, No. 30*, p. 22.
8. Ibid., p. 23.
9. Ibid., p. 27.
10. Ibid., pp. 27-8.
11. This power was given by Sec. 1.3 Industry Act 1975.
12. *Daily Mail,* 3 Mar. 1977, p. 9.
13. *Daily Mail,* 17 May 1977, p. 15.
14. *Daily Telegraph,* 2 Mar. 1976, p. 17.
15. The episode is described in Michael Edwardes, *Back from the brink* (Collins, London, 1983), at pp. 213-16.

6
Firms Aided by the NEB as Venture Capitalist: Case Studies

It will be the purpose of this chapter to provide case studies of the relationships prevailing between the NEB and quite a few of the undertakings to which it provided venture capital. The reader will see here and in Chapter 7 the extent to which they were not able to obtain aid from traditional sources of financing and private venture capitalists; and which of them would have gone out of business or remained tiny had it not been for Board assistance. The case studies will reveal, too, how frequently the Board acted like many other venture capitalists[1] and revamped the management or the accounting techniques of its investments. They will also indicate the degree to which the Board was wont to suffocate its clients in red tape; how far it co-operated with other public and private agencies in providing venture capital; and how active it was in seeking customers. They will, likewise, give some idea of the success of the NEB in creating jobs and exports. In order to preserve my pledge of confidentiality to the men I interviewed, I shall not (except in one case) furnish the real names of the companies I depict and shall give only approximate descriptions of their location.

Able Company

This is a firm located in the south of England that designs and supplies electronic equipment for data handling, message preparation and message switching. It was founded in 1969 and by the mid-1970s needed cash for expansion. Able could not get bank financing because it did not have enough security for a loan. At that time, moreover, the only real source in the UK for private venture capital was Industrial and Commercial

Finance Corporation (ICFC, now, as seen, part of Investors in Industry (3i) group). The NEB approached Able for purposes of investment because it wanted to expand the application of microcomputer technology in the UK. It gave the company the cash it needed for its growth by taking an equity holding in it. The funding was provided quickly, without much red tape. Though the Board did not intervene in the day-to-day management of the firm, it made it appoint a finance director: the founder of the enterprise was an engineer, not an accountant, and did not have the time or expertise to ensure that the plant operated efficiently. The NEB also picked two non-executive directors to sit on Able's Board of Directors. (The role of this type of director will be discussed in the next chapter. All the directors appointed by the Board were non-executive.) One made good suggestions about planning for growth and the other provided good ideas about marketing: both had experience in industry and were not dogmatic. The NEB never vetoed any of Able's proposed transactions; though it eyed with suspicion its purchase of a building. This structure was ultimately financed by a bank loan made possible only because the NEB had obtained an equity stake in Able: the larger the equity invested in a company, the more willing are ordinary banks to lend to it. The Board has sold its shares in Able at a nice profit: without the Board's help it never would have grown. When the NEB took its stake in 1978, it had 40 employees and was, as its founder described it to me, a 'struggling company': in 1985 it had 250 individuals working for it. In 1978 it had sales of about £1 million: in 1983 its turnover was £4.6 million. In 1986 it and another firm merged to form a group in which each participates equally and which had £17 million in gross receipts. Its head feels that the relationship between the Board and it was basically quite good during the years in which the latter was one of its owners.

Baker Company

This firm, located in a northern city suffering from high unemployment, is probably the smallest undertaking in which the NEB ever invested, featuring only a director and a secretary. Before setting up this enterprise, the former had been working towards his MBA at the local university. The city's

Chamber of Commerce asked him to study the problems of small business in the area. Consequently, he interviewed about 90 one- and two-person enterprises about their problems and discovered that most had difficulty finding adequate space. More specifically, they were being forced by landlords to take long-term leases at a stage in their development when they could hardly afford to be locked into an expensive commitment. He concluded, accordingly, that what had to be done to help these ventures and thus save jobs was to provide 'flexible space' for them by allowing them to rent locations in a large building, spots they could vacate at any time simply by giving 90 days' notice. Moreover, he declared, there should be very small units available in these quarters, units which at a rental computed per square foot would be reasonably cheap. In addition, the tenant should be able to move from a room of one size to one of another as his/her needs changed.

He then did a market research and feasibility study and found that for £200,000 an unused mill could be converted into rooms of different sizes for a myriad of small businesses. He first asked the City Council for the money, which responded that it would seriously consider his request only when the private sector guaranteed him some support. About 25 private individuals then contracted to invest between £500 and £2000 and a bank consented to provide a loan. The ICFC division of Investors in Industry said that it would put in equity funding if another reputable party also would. Then he contacted a regional office of the NEB, which within a few weeks agreed to buy an equity holding and quickly took care of the necessary formalities. The City Council kept its word and handed him £36,000. He was thus able to form Baker, which leases a portion of an unused mill and has converted it into the type of area that he feels that small, non-retailing enterprises need. Businesses subleasing its units include a car repairer, plumbers, a music teacher, woodworkers, wholesale distributors, an electrical contractor, and an insurance consultant. In addition to space, Baker provides on-site services that small concerns often cannot afford on their own, e.g., typing, photocopying, a cafeteria, message-taking, bookkeeping, scrap removal and professional advice. The units are, moreover, accessible 24 hours a day.

Before getting NEB funding, Baker had to submit business documents and cash flow forecasts that had been prepared by an accountant. The Board reserved the right to appoint someone to Baker's Board of Directors; but it never exercised this prerogative. Baker, as a condition of getting the assistance, had to keep the Board informed of its progress and sent it the minutes of its monthly Board meetings and its monthly reports. NEB staff phoned every six months or so. No more contact was necessary because Baker regularly fed it with information. During 1985-86 the NEB transferred its holding in Baker to a wholly-owned Board subsidiary.

The units in Baker's mill (refurbished with ICFC and NEB money) witness a high turnover of small businesses. Some of these have prospered and left for more spacious premises. There are about 75 enterprises in the factory that *in toto* employ about 150 persons. Their combined turnover is between £3 and £4 million a year. In the few years since the mill's rooms were opened between 500 and 1000 men and women have worked in them; and visitors come from all over the country to study Baker's operations.

Charlie Company

This is a company located in a northern city of high unemployment that develops software to produce visually-arresting two- and multi-dimensional pictures of mathematical, scientific and technical data. The pictures include graphs, contour plots, and rolling surfaces with peaks and troughs. The Managing Director of Charlie and his wife were originally employed by the local university. She produced software for its use, which was originally given free of charge to other academic institutions. An article describing her work was published in a magazine for electrical engineers and got a big response from all over the world. Shortly afterward, she and her spouse decided to revise the software completely and have it marketed by a software publisher. But at the time it was impossible to distribute software that way in the UK.

At this point a representative of the NEB visited the industrial relations liaison person of the University to ask whether it had any projects underway that might form the basis of a company that the Board could support. By chance, the future Managing Director of Charlie was in the room at this time; and so it was soon decided that he and his wife would found this firm to market their software and that the Board would take shares in the new entity. The industrial relations person handled the negotiations with the Board. He and the Managing Director had to demonstrate that the company had a potential market, which was easily done, and to draft three year plans.

After Charlie was set up, the Board had the right to place someone on its Board of Directors; but it never exercised this right. Until the NEB's stake in it was recently hived off, it had to make monthly reports to the agency (which was happy with it as it had been making a profit almost from the start). Charlie has a specific niche in the UK software universe and would like to expand its export market to the continent, Japan and North America. The Managing Director described the NEB as 'very supportive' of his enterprise. As a courtesy, the Board was invited to send a staff member to Charlie's monthly Board meetings, which the NEB suggested it should hold. One NEB visitor recommended that Charlie hire a public relations firm to improve its marketing; but did not insist on this. All the NEB staff who sat in on these meetings were, in fact, pleased with its commercial and technical achievements.

The funds from the NEB's investment were used to hire personnel, rent premises, purchase equipment, and pay the Managing Director a salary so that he could leave the university and devote full time to his young enterprise. At first, it had only two full-time workers and one part-time employee. It now has seven and will doubtlessly hire more in the near future. Had it not been for the state body's prodding, the Managing Director would in all likelihood never have established Charlie but, rather, would have remained in academia. He and the university's industrial relations liaison person never tried getting financing from a private bank because the NEB was literally present when the idea of the company was broached to the man who was to become its founder -- and also because it made him a good offer of aid. In 1985-86 the Board share in Charlie was turned over to the NRDC. In the future, therefore, Charlie will have to use its own income and cash from banks, private venture capitalists, and the Department of Industry to finance most of its future expansion.

David Company

This company, located in a city in the east of England, makes electric motors for a device in common use in large buildings. When the NEB came on the scene, it was owned by a US corporation. The electric motor factory was losing money, partly because it had seen too many changes in chief executive; and in 1977 the American parent was planning to close it down. At the time, it had between 450-500 employees and was one of the largest employers in the town. Seeing that its owner was not finding any bidders, the unions to which David's workforce belong approached the local Member of Parliament to see if the NEB would buy it and thus preserve jobs (and exports, since 50% of its sales are outside the UK). Accordingly, the Board became its sole shareholder and proceeded to recruit a completely new management team. In addition, the public body obtained and exercised the right to appoint two non-executive directors to David's Board of Directors. David had to submit to the NEB its monthly reports plus an annual plan and a five year plan.

During 1978 and 1979 David for a variety of reasons lost £700,000. It had leased property on unfavourable terms and owed considerable amounts for breaches of warranty. The NEB-appointed management whittled down the workforce to 170 employees. (About 210 persons are now working for it.) However, these firings did not immediately save the firm money because it had to make redundancy payments to the discharged employees. The union did not protest these severances, because it realised that they were necessary to keep the factory from bankruptcy. The funds put in by the NEB over a period of years thus were utilised to meet warranty claims and redundancy costs. It also guaranteed a bank loan drawn in favour of its subsidiary.

It was during these years that strife erupted between the NEB and the management it itself had appointed for David. The Board hired consultants who made optimistic projections; and the NEB, accepting these, wanted David to start selling quite a few more motors and became unhappy with the factory's management when it said that it could not dispose of too many. David's management was also of the opinion that the NEB representatives on its Board were of little use. They felt that the latter stayed in the position only for a short period of time and then left to take good jobs in private industry; that they did not know anything about electric motors; and that they did not grasp the complexities of financing exports. In addition, the NEB policy *vis-à-vis* the Board was perceived as inconsistent: one officer of David went so far as to refer to it as 'chameleon-like'. For example, the state body decided that it would be a good idea for David to resume exporting its motors to the US, as these were technically superior to those made by its American competitors. The Board added that it would purchase a US company to act as marketing agent for David across the ocean. However, by the time the contract was to be signed, the Board had come to the conclusion that the US endeavour would be costly and unlikely to realise a significant profit. It thus killed David's plans to acquire an American presence although it itself had kindled these. (I must add that the two officers of David whom I interviewed split on the question of the desirability of the transatlantic operations.)

During 1980 and 1981 the company continued to do poorly. Management had to engage in some fancy financial footwork in order to keep it out of receivership. They asked the NEB for more money, which was finally forthcoming but not, at least in David's eyes, when it was most needed. The aid was finally granted because the Board became convinced that David was a viable company that needed just a bit of tinkering to make it attractive to the private sector. (It was privatised in 1985.) The NEB's perceived slowness in providing the funding to keep David viable created further tensions between it and the undertaking's management. These were augmented by the fact that they sometimes were unable to contact anyone at Board headquarters; that the person to whom they talked in May often had departed by October; and that the agency kept postponing decisions on the approval of the corporate plans the firm was submitting to it. (Turnover on the Board was high because by these years it had become clear that the Thatcher Administration was planning to severely contract the scope of the NEB's operations.)

David finally became profitable in 1982 and has remained in the black since then. Its revival is due partly to the fact that it makes an excellent product; partly to its knowledge of overseas markets; partly to the fact that the workforce has been significantly reduced in size; and partly to the improved accounting procedures initiated by the NEB-appointed management. One person connected with David said that it might have been better to put it into receivership rather than have the NEB rescue it because its success has threatened the viability of its UK competitors. On the other hand, he admitted, it handles its export business more competently than do those other firms (and, we may add, wins orders at their expense probably because its motors are of a higher quality).

Elspeth Company

This group was formed by the NEB out of companies involved in working with the UK's offshore oil industry. Elspeth's main job is servicing and maintaining offshore oil rigs, especially those portions of these rigs that are underwater. Elspeth's predecessors could not get private financing for several reasons. First, the business is cyclical, i.e. it increases or decreases with the worldwide demand for oil. Second, it is capital-intensive and its capital needs are continually changing, with the result that the expensive equipment it buys in one year might well be outmoded by the time that the next twelve-month period rolls around. For example, it orginally used manned undersea craft but these were soon replaced by unmanned vehicles (which are the only ones that can be used at great depths). And unmanned subs are getting more and more sophisticated all the time. Therefore, if Elspeth had not been established and given NEB assistance -- the agency took equity shares in it in 1979 and increased its holdings in 1980 -- at least some of the concerns out of which it was formed would have gone out of existence. This would have hurt the UK's balance of payments, as these firms were the only UK-owned enterprises repairing underwater offshore oil equipment. Because of the technical problems facing any company in its line of work, Elspeth has had years of loss as well as years of profit since it was founded. Nonetheless, it now employs 700 persons and the NEB has been able over the last few years to sell all its holdings in it.

Elspeth had to submit reports and plans to the NEB, which had one representative on its Board of Directors. He usually attended meetings but he, and the NEB as a whole, usually played only a passive role with respect to the company. However, the agency aided Elspeth in selling some assets that had to be disposed of to redeem various bonds. Furthermore, it tried to help the firm develop good relations with institutions such as the Department of Energy and informed it of possible sources of financial assistance.

Fred Company

This is a major UK software and systems design concern located in the London area. Formed in 1962, it was tapped by the NEB to be one of the partners in Insac, the venture set up to market UK software overseas. (The Insac experiment will be detailed in a later chapter.) The Board desired to obtain a stake in each of the Insac partners; and Fred agreed to NEB funding (which it did not need for survival) because it was engaged in developing what it thought would be a standard language for microprocessor-based systems. To refine this language considerable cash was needed. Unfortunately, despite the NEB help, Fred was unable to complete this project successfully. Both the Board and Fred's management wrongly predicted that the language would become commercially popular: there is some feeling at Fred that the NEB did not push the firm hard enough to vigorously market it.

Fred then needed refinancing; the NEB participated with other institutional investors in this process. The Board had a role in appointing new management at this time. The company soon became, and remains, quite profitable: in 1984 the NEB sold its shares. The connection between the NEB and Fred was always a strained one. The company's management had little respect for the state body's representatives on its Board of Directors, feeling that these asked irrelevant questions and were afraid to make decisions at Directors' meetings, always claiming that they had to go back to the NEB for further instructions. They criticised Fred's operations; but the firm's officers believed that these censures were off the mark and paid little attention to them. At first Fred even refused to submit a corporate plan to the NEB. However, it eventually surrendered on this matter and admits that drafting the plan forced it to become more efficient. In general, its management preferred dealing with the delegates of the private shareholders that had invested in it, believing that it was easier to know what they wanted than what the NEB desired. Fred, a company with 1300 employees (about 500 when the NEB appeared on its horizon) is glad that its relationship with the state concern is at an end.

Graham Company

Like Fred, this is a quintessential high tech company located in the London area. It manufactures devices that connect computers to one another and to other units that transmit, receive or manipulate data. The NEB was never deeply involved with Graham, a concern that has expanded from about 100 employees in the mid-1970s to 1500 in 1985, over 1000 of these working in the UK. The Board purchased its shares in 1978 and sold them in 1980: while an equity holder in Graham it owned slightly under 30% of its stock. In 1978 the NEB was seeking to build up a good high tech portfolio and asked Graham's management if it would be interested in financial assistance. Graham at that moment did need money for expansion. Though it could have obtained this from the City even at this time when private banks in the UK were wary of investing in ventures that specialised in 'newfangled' technology, it accepted the NEB offer because the Board was willing to provide a significant amount of financing at a good rate. The money received from the Board made it possible for Graham to export a considerable percentage (30%) of what it produced. Part of the NEB funding went into fixed assets; the rest into working capital. Graham, incidentally, has no important UK-owned competitor: nearly all its counterparts operating in the country are subsidiaries of American companies.

The NEB during its short-lived relationship with Graham had one representative on its Board of Directors. He took no active role in the management of the company and Graham's officials felt that he was not very helpful. Most of the contact between the agency and the firm took place through him, though the two organisations had discussions about Graham's joining Insac. Eventually nothing came of this idea as Insac wanted to market software only.

Harlan Company

This enterprise, located near London, is the UK's largest biotechnology company. It has not yet become profitable; but undoubtedly will soon be so as it has a worldwide reputation for quality and excellence. Its major (though not its only) wares are monoclonal antibodies and monoclonal antibody products. Monoclonal antibodies can be used, e.g., in identifying toxins in food, in blood typing, and in manufacturing reagents for the purification of human interferon. (Various types of human interferon may turn out to be useful in the treatment of cancer.) In 1986 Harlan, founded in 1980, did almost £4 million worth of business (up from £0.826 million in 1983); and 90% of its sales were overseas.

Harlan was formed on the initiative of the NEB. The current chief executive of the firm was formerly on the Board's staff and he (with his degree in biochemistry) and some of his colleagues felt that there existed an opening for a UK biotechnology firm. This concept could not be put into practice immediately because of NEB internal problems that resulted from the Tory victory in 1979. It proved difficult to find good people to lead the contemplated venture. As a result NEB Chairman Sir Arthur Knight suggested that the NEB staff member become the head himself. He attracted an important scientist to work for the new enterprise and then got a unit of the government-funded Medical Research Council to allow the company to commercially exploit the monoclonal antibodies developed in the unit's labs. The researchers there were happy to see a UK rather than a US company refining and selling the end-results of their hard work.

At Sir Keith Joseph's insistence, private companies as well as the NEB participated in the initial funding of Harlan. It might have been possible for it to receive all its financing from private sources, for at the beginning of the 1980s biotechnology was a 'trendy' area. However, it is quite conceivable that no replacement for the NEB could have been found when the decision to set up Harlan was taken. Once again, there were few UK venture capitalists at this time and these were especially suspicious of 'start-up' endeavours. Each original investor had one member on Harlan's Board of Directors. The person appointed by the NEB was not one of its staff but acted on behalf of it. The Board applied some pressure on Harlan to achieve short-term results at the probable expense of long-term gains, but its own appointee helped the firm resist this urging. (He now holds an important position with the firm.) Harlan is extremely optimistic about the future; and has moved to a larger site in its community. By 1986 (when the NEB disposed of its Harlan shares) it had become the world's largest producer in bulk of monoclonal antibodies and had obtained the first license from the US Food and Drug Administration to manufacture these in bulk in America.

Ivy Company

This is one of the largest independent computer-peripheral manufacturers in Europe. Beginning in 1956 with 30 workers, it now employs over 2000 persons and, in 1983, sold over £70 million worth of products. In the mid-1970s it got into financial difficulties. No private banks would lend it money -- they claimed that it was too much in debt. Nor did it want to borrow money from the Department of Industry directly, as the rates charged were too high. So it went for financing to the NEB, which was happy to take a controlling shareholding in order to carry out its plan to play an important role in the development of UK high technology. And, in fact, without NEB aid, Ivy might well have gone out of business.

None the less, relations between Ivy and the NEB were stormy and harmful for the private firm during the first few years of the connection. An imaginative, forceful member of the NEB's staff wanted Ivy to enter into a joint venture with a major American high tech company to manufacture certain goods. The American concern was to contribute the products and management while Ivy was to put in the initial working capital and give the Americans a management fee. The US partner ended up delivering only two products to the new entity, one of which was a flop. Ultimately, it received £8 million in royalties on the article that was a success: Ivy paid three-quarters of this sum. Ivy was opposed to the whole deal from its inception but had to agree to it because of an NEB threat to cut off aid. The partnership incurred many costs over which Ivy had no control and so Ivy lost almost £10 million during the two year period 1980 and 1981.

By this time new people on the Board's staff were dealing with it. They were very supportive and agreed that the co-operative effort with the Americans had been a disaster from its point of view. The Board thus made payments of £12 million during 1982 to Ivy to reimburse it for some of the losses it had incurred because of the partnership. In 1982 it returned to the black and in 1983 made even more money. It remains profitable; and in 1984 a considerable percentage of the NEB's holding was sold to private investors.

Aside from the one debacle described above, the NEB maintained a hands-off attitude towards the management of Ivy. It had to submit one- and five-year plans to the Board; but not one of these ever was vetoed. The NEB never suggested new products for it to make but did urge some applicants for Board aid to talk over their ideas with Ivy instead. Finally, the Board could argue with some reason that despite the poor results, Ivy's collaboration with the American firm was a sensible idea: the latter is one of the world's pre-eminent high tech firms and it was not irrational to expect that its inventiveness and expertise would ultimately prove to be of benefit to its UK colleague.

Jane Company

This company is one of the few UK concerns making auto-engine testing equipment. It was founded in 1972 and by 1979 needed additional finance to purchase an adequate plant and bring in a new generation of products. It wrote to both the Board and ICFC asking for assistance. It accepted the Board's terms because it preferred having equity taken in it to borrowing money. This east-of-England undertaking could not get loans from local banks because its assets did not cover the amount it wanted to borrow and its directors were unwilling to give their personal guarantees for this indebtedness.

It did take a certain amount of time for the NEB to decide to aid Jane; but this was due to the climate of uncertainty emanating from the Tory victory in May 1979. Once it became clear that the Conservatives were not going to immediately abolish the NEB, the funding came quickly. The Board had the right to veto Jane's large capital expenditures and its dividend payments; but never exercised these prerogatives or in any manner seriously limited its freedom to act.

As seen in Chapter 1, in 1981 a firm known as Grosvenor Development Capital was established as an instrumentality for transferring the NEB's holdings to private hands. Three City institutions, including Equity Capital for Industry, together took about 70% of the stock, leaving the NEB with 29.5%. Eight NEB investments were moved to Grosvenor, Jane among them (somewhat unwillingly, since it was pleased with the Board). When the NEB took shares in Jane it had 15 employees; it now has slightly under 40. It then did no export business; but now it is beginning to ship to the far east and the Common Market. Then it made car-testing equipment only; now it plans to move into the medical electronics field in partnership with a German firm.

Krumpet Company

This firm, located in the unemployment-stricken northeast of England, makes storage tanks of up to twelve feet in diameter and up to 36 feet high. It also manufactures large paper cylinders used as components in electrical transformers. (The same material is used in the fabrication of both tanks and cylinders.) Its factory had been tailor-built for the tank-making venture by the town in which it is situated, the enterprise receiving aid both from the town council and the Department of Industry (under Section 7 of the 1972 Industry Act permitting the Department to subsidise companies located in economically-depressed areas). In 1978 it went into receivership; and the receiver sought a purchaser for the plant. He approached a large engineering concern a subsidiary of which assembled the paper cylinders for transformers. The engineering group became interested in the offer and began negotiating with the DOI, the town council, and the Northern Regional Office of the NEB.

Ultimately, the NEB and the engineering company agreed to create Krumpet on the site of the tank-assembly firm; the agency taking 40% of the equity and the private firm the remainder. The paper cylinder operations of the latter's subsidiary were removed to this locale with the aid of the funds coming from the state body. (DOI grants were also used for this purpose.) Before the NEB sold its shares to its colleague, it had two members on Krumpet's Board of Directors. These made constructive criticisms about marketing and other matters. Krumpet sent the Board its monthly profit-and-loss figures, as well as its one and three year plans. As at first it was not profitable, the NEB delegates on its Board wanted to close it down. However, the private investor had more of a 'risk-taking' attitude in this situation; saw some light at the end of the tunnel; and successfully pushed to keep it open. (Krumpet was set up just before the Thatcher victory in 1979; and thus the relationship between it and the NEB existed during a time in which the Board had to watch its step.) Krumpet is making a small profit now and plans to increase its export business (currently about 10%-15% of its turnover) and diversify its product range. It still has the number of employees it had when set up, i.e. about 40.

Lulu Company

This firm is located in an unemployment-stricken city in the north of England. The street on which it fronts used to be full of thriving industrial concerns: it now is lined only by Lulu, vacant space, and several enterprises furnishing services rather than producing goods. Before the mid-1970s Lulu concentrated on producing machinery for the tyre manufacturing trade; but this sector turned sour with the decline of the UK auto industry -- and Lulu's profits began a downward slide. Its management felt that if it were to survive it had to look to completely new products.

Its own merchant bank proved of little help. It first tried to discourage it from borrowing any new funds and then steered it to the ICFC. However, this occurred late in 1976 when ICFC had just been merged with Finance Corporation for Industry to form Finance For Industry. ICFC was, therefore, not too encouraging. Lulu did get a loan from the DOI and subsequently went to the NEB. The Board offered it an excellent financial package unencumbered by any red tape. Lulu dealt mainly with an NEB regional office: the director there did not give it much in the way of forms to fill out but simply said 'state your case'. Throughout, the interface between the public body and Lulu was excellent. The Board made a fast decision to grant financial assistance and quickly provided Lulu with cash and a loan guarantee in order to purchase the machinery needed to fabricate its new goods. It sent the Board monthly reports, annual budgets, and a three year forecast. Sometimes it fell behind on preparing these documents; but it agreed with the Board that when this happened the NEB would simply send an accountant to its office to get the information from it orally. The Board never interfered with its product development. Its non-financial support was, rather, on the bookkeeping side, helping the concern, for example, install a better system of cash flow forecasting. In order to stay alive, Lulu had to reduce its UK workforce from about 900 to about 350 and close its overseas subsidiaries. Though the suggestions for taking these steps did not come from the Board, neither it nor Lulu's union objected to them. The unions recognised that this surgery was necessary and that it was especially distressing for the Managing Director to have to hand out the pink slips, because he and those he fired all live in the vicinity of the plant.

Lulu's own bank finally did give it an overdraft with a high rate of interest. When it became impatient at Lulu's lack of profitability it demanded 'action'. To safeguard Lulu against any adverse moves by the bank, the NEB guaranteed £250,000 of the overdraft free of charge. The Board understood much better than the lender the problems of a firm converting from one article to others: the creditor naïvely believed that this conversion would make Lulu an instant hit. Moreover, the NEB regional director with whom Lulu dealt was an individual well versed in the ways of industry who also wanted to crusade for this economically-depressed but once mighty region. Some believe that Lulu will never become a big money-maker and thus that it might have been better to close it down in the mid-1970s. However, a private firm thought enough of its prospects in 1982 to acquire the NEB's holdings in it.

Morton Company

This is a small high tech concern located in a northern English town that has seen more than its share of economic tragedies in recent years. The city's major factory closed a few years ago and the rail line connecting it to the regional metropolis was recently abandoned. Morton's founders were two academics who originally got a loan from a well-known English bank to start in business. They soon needed between £50,000 and £100,000 more for research and development. Even though the date was the early 1980s UK venture capitalists were unwilling to deal in sums this small and the original lender was not happy about supplying Morton with more aid at this stage of its history. So the regional development agency suggested that Morton obtain funding from the NEB, which took 28% of the stock. It began talking seriously to the Board in January 1983 and by March of that year had received cash from the agency. It is uncertain what would have happened to Morton had it not been able to secure Board assistance: as seen, other sources of finance were not independently available at that particular moment. The NEB insisted that it would not invest in Morton unless its bank increased its loan. This it did, mainly because the NEB was now a partner in the enterprise. The Board made Morton produce a business plan and helped its directors, persons with little business experience, draw one up. The Board wanted it to show in this plan that there was a market for its products; but because it was a start-up company making an article about which not much was then known, it could not provide this demonstration. Nevertheless, the Board purchased equity anyway. In summer of 1983, when Morton needed more money to obtain the rights to a new operations system, it asked the Board for £25,000 more; and got this without any fuss.

The Board never exercised its prerogative to put a member on Morton's Board of Directors. The firm always sent the Board a monthly report. As its turnover was increasing rapidly and as it was showing a profit, the NEB never harassed it. Board employees spoke to its officers via telephone occasionally but never vetoed any proposed step they had a right to halt, e.g., a rise in the Managing Director's salary. The latter got along quite well with the Board representative with whom he usually dealt, though Morton felt that the dividends it had to pay the state body on its shares were too high.

In autumn of 1983 the Thatcher Government, as seen, announced that the role of the Board was to be severely contracted and that its regional offices were to be locked. Morton had been dealing with one of these exclusively and did not want to have to be in constant communication with the NEB's London bureau. So it decided to buy out the Board's investment and sell this to a private venture capitalist. Morton is very optimistic about its future: when the NEB came to its support it had only six employees but two years later had 15. It will increase its product range and try to export, especially to North America. The fulfilment of its ambitions would be a godsend to a community that reels from one crisis to another.

Ned Company

This electronics firm is also located in a depressed area in the north of England. It makes small transformers, including some used in computer games. Formed in 1965 by two friends, it was sold to a larger company and went into receivership. A member of the union representing its workers approached an NEB regional office. The personnel there decided that it had a bright future and had the Board purchase stock in it to resuscitate it. The director of the regional office moved much more swiftly than a bank would have to develop the financial package that saved Ned. (It is far from certain that a bank would have given it any help then.)

Before the NEB arrived on the scene, Ned had been the victim of crooked dealings. One of the directors of the private company that had owned it sold the land on which it is located in a rather questionable transaction. (Even today, it is unclear whether it holds title to this site.) When Ned became the NEB's subsidiary, the Board appointed a three man Board of Directors for it: the head of the NEB regional office, a person from the regional office staff (who is currently its Managing Director) and the company's then-Managing Director. Though the two NEB representatives looked at the monthly reports that Ned had to submit and attended the monthly meetings of the electronics firm's Board of Directors, they had no time nor any authority to supervise the day-to-day management of the company. Thus it was not until late 1979, more than two years after the Board had taken Ned over, that they began to suspect that the man they had appointed as Managing Director was a thief. Finally, a team of auditors discovered that he was stealing Ned's customers by steering them to a phoney outfit he controlled. After he was fired and jailed and the current Managing Director took over, Ned became profitable, thanks in part to a further infusion of £50,000 from the Board. By June of 1984 it was doing so well that the NEB holding in it was sold to a private corporation. The factory has almost 120 employees, most of whom are female assembly-line workers; and remains one of the largest employers in the town in which it is located. (When the Board acquired it, it had a staff of slightly under 100.)

Olga Company

This London-based enterprise is one of the UK's major developers of software. The NEB approached it in 1979: the initiative here came from the Board and not vice versa. The Board had several reasons for desiring to take a stake in Olga. It wanted to fund the development of a word processor by Olga that would be part of the fully automated office marketed by Nexos. More generally, it hoped to increase its stake in the high tech arena and acquire credibility by purchasing a company that was profitable and well-regarded. Before the Board purchased a holding in it, Olga had been owned by a US corporation that had wanted to move more and more of its operations across the Atlantic and to keep it small. The Board paid the Americans a good price for its shares but permitted Olga's staff to acquire the bulk of the equity. Though Olga at this time probably could have obtained private financing, it would not have received nearly as good a deal as the Board gave it -- and without excessive paperwork, by the way.

As we shall see later in our discussion of the Nexos quagmire, relations between the Board and Olga became quite strained despite the happy start. Moreover, the NEB representatives on Olga's Board of Directors did not know much about high technology. They certainly did not try to exercise day-to-day control of the company but posed questions at Olga's Board meetings that seemed to the firm's management not very helpful. During 1983 the NEB sold its shares in Olga, then a rapidly growing concern. In 1979, when the Board made its investment, it had about 600 employees; in 1985 it had 1400 workers in the UK and another 600 overseas. About half its business is export.

Pet Company

This now-profitable south-of-England company manufactures advanced electronic photo-typesetting machines. In the mid-1970s it was the largest -- and now is the only -- firm of its sort in the UK. It ran into financial difficulties, partly because it was overstaffed and partly because it had been too slow to adapt to new technologies. The Department of Industry called the NEB and suggested that Pet be bailed out as it was having difficulty getting finance from the private sector. The Board in partnership with one major bank took stock in and made loans to Pet. The state agency brought in a new manager and, as did the bank, obtained two seats on the concern's Board of Directors. The NEB members on that Board were active and able people. They had a background in industry and made useful and constructive criticisms. Both they and the bank representatives convinced one of Pet's major customers that it was not about to expire. They did not, however, take a part in the day-to-day management of the undertaking by, e.g., participating in determinations as to what services to offer its customers.

Over a year after the NEB-bank takeover, Pet was still an economic disaster zone. Therefore the NEB replaced its first manager with the individual who as of this writing is Managing Director of the company. This person felt strongly that it would go nowhere until excess staff were shed. When he was appointed over 1150 men and women worked for it: within a few years this number had shrunk to 545, though by 1985 it had risen to 650. In addition, he closed a plant in Scotland. Despite union unhappiness with these steps, the NEB backed him to the hilt even though it was not it who had originated the idea of the sackings or the shutdown.

If it were not for the aid provided by the Board and the bank Pet, 80% of whose business is exports, would probably have gone under or moved to the US. It should be emphasised that it was the NEB that persuaded the bank to participate in salvaging Pet. Moreover, in 1981 the Board and bank provided another tranche of assistance to help the company meet the redundancy payments triggered by the discharge of staff and to compensate it for exceptional write-offs of certain of its assets. Without this slice of funding, the firm would have collapsed.

Relations between Pet and the Board were generally very good, as seen. However, they did not run perfectly smoothly. As was usual for an NEB venture, Pet had to submit its budgets and annual and five year plans to the Board. The agency scrutinised these very closely and was, in the eyes of persons connected with Pet, too concerned with its profit-and-loss numbers and unwilling to make enough of an effort to understand the nature of its business and what steps it was taking to improve its affairs. In other words, Pet's head office believed that NEB staff were too much the accountants and not enough the industrialists. However, the NEB representatives on Pet's Board of Directors smoothed things over to some extent. (The Board disposed of its holdings in Pet a few years ago.)

Powerdrive PSR (Real Name)

This is the Midlands company that came into being when the NEB financed the purchase of a division of a large US corporation by the management of that unit (which the Americans wanted to close). The management buyout was described earlier in this book in the course of our discussion of how the press treated the NEB. As will be remembered, the firm makes air-operated clutches and brakes for industrial machines. It will also be recalled that the managers went to both clearing and merchant banks and to the ICFC for a deal under which they (the managers) would be able to obtain a controlling shareholding at a reasonable price. Only then did they turn to the NEB, whch quickly worked out a satisfactory package. The company during the negotiations dealt with three NEB persons, all of whom it felt were top-notch. All had backgrounds in industry and one was an engineer, a qualification that no banker they spoke to could claim. The NEB people thus could understand Powerdrive's problems and needs. Within two or three weeks, all formalities were completed despite the fact that the founder had to submit a company history, a five year plan, and a description of its products and chief personnel. The Board was, in fact, quite impressed with all these documents.

The NEB aid was used, of course, in the acquisition of the subsidiary that made Powerdrive an independent corporation. After the new concern was underway, the NEB had two non-executive directors on its Board -- both people with whom it had originally dealt -- but these people did not involve themselves in the day-to-day running of the firm. Powerdrive had to submit monthly reports and annual plans; but these were never criticised. The fact that the Board was an investor made it easier for the concern to get loans from private banks.

It is uncertain what would have happened had Powerdrive not received financial assistance from the NEB. It is quite possible that the American corporation would have carried out its threat to close it down. Powerdrive has been profitable from its inception and was transferred to Grosvenor Development Capital in 1981. In 1983, Grosvenor sold it to a larger group, whose subsidiary it remains today. Its executives have, to put it mildly, very fond memories of the NEB connection.

Quirk Company

This firm, engaged in the manufacture, leasing and repair of high-pressure water pumps, has its plant in a valley town in the north of England. The city is in an area of considerable unemployment but is not as badly off in this regard as many of its neighbours. In 1981 the company decided to change from selling pumps to manufacturing them. However, recession intervened and the conversion proved expensive. Consequently, it needed external financing to develop its production capability. The local banks were unwilling to lend to it until more equity was put into the firm. It had discussions with both the ICFC and the NEB; but outside accountants thought the state agency was offering a better deal.

Relations between Quirk and the NEB were beset by friction. The Board was dissatisfied with the financial material that Quirk submitted to them in its application -- it wanted better market forecasts and updated accounts. Finally, Quirk had to use a firm of accountants to do the job and pay, as well, for the accountants used by the Board and the lawyers employed by both sides. The total bill came to £17,000, which Quirk feels is quite a bit for a small firm to have to expend. It took eight months until the NEB funding came through: the firm's chief executive had to spend a considerable amount of time during this period talking to a Board staff member. This man was permitted to attend Quirk's Board meetings: though he is an innovative, dynamic individual he said little during these meetings themselves.

Soon after the Board invested in the company the regional office with which Quirk had been dealing was shut. This means that it had to begin working with Board people in London whom it did not know. Also, the rapid turnover in the London office meant that it did not develop any permanent relationship with any Board staff members there. The Board, which by now has disposed of its Quirk stock, required the company to submit a monthly financial report but imposed no conditions on its way of doing business and did not interfere in its day-to-day management. When it was considering whether to support Quirk, it concluded that its chief executive was overworked and wisely and successfully persuaded him to hire a full-time accountant. The firm has been profitable since the NEB took its equity holding and has expanded its workforce from 60 to 95. It hopes to begin exporting its pumps to the US and the Common Market. (At present, it is in the hands of an NEB-owned subsidiary, which is trying to privatise it.)

Richenda Company

This is a paper-making firm one of whose major mills is located in the southwest of England. In the mid-1970s the concern began losing money, thanks mainly to problems at that site. These resulted from the fact that the glazed paper produced there was made by old machines, which were costly to operate and thus put Richenda at a serious competitive disadvantage. In 1970 the firm had purchased a modern glazed paper-making device from Finland for the mill; but it had never been installed and remained in cartons. Richenda realised that the only way it could be brought back to profitability was to get that new machine working. However, it found that private banks did not want to lend to it and that nothing came of its discussions with the then-fledgling Equity Capital for Industry. Thus it decided to approach the NEB, recently set up and well-publicised.

Richenda engaged in lengthy and at times rather stormy negotiations with the Board. After a tentative agreement had been reached, the share price of Richenda's stock kept falling, which frightened the NEB. It therefore brought in a well-known merchant banker to help it renegotiate the initial contract in the light of the lower price. Ultimately, it agreed to purchase its shares at slightly above the market rate; and also loaned Richenda £620,000.

Once the transaction had been consummated, relations between Richenda and the Board became very good. The individual who had proven difficult during the negotiations was transferred to another NEB division and his successor was easy to work with. The agency never appointed a director to Richenda's Board though it had the right to do so. It never attempted to intervene in the day-to-day management of Richenda but wanted to see its monthly and annual corporate plans. In addition, the firm had to submit a five year plan to the Board. In practice, the only other contact between the two was a bimonthly meeting in London between the agency member responsible for Richenda and an officer of the firm. At these conclaves the monthly plans were discussed. After the five year plan had been submitted, that officer went before the Board to lay before it Richenda's plans for expansion. Though the new machine was not yet fully operative and the mill was losing more and more money, the Board treated him with courtesy. In late 1977, soon after that apparatus began running full speed ahead, Richenda held an open house to show it off. Princess Alexandra visited as did a delegate of an American multinational who was so impressed by what he saw that he made a bid for Richenda. Sir Leslie Murphy, the new NEB chairman, accepted the offer; and the firm remains under the control of this US holding company today. Had it not been for the NEB assistance that got the machine in working order, Richenda might well have closed the doors of the mill where it was sited. (Richenda was the first of the NEB's companies to be privatised; and it should be noted that this step was taken while Labour was still in power.)

Sam Company

This is a very small firm (two-and-a-half employees) located in a depressed industrial town in the north of England. It makes a high-quality screen for use in colour printing. The NEB and the enterprise board of the city were enthusiastic about the product and both took equity stakes in it when it was set up. It has never proven profitable; but the ex-NEB official who handled the negotiations with its founder still has confidence in the article it makes and feels that it may become more popular in the future. This man visited quite a few potential customers for the screen. Most liked it and predicted that it would find an extensive market. Some said that they were likely to order it themselves. However, few did as they remained content with more tried-and-true devices. Sam is still in existence because the founder (who is also its current head) does not draw much of a salary and because it is increasing its transatlantic business. In 1985-86 the NEB equity in it was transferred to a wholly-owned NEB subsidiary which will attempt to sell these shares.

Tamsin Company

This concern, founded in 1969, orginally concentrated on developing computer-aided-design equipment. In this connection, it entered into a joint venture with the National Research Development Corporation, ultimately to become the NEB's partner in the British Technology Group. Tamsin needed cash for research and development. It never attempted to get this from a private source, as this probably would have been a futile step. The NRDC suggested that it get assistance from the NEB, which took an equity stake in it. Though the NEB money was used for R and D for new high technology products, the company soon found that these manufacturing efforts were unprofitable and halted them. In 1979 it had 350 employees: in 1985 only 220. It currently focuses on the less glamorous areas of marketing and servicing computer hardware and selling and supporting software, most of which comes from Japan and the US. It is one of the largest firms of this genre in the country. After a few losing years in the early 1980s, it was totally privatised in 1985 and returned to profit in 1986.

Tamsin is happy about its experience with the Board. The agency had a representative on the firm's Board of Directors and the company had to submit to it a monthly report; but the NEB did not intervene in the day-to-day affairs of this investment. The first NEB director would ask frequent questions and initially turned up at all the Board of Directors' monthly meetings. However, his suggestions were never intended to pressure or force the company to take any particular step. Soon he and his successors developed the habit of attending only every third or fourth session. When the NEB took its equity it required that Tamsin submit a five year plan, which its directors feel was not worth very much. The Board had a major accounting firm conduct an audit and itself did a market analysis for Tamsin. All in all very little paperwork was required before the investment was approved: the concern was not even required to make its own market predictions. The NEB aid was quick in coming. Both Tamsin's management and the NEB people who dealt with them were knowledgeable about high technology and so developed a good and understanding relationship.

Ulysses Company

This is a pharmaceuticals company, with headquarters in Wales, that has recently moved into biotechnology. Its research scientists discovered a pig's blood derivative of use in treating certain human haemophiliacs. Management then started looking for funding to make possible the manufacture of this product. It was unsuccessful in obtaining financing from conventional financial sources. It next sought out the NEB and Prutec, the high tech investment company funded by Prudential Assurance that has just folded its tents. Both of these institutions agreed to take shares in Ulysses. Without this assistance, the commercially-practicable version of the blood derivative never would have been developed; or, at best, a foreign concern might have brought it to market. In fact, Ulysses might even have gone entirely out of business.

Prutec and the NEB imposed certain conditions upon Ulysses' receipt of aid. Each was to have a delegate on its Board of Directors. Moreover, an independent chairman and a financial controller had to be appointed. Soon after the investment,

Ulysses began losing money at an alarming rate and faced a cash flow crisis. Its financial controller thus had to remain in close and constant contact with both institutional investors. Some persons aware of Ulysses' problems feel that neither had taken a close enough look at the plans presented to them in support of the funding. However, though the concern has not yet become profitable and its staff has had to be reduced from 70 to 50, it has high hopes of entering the black and was sold to a private corporation in 1984. Ulysses has helped a major American biotechnology company synthesise (via genetic engineering) a product related to its original anti-haemophilia find; and both the porcine and the synthetic medicines should be free from diseases such as hepatitis and AIDS that might well be lurking in the counterpart obtained from human blood.

Velma Company

This is a rapidly growing high tech firm located in the south of England. In 1978, when the NEB first invested in it, it had only 200 employees. It now has 1300, 900 of whom are in the UK. (Part of this increase was due to a merger with another NEB-funded high tech concern.) Until recently, about 30% of its market was exports; but this has just increased to 50%. Even in 1977, when it approached the NEB, it could have received finance from conventional sources. If Velma's officers had not contacted it, it surely would have written or telephoned them, as it wanted to (and did) secure their participation in its Insac project designed to market UK software abroad.

The Board had one representative on Velma's Board of Directors. Velma's management feels that he made no positive contribution to its functioning; but admits that he took no steps to hamper it. As Velma has always been quite profitable, there was no scope for the NEB to bring about improvements in management or accounting techniques; though it had to file monthly reports and annual plans. The state body did not intervene in Velma's day-to-day affairs: relations between it and the firm were on the whole cool but not extensive. When an offer was made to the NEB for its shares, it accepted without complaint. Velma wanted to see the NEB out because the Board's presence might have made it more difficult for it to sell its stock to the public and also because it feared that the Tories would stop the NEB from granting it any more financial assistance.

William Company

This is a high tech firm located in a large town in the north of England. It produces computers, computer peripherals and software. Until recently, it was one of the largest UK manufacturers of business computers. It was begun in 1973 by an imaginative, dynamic individual who was not the world's most efficient manager. The NEB invested in it in 1977 as part of its plan to increase the UK's high tech capabilities. The concern needed money to expand but the City was not willing to provide it. For a while after it came under the Board's wing it was profitable but it ran into difficulties in the early 1980s because it built (with Department of Industry assistance) a new, huge factory and because some of its overseas operations were hard to supervise and ultimately sunk into the red. In 1983 it underwent a capital restructuring and some interest payments were forgiven. However, by 1986 its workforce had shrunk from 1300 to 250; its modernistic plant had been sold; and many of its assets had been transferred to a US company, which did hire about 150 of its former staff. The Board had one seat on its Board of Directors but the various incumbents never interfered with the day-to-day management of the company. It proved, however, very useful to William in talking to other government agencies on its behalf. (The NEB's stake in the firm was disposed of a few years ago at a loss of £2.2 million.)

Xerxes Company

This is a computer-aided-design company located in the Midlands. It formerly was a division of a much larger UK corporation; and its present Managing Director had been hired by that firm to put this section on its feet. Then the parent decided to sell it, a resolution which presented its supervisory staff with the opportunity for a management buyout. The owner assented to this arrangement; but the managers needed cash. They first went to ICFC but did not get much satisfaction there because this private venture capitalist wanted Xerxes to reach profitability earlier than its hopeful owners were projecting. Finally, the future Managing Director put up some savings of his own and received some funds thanks to a government-guaranteed loan scheme for small firms. A big UK commercial bank offered to make a loan on condition more equity was put into the venture. So Xerxes' organisers went to the NEB (which it had heard of through its dealings with another Board-aided firm) in the hope that it would acquire some shares in the new company. The NEB took its time making a decision, which created great tension among the organisers because Xerxes had already begun operations and needed the additional money to keep its employees from leaving.

The NEB's attitude was basically a sympathetic one but it wanted a better business plan submitted. Finally, an expensive but high-quality one was drafted and Xerxes received Board assistance in 1982. However, it immediately met with financial difficulties even though it reduced its staff from 50 to 18. Because of a computer that was too large for its needs, it had to charge a non-competitive price for its product and soon lost many of its old customers. To keep afloat it had to curtail its sales and marketing division. It thus was in dire need of help to reopen this section, to buy a smaller computer, and to meet the costs of necessary research and development. It found it difficult to get this additional finance from anywhere, including the NEB. The problem was that it was not meeting the targets embodied in its business plans, which it had to continue to submit to the Board.

It was here that the two directors that the NEB had placed on Xerxes' Board came to the rescue. Very competent individuals, they did not interfere in the day-to-day management of the company but did convince the state body that Xerxes would soon become profitable if adequately supported. So it gave Xerxes an extra tranche of money and guaranteed loans made to it by various banks. The sales and marketing office has been reopened; and the firm has 20 employees as of this writing. It plans to hire ten more and increase the export share of its business from the current 5%. The quality of Xerxes' products is high; it has highly-trained scientists on its staff and a tight management team; and thus its future is promising. Were it not for NEB assistance, it would not be open for business today.

Yolanda Company

This is a small company located in a large northern city. Like Xerxes, it is in the business of computer-aided-design but has only two full-time and two part-time employees. The founder (the current Managing Director) had been working for the local university in the early 1980s but decided to leave to establish his own firm when that institution was hit by government cutbacks. He went for aid to the NEB partly because in the past he had had projects funded by the NRDC, the NEB's partner in the British Technology Group; and partly because he knew he could not get assistance from regular banks, which usually shun start-up ventures. He also felt that ICFC and ECI would not give him and his partner as good a deal as would the NEB. So they dropped in at the Board's regional office, which told them that they had only to supply a business plan and a list of customers who would be interested in Yolanda's product. The Board checked with the companies whose names they furnished and found the plan satisfactory. The organisers had to hire a lawyer and an accountant to draft the plan and the NEB contract; but they felt that this was an eminently reasonable precondition of government aid. It took a bit over six months after the plan was submitted for the NEB moneys (used, e.g., to buy software and carry out a market survey of the US) to start flowing.

A good deal of time elapsed before Yolanda made its first sale and during this period it naturally had money problems. When it informed the Board that its management could not afford to attend an important trade conference in Italy, the NEB supplied a £10,000 loan. Its first order was received as a result of this exhibition and, as a consequence, it was able to pay off some of its creditors. It had to submit short reports to the NEB every two or three months and, when I visited its headquarters, the agency was insisting that its plan for the next year be turned in as soon as possible since it was late: the Managing Director admitted that the Board's importuning was justified. When the NEB's regional bureau was in operation Yolanda often phoned it to ask questions about financial or accounting (as opposed to marketing or product development) problems. The Managing Director was happy that this office was available to give suggestions on these matters and indicated that the advice it gave often turned out to be quite helpful (e.g., the employees should take less in salary but the company should buy a car). After the regional headquarters was phased out, a visitor from the NEB in London would arrive every so often. Yolanda was very pleased with the Board and feels that it is an institution that greatly benefits the country. The firm has just become profitable and makes a fine product; and so the future looks bright for it. Without NEB aid it might well not be in existence today. (In 1985-86 the Board's stake in Yolanda was turned over to a wholly-owned Board subsidiary which will try to market this stock.)

Zelda Company

This is a highly-successful enterprise that exports UK know-how in the health service field to other countries, particularly in the Middle East. It superintends hospitals abroad and also delivers medical supplies and hardware to other countries. It came into being after the NEB, in partnership with a private firm managing hospitals in the UK and elsewhere, set up in 1977 a company to sell medical provisions overseas. Several months later, Zelda was formed by a merger of the medical supply company and the hospital-managing firm. Under the merger agreement, the NEB took 70% of Zelda and the three institutional shareholders that had owned the firm took 10% each.

The deal founding Zelda was popular neither with those Tories who continually sniped at the NEB nor with the left wing of the Labour Party. The journal *Private Eye* claimed that the hospital-manager ancestor of Zelda had won a major hospital-superintendency contract in the Middle East by bribing the government of the relevant country, which alleged graft left wing Labourite MP Dennis Skinner referred to as a 'sleazy episode'. The Government merely and weakly responded that the hospital-managing concern denied the bribery charges.

The NEB decided to purchase the hospital-managing firm after it had obtained that contract mentioned above. No one would write a performance bond for the deal even though it

111

appeared to be a profitable one. Then an American concern made overtures to buy the company. At this point the NEB decided that the loss of its export business would be a tragedy for the UK and thus made its offer. After the NEB takeover Zelda executed the agreement without putting up a performance bond. Had Zelda not performed its end of the bargain the Board would have suffered a £6 million loss; and so it did take a big and ultimately successful gamble in backing its subsidiary. (One of the leading figures on the NEB, even before he joined it, had thought up the idea that it should back a firm like Zelda.)

The NEB appointed one of its staff as Zelda's Chairman. One NEB employee spent six months drawing up a budget for it, as its hospital-management progenitor never had had one. This man soon left the Board and went to work for Zelda, whose Finance Director he remains. Zelda had to submit the usual plans and reports to the NEB, which had a representative on its Board of Directors. He understood its problems and neither he nor his superiors ever tried to get control of its day-to-day management. There was one major clash between the NEB and the firm, a fight that was based solely on political grounds. Zelda wanted to build private hospitals in the UK to compete with American firms that were doing this. As these private infirmaries might have siphoned off patients from the National Health Service, whose viability the Labour Government wanted to safeguard, the NEB refused to let Zelda acquire private hospitals in the UK while that Government was in power. After the Tories took over, it was permitted to build some in Britain. Zelda was privatised in 1983 and, at present, manages more hospital beds in the Middle East than any of its competitors. It hopes soon to do business in France and the Canary Islands.

Ailsa Company

In the late 1970s the major NEB rescue operation, British Leyland automobile manufacturers, was beset by lagging sales, strikes and inflation. Its dealers gave it a deposit for the BL cars they had in stock; but this payment was rather low. This contributed to a cash flow crisis at the company. A major British merchant bank devised a scheme under which a firm would be set up that would place a reasonably large deposit with BL for each finished car leaving its factories, The firm, in turn, would be reimbursed through collecting from the dealers a 'display charge'. The scheme benefited BL by increasing its cash flow by £30 million a year. It helped the dealers, as well, because they had been receiving interest of only 1% on their prepayment to the car maker.

The scheme came to the attention of BL, which liked it. It suggested that the NEB become one shareholder in the concern that would be incorporated to put it into effect. The NEB agreed and thus took a more than 75% holding in Ailsa, formed in early 1979. (The National Coal Board Pension Fund was another investor.) BL wanted the NEB to participate because it realised that it would be difficult securing from private institutions the cash needed to start Ailsa. The NEB selected Ailsa's management and also had two members on its Board of Directors. The crucial decisions were made by its Chairman and Managing Director, who occasionally consulted with the NEB and the other shareholders. Relations between Ailsa and the Board remained good until it was privatised in 1984: one reason for the lack of tension was that Ailsa, unlike BL, was profitable from the start. It had great freedom to determine how to report its activities to the Board: in practice, it forwarded only monthly reports. If Ailsa had not come into existence, some feel that BL would have folded in 1979 due to the above-noted shortage of cash. Ailsa thus has helped keep this giant alive, though it itself is relatively small -- starting with five employees and engaging 20 in 1985. Its new owner hopes that it will be able to develop relationships with auto manufacturers in addition to BL.

Bruce Company

This is a Midlands concern whose main product is a special type of battery that is used by the UK military. It was formerly the advanced products division of the UK subsidiary of a US multinational. This subsidiary was then taken over by a UK corporation, which indicated that it wanted to shut the advanced products unit. When this projected closure was announced, the division's management in 1982 approached the NEB to arrange a management buyout. They chose this route because they were fairly sure that they could not get much in the way of private venture capital: UK venture capitalists were reluctant to finance the transfer of laboratory technology to production, especially in a start-up situation. The Board worked with a brokerage house to find two private institutional investors to join in the buyout: a deal was arranged whereby the Board and these two private firms took equal shares in Bruce.

In order to get this public-cum-private investment, Bruce's organisers had to prepare business plans, which were perhaps a bit too optimistic. They also had to incur considerable expenses to hire accountants and solicitors to help them in the negotiations with the Board and the other venture capitalists; but these professionals have been useful since Bruce came into being in 1982 with 26 employees. (At one time, the division had 80 persons working for it.) The money from the investors was used to purchase the plant Bruce currently occupies and to obtain working capital.

For the first few years of its existence, the firm decided to concentrate on producing batteries for the Ministry of Defence, which had promised its founders orders even before its establishment. It now also works on research and development contracts, especially for the armed services. After losing money (as predicted) during 1982 and 1983, it became profitable in 1984 and now employs 108 persons and hopes to begin exporting to the Common Market soon. During 1985-86, the NEB's equity was transferred to the NRDC.

Relations between Bruce and the Board were extremely good. The NEB selected the Chairman of the company; and it and the other institutional investors had representatives on its Board of Directors. The spokespersons for the other two investors pushed it to expand too quickly; but the NEB's delegate was more realistic. The NEB-appointed Chairman was also opposed to having it grow too swiftly. It had to submit to the Board monthly reports, a three year plan and a yearly budget. The public agency commented about these but never demanded that they be revised. For practical purposes, Bruce dealt with only one man at NEB headquarters and the firm found this continuity a great help.

The three institutional investors during the years when Bruce was in the red were interested mainly in its profit and loss statement; but, after it turned the corner, they switched their attention to whether it was marketing its product properly. However, they never helped it improve its selling efforts and none had people who were thoroughly *au courant* with the technology that it employs. It found that customers were attracted to it because it was backed by the Board, which was equated with the UK government. In the words of one of its directors, it found there was a 'cachet' in having the NEB as one of its owners. Thus Bruce has good reason to be grateful to the Board: without NEB assistance it would never have taken off.

Carol Company

This company is located in a medium-sized town in the north of England. Its main product is rubber sheets that are used for various purposes. It had once been part of a firm employing 2000 persons that was taken over by another large UK company during the 1970s. This undertaking then sold this division to a competitor, which immediately announced that it would lock its doors. Its managers had been anticipating such an event and had spoken to a business contact of theirs who had been a member of an NEB Regional Board. He in turn suggested that they go to the NEB's regional office for assistance in purchasing their division. (They could not initially borrow from local banks.) The county enterprise board also expressed its willingness to help; and the NEB created a package under which it, the county enterprise board, and the ICFC would fund this management buyout. Before the Board and the others gave them assistance the organisers had to furnish a cash flow forecast. The three potential investors commissioned a market survey and an independent accountant submitted his own financial appraisal. The founders did have to hire solicitors and an auditor to help them prepare the documents they had to provide.

Carol was formed in March 1983 and began trading in May of that year. (The NEB sold its stake during 1985-86.) It needed and used the NEB and the other investors' money to relocate all its equipment to one site on the industrial estate on which it is located. These funds were also used to buy materials and modernise the equipment used in production. Carol soon got a loan from a commercial bank; but only because it was backed by the Board and the other institutional investors. The Board never exercised its right to put a representative on Carol's Board of Directors. The company is well organised and has been profitable since its founding. It sent the Board monthly a set of accounts and reports; and every three months its officials met with various representatives of the institutional shareholders. These latter did not intervene in its day-to-day-management: they did not, e.g., suggest new customers and products. They would have wanted to be consulted, however, if Carol had desired to make a big capital expenditure or raise significantly the salaries of its management. Carol now employs 40 people; and hopes to expand into the service sector. Without the Board's help, Carol probably would not exist today.

Daisy Company

This is a small company located in the north of England that was another venture negotiated by a regional office of the NEB. It is a software concern that developed an excellent program for recording product sales instantly. Its research activities drove it to the edge of bankruptcy and it found it difficult to get assistance from a commercial bank. The firm continued to meet with financial woes after the NEB stepped in. So the Board had to fire its old chairman and replace him with a man who was then a member of its own staff. The new executive had to effect economies -- e.g., discharge three senior people to save £20,000 a month. He also worked hard to secure three new contracts for Daisy: the ex-chairman was good on product improvement but weak on marketing. Because of the second head's efforts and, more generally, because of the NEB presence in the firm, a commercial bank was induced to make Daisy a loan. Though it is still in the red, its product is so good that it is highly likely to turn a profit in the very near future. (It is now in the hands of a fully-owned NEB subsidiary.)

NOTE

1. US General Accounting Office, *Government-industry cooperation*, p. 18.

7

Highlights of the Case Studies

This chapter will spotlight the major points revealed by the case studies of the NEB as venture capitalist appearing in the last chapter and evaluate several specific matters about the Board disclosed there. Later, Chapter 16 will weigh the Board's accomplishments as venture capitalist in the light of all the data of Chapters 1 through 15.

One striking fact uncovered by the case studies is how difficult it has been in the UK for new companies, or for firms that are making a fine product or delivering a valuable service but are having financial difficulties, to get help from banks. We can note as examples Elspeth Company, repairing the nation's offshore oil rigs; Ivy, the large computer-peripheral manufacturer; Jane, the maker of auto-engine testing equipment; Lulu, the old northern company that used to produce machinery for the tyre industry; Pet, the specialist in advanced electronic typesetting equipment; Powerdrive, the fabricator of air-operated equipment for industrial machines; Quirk, the high-pressure water pump concern; Richenda, the paper-maker; Ulysses, the biotechnology firm; Xerxes, the computer-aided-design people; Carol, the rubber-sheet maker; and Daisy, the developer of an imaginative computer program. All these undertakings either could not obtain any support from commercial or merchant banks (e.g., Elspeth, Ivy) or only received this after the NEB had taken or promised to take an equity holding in them (e.g., Pet, Quirk). In addition, electronics firm Able could not get private bank help for its projected expansion. In some cases (e.g., Yolanda, another computer-aided-design venture; Tamsin, the servicer of computer hardware and software) the concern never even attempted to seek assistance from the banks, knowing that this would be useless. Only a handful of

117

the companies covered in the case studies (e.g., software houses Olga and Velma) could have received bank funding in the absence of an NEB presence. Morton, the recently-founded high tech company located in the north, did initially negotiate a bank loan; but could not acquire any more funds from that source until the Board had taken an equity stake. Harlan, the major UK biotechnology concern, might have been able to receive private financing without NEB intervention, but this is far from certain. Grylls and Redwood's contention[1] that there was during the NEB's heyday no real 'market gap' for small, risk-taking firms is simply not borne out by the facts.

It is true that ICFC (merged, as seen, to form Finance For Industry, which is now known as 3i) and Equity Capital For Industry (ECI) were available throughout the 1976-1984 period to aid these enterprises. But the NEB proved bolder in supporting them than did either of these private venture capitalists. Thus Baker Company, the concern that rents space to one-or-two person enterprises in a converted mill, found that ICFC would look at it only if the NEB would. Jane and Quirk received better offers from the Board than from ICFC. The latter did not provide much encouragement to Lulu or Powerdrive; and ECI was not of much help to Richenda. It was the Board that took the initiative in convincing ICFC to join in aiding Carol, not vice versa. Xerxes was told by ICFC that it would have to reach profitability earlier than its incorporators thought possible. Tamsin's founders had heard enough about ICFC and ECI to realise that they would not give them as good a package as the Board was willing to arrange. It is not my purpose here to 'put down' ICFC or ECI, both of which have played -- and still have -- an important role in financing UK corporations that have trouble getting conventional financing. I simply want to demonstrate (1) that there were firms that they first turned their backs to that the Board supported, which further indicates that at least in the recent past there was a niche for a venture capitalist such as this public agency; and (2) that (as a member of the Tory Party I interviewed emphasised) in some situations where the Board and one or both of these private venture capitalists were willing to step in, the Board assistance was offered on better terms.

Contrary to the general assumption about the behaviour of public institutions, the NEB did not require the firms it was considering for aid to file with it an excessive amount of paperwork. It is true that every enterprise it contemplated had to submit to it evidence of its financial condition and prospects and that every firm it supported had to file monthly reports and long-term plans. However, this is standard operating procedure for any venture capitalist. An undertaking of this type that does not study thoroughly the present state and future possibilities of the companies in which it seeks to invest would indeed be behaving bizarrely. What would we think of a private person who threw £100,000 into a corporation without knowing anything about it! And it would have been even worse for the NEB not to demand both evidence of the outlook for the companies it proposed to succour and a flow of data about the concerns in which it had taken a stake. For, as its critics always reminded us, it was using public money. They who negligently toss their own funds into a outfit about which they know little are simply being stupid on their own account; but directors of a state body that behaves in a similar fashion are betraying a trust reposed in them by the community.

On a matter somewhat related to the red tape problem, it will be remembered that Quirk complained that it had to spend quite a bit of money hiring a firm of accountants to do a better market forecast for the Board and also pay all the lawyers' and accountants' bills resulting from the negotiations. Some of this lament appears justified. Though it was very reasonable for the NEB to compel Quirk to hire professionals to draft the business plan that would enable it to determine whether Quirk was a sensible investment, requiring a small, recession-hit concern to pay the solicitors for both sides seems a bit much.

Firms usually received NEB financing within a reasonably short time after they had applied for it. Examples include electronics firm Able; mill space renter Baker (aid received within a few weeks after request); Lulu; Morton (only two months elapsed between beginning of serious negotiations and the aid); Ned (the maker of small transformers); and Powerdrive (formalities completed in two or three weeks). It should also be remembered that, under certain circumstances, taking a long time to make a decision was a desirable *modus operandi*. This was certainly true, for instance, with respect to computer-aided-design partnership Yolanda. It took about a half year after the business plan was submitted before the NEB's cash was forthcoming. However, this venture had been founded by two persons who had no business experience and no guaranteed sales. Therefore, the NEB was well within its rights holding off the financing until it had checked with potential customers. Xerxes, the other computer-aided-design undertaking helped by it, needed its public money desperately and became very tense when this was not handed over immediately. The reason for the delay was that the Board wanted another business plan submitted. Given that this was a management buyout and that the plan originally filed was not satisfactory, the Board's caution was understandable even though the firm needed funds to retain its workforce. Richenda was annoyed that the NEB insisted on paying a lower price for its shares than that stated in the tentative original agreement between the parties. However, this obdurateness was sensible in the light of the continually-falling price of the company's stock: one can imagine the howl that would have emanated from the press and the Tory right had the NEB paid a price far above the market price on the date when it actually became an equity holder. (Admittedly, it did perhaps delay a bit too long in providing extra funding for electric motor assembler David when that firm was on the brink of bankruptcy.)

The Board was not reluctant to provide firms with more competent leaders and/or to improve their management practices. When David was purchased, it was losing money at least partly because of frequent changes in chief executive. The NEB put in a totally new management team that, while the firm was wallowing in red ink, was expert enough to use clever financing devices (e.g., selling assets and leasing them back) in order to avoid bankruptcy and steer it back to profitability. When the Board had difficulty finding a good person outside its ranks to head start-up biotechnology company Harlan, it picked as chairperson a very able man from its own staff. When engine-testing equipment manufacturer Jane was falling short of its business targets, a more capable Managing Director was hired by the Board. The first NEB-appointed chief of electronic photo-typesetting equipment fabricator Pet proved weak; but his NEB-chosen successor turned the company around. The Board compelled Quirk's overextended director to get a full-time accountant for the firm. It made Yolanda contract with professionals to prepare its business plan and itself gave it good advice on financial and accounting problems. The ancestor of health care know-how exporter Zelda had never bothered to draw up a budget; but the NEB forced Zelda to do so and had one of its own staff assemble the first one. Though it was expensive for battery-maker Bruce to engage accountants and solicitors to help it in its negotiations with the Board, these persons proved valuable to it in later years. The Board had to replace Daisy's first chairman, who was no good at marketing, with one of its own staff who was a more experienced manager: this saved the venture from bankruptcy. It is true that the first NEB-nominated Managing Director of small-transformer manufacturer Ned proved to be dishonest; but the firm has prospered under the individual the Board hired to succeed him.

The NEB behaved like other venture capitalists in usually eschewing participation in the 'substantive' management of its companies, i.e. in their day-to-day decisions and their mid- and long-range policy making. That is, it rarely intervened in judgements about what and how much to produce, what customers to search out, whether to increase exports, whom to promote and hire, where to locate, whether to acquire new machinery, etc. (We are, evidently, distinguishing here between the Board and the managing directors it placed in charge of its firms.) There was a handful of instances, however, where it did become heavily involved in making substantive decisions for its undertakings. It will be remembered that electric motor manufacturer David was pressured by it to re-enter the US market. At least some of the firm's officers were opposed to this idea; and ultimately the Board itself turned against the project. (One can argue that the NEB looked foolish first urging a step and then speaking out against it. However, one can defend it by noting that switching policy was a much more sensible course of action than insisting on conduct that it came to believe would lead its subsidiary to ruin.)

The second occasion on which we saw the Board intervening in the substantive management of one of its companies was in the case of Ivy, the large manufacturer of computer peripherals. Here, as seen, it threatened to cut off aid unless Ivy entered into a joint venture with a well-known American high tech company to manufacture certain products. As also noted, the venture proved financially disastrous for Ivy even though the US concern was and is a highly reputable one. Third, the Board unsuccessfully tried to push biotechnology firm Harlan to achieve short-term results. And, fourth, we saw it in the days when Labour was still in power force Zelda to scrap its plans to acquire private hospitals. That substantive management decision was, of course, made for political rather than economic reasons. But NEB substantive management decisions were, to repeat, the exception rather than the rule: normally, the Board did not formulate or veto its companies' proposed major projects though it often had a contractual right to do so.

There is, naturally, nothing *per se* wrong for a venture capitalist such as the NEB to on occasion take a close look at its investments and even make substantive policy decisions for them. Actions of this sort are especially necessary when the subsidiary is losing money, though not all of the examples we have cited can be justified on that particular ground. There is, actually, one company that it should have kept under closer surveillance. This was William, the producer of computers, peripherals and software. It sprouted wings the first few years after it entered the Board's nest; but then its founder neglected its efficient management and had it move into quarters that were too big and expensive. Consequently, it came upon hard times. Surely, the NEB's central headquarters or the NEB representative on William's Board of Directors should have asked piercing questions and fought hard to delay the construction of the new building. (The NEB alone could not have postponed the erection of the new edifice, for it did not own a majority of the firm's voting shares.)

As will be remembered, the Board had one or more non-executive directors on the boards of directors of many of the companies in which it had an equity share. (A non-executive director is not responsible for the day-to-day management of the company. He/she is, rather, part-time and supposed to bring her/his objectivity, independence and experience to bear upon the firm's proposed actions. He/she does have the right to vote at Board of Directors' meetings.[2]) Generalisations about the quality and the role of the NEB-picked non-executive directors are impossible to make. Some were competent and some were not. Some asked few questions and/or had little advice to give; and some asked many questions and made many recommendations. Some took the part of the NEB and some identified at least as much with the firm to which they were appointed as a director. As we saw, for example, the two NEB directors of Able made good suggestions -- one about planning for growth, the other about marketing. Those on David's Board were viewed by the company as of minimal help: they seemed to know little about electric motors or the financing of exports. The NEB person who sat on Elspeth's Board was usually passive. His counterparts in Velma and William also were of little assistance. Those on Fred's Board asked what were seen as irrelevant questions and were afraid to take decisions at Board meetings. On the other hand, the NEB representative at Harlan helped the company withstand Board pressure to achieve short-term profits at the expense of long-term results. One NEB director of Jane was responsible for its obtaining a more competent Managing Director and a good accounting system. The NEB people at Krumpet wanted to close it down and those at Olga posed what were perceived to be naïve queries. But those on Pet's Board made constructive criticisms and convinced an important customer that it was not about to go under. The first NEB director of Tamsin showed up to most meetings and made many suggestions. Later, he became less active, a precedent followed by his successors. Those on Xerxes' Board retained their faith in the firm even in its worst hour and convinced the NEB to give it extra cash. And the person on Bruce's Board fought attempts to have the concern expand too rapidly.

One type of NEB refusal to interfere with the substantive management of its firms might surprise the reader if she/he stereotypes government officials as pro-union, especially the employees of an agency set up by a British Labour Government and given job creation as one of its roles. But (with the possible exception of the British Leyland refrigeration subsidiary Prestcold mentioned earlier and its push for a delay in closing a Ferranti plant) the NEB backed attempts by the managements of its companies to effect economies by severe cuts in staff. David's workforce decreased from 450-500 to 170; Lulu's from 900 down to 350 and Pet's from 1150 to 545 -- all without Board disapproval. Likewise the NEB staff member who became head of small software firm Daisy discharged three of its senior people to save £20,000 a month. We also shall see that the Board backed BL's shrinking of the number of employees working in its automobile divisions and Fairey's closing of one of its subsidiaries. Not even the union members on the Board itself made attempts to stop any of these workforce reductions.

The case studies give us several examples of inter-institutional co-operation. (Co-operation is a social phenomenon that will play a major part in the last chapter of this book.) In several instances, the Board, a private institutional investor, and/or another public body worked jointly to foster or save a company. (Remember that after the Tories came to power they insisted that new NEB investments normally be conducted jointly with private sector participants.) Thus those taking shares in Baker Company, the lessor of small units in the reconverted mill, included the NEB, ICFC, the city council and even public-spirited private citizens. The Board and other institutional investors joined together to refinance major software house Fred when it was on the rocks. Krumpet, the storage tank and large transformer manufacturer, had a major engineering group as well as the Board as its equity holders; and also received grants directly from the Department of Industry. The local developmental authority leases its site to it at a low rental. Small but promising high tech firm Morton's bank increased its loan to it when the NEB became one of its shareholders. Pet, the specialist in electronic photo-typesetting equipment, was rescued by the Board in partnership with a bank. The Board and Prutec, Prudential Assurance's former high tech-investment subsidiary, aided biotechnology company Ulysses. Though the Board took 70% of hospital-management firm Zelda, three private shareholders obtained 10% each. The NEB and the National Coal Board Pension Fund took equity in car-sale financier Ailsa; and the Board worked with a private brokerage firm to mould a package under which itself and two private instititions supported battery-manufacturer Bruce. It plus a county enterprise board and the ICFC aided the management buyout that gave birth to rubber-sheet maker Carol.

On the whole, as seen, firms came to the Board for assistance and not vice versa. However, there were several occasions on which it followed what a man who has been connected with it for a long time terms a 'proactive' strategy. This means (1) that the Board went to a going concern and asked if it could assist it, (2) that it formed an undertaking on its own initiative or (3) that it fought off private competitors for control of a holding. In a major salvage operation that we have not yet discussed in detail, the Board outbid a private investor for the control of the Faircy engineering group after it had gone into receivership. Insac and Nexos, which also will be analysed later, were NEB ideas. Scientific-data software firm Charlie was created because its organiser happened to be in the room when a Board representative asked an official of the local university whether it was sponsoring new projects that the Board could support. Electronic equipment producer Able was approached by the NEB because it wanted to expand its high tech interests. It purchased stock in Graham and Olga for the same purpose. Shares were acquired in Fred because the Board wanted holdings in all the firms in the Insac venture. Hospital-manager Zelda was brought into being because a high-ranking official of the Board felt that the UK should continue to export its expertise in providing health care. The Board created offshore-oil-rig servicer Elspeth out of several concerns that were engaged in one aspect or another of this business. Leading UK biotechnology company Harlan was the brainchild of several NEB staffers, including Harlan's current chief executive. Professional anti-government ideologists may deem the examples listed above to be instances of an empire-building instinct common to all public agencies. However, more objective individuals could reasonably label them demonstrations that government officials can be just as imaginative in conceiving and supporting projects as individuals in the private sector!

There were a few occasions on which the NEB provided services for its venture capital investments that a private venture capitalist might have been unable to furnish. William, the computer and computer peripheral assembler, benefited because the Board talked to other government agencies on its behalf. The Board likewise helped Elspeth develop relations with government agencies and informed it of sources of financial assistance. One wonders whether its private counter-parts would have been as successful in 'running interference' for their investments in their dealings with public bodies.

It is always dangerous to engage in 'but if' history; but in appreciating the NEB's role as a venture capitalist it is important to indicate the firms that probably would not be in business (or would be smaller) today were it not for its venture capital aid; and also to tot up the complete number of persons who are working in these firms thanks to this assistance. Of course, in most cases we cannot say for certain that this or that undertaking would not have got off the ground, would have collapsed, or would have remained minuscule in the absence of the Board's efforts. Many of the men I interviewed were uncertain about what would have happened to their concerns if the NEB had not stepped in; and these were all high officials of the companies surveyed and more often than not working with their enterprise when it received the funding. If they cannot be sure what would have been the fate of their undertakings were it not for the subsidy from the Board, we obviously cannot be dogmatic either. Yet we have to make the attempt and shall thus furnish a roster of firms (or units thereof) of which *it can reasonably be said* that they would not be in existence now, or that they would not have grown, but for the Board's subventions.

Able, the electronics equipment assembler, could have struggled on. However, it would have had great difficulty expanding without the NEB's cash. When the Board invested in it, it had 40 employees; in 1985 it had 250. It is fair to attribute 200 of these to the Board. About 200 of the group of 400 workers who have stayed with William or moved to the company that bought most of its assets can be credited to the Board's account. (William had only about 200 posts when the NEB gave it assistance so that it could expand.) Though Baker, the renter of space in the converted mill, has only two employees, between 500 and 1000 individuals have worked in the enterprises run by its lessees. Exactly how many of these tenants would not have found space had it not been for Baker is unclear, but it is plausible to conclude that ventures with a total workforce of 50 fall into this category. Charlie, the producer of software for displays of technical data, would not have been set up without Board prodding: it now has seven

126

employees. David, the electric motor manufacturer, would almost certainly have vanished into thin air without Board help: its 210 current employees thus owe their positions to that agency, though this is half the staff of its halcyon days. Elspeth, with its 700 men and women, is a creature of the Board. It cannot be definitely determined how many of its constituent companies would have lasted without Board assistance; but let us chalk up 450 of the 700 jobs to the NEB's initiative. Despite its bitter feud with the Board, Ivy with its 2000 employees would probably be extinct if the public body had not propped it up. Krumpet, the storage-tank and transformer assembler with its 40 workers, would most likely have fallen by the wayside without Board aid; as would Lulu with its 350-strong workforce, Ned (maker of small transformers) with its 120, and Pet (electronic typesetting machinery) with its 650. Probably the 280 individuals employed at the mill where Richenda's new paper-making machine was installed would not be there if the NEB had not supported the assembling of that piece of equipment. The management buyout that saved Powerdrive and its 45 workers probably would never have taken place without NEB help. Xerxes, Ailsa and (most likely) Yolanda owe their existence and approximately 40 total jobs to the Board. The same is true of Bruce and Carol with about 150 positions in all. Probably 20 of Ulysses' 50 posts are due to the NEB's support of that company's turning into a marketable product the animal-blood derivative its scientists discovered.

The total number of jobs that the above paragraphs indicate was probably created by the NEB acting as venture capitalist was about 4800. This seems like a drop in the bucket; but it should be noted that it does not include the workforces at the NEB-backed firms with which I was unable to secure interviews. It also does not include the personnel at Inmos or Fairey, which companies will be discussed later. Moreover, the reader should realise that some of the firms mentioned above have a very bright future and may soon employ many more men and women than they do now. I refer especially to computer-peripheral manufacturer Ivy, electronic photo-typesetting equipment assembler Pet, biotechnology venture Ulysses, technical software producer Charlie, and computer-aided-design concerns Xerxes and Yolanda. Also, I would put biotechnology enterprise Harlan with its potential growth into one of the leading companies in its sector on the list of the NEB's employment-generating offspring. Though it might have received funding elsewhere, it owes its origin to the foresight of NEB staff. Thus adding its 200 posts to the total number of jobs due to the efforts of the NEB gives us up to this point a figure of about 5000. (Obviously, it would be improper to add the workforces at the lame ducks rescued by the government and then transferred to the Board to the sum total of the jobs created by the NEB as *venture capitalist*.)[3]

One of the purposes for which the Board was founded, it will be remembered, was the promotion of 'international competitiveness'. Several of the firms that probably would not have existed (or that would have been smaller) but for the NEB's becoming a venture capitalist do a considerable export business or save the country imports. Were it not for Elspeth, UK offshore oil rigs might well have to be kept in working order by US firms. Half of electric motor manufacturer David's sales are outside Britain; and the analogous figure for Harlan is 90%. 80% of electronic photo-typsetting equipment builder Pet's business is overseas, including the US. Moreover, the 20% that is domestic would have to be imported from abroad were Pet to shut its doors, as it has no UK competitors. Ulysses' animal blood derivative for treating haemophiliacs probably would have to be brought in from the US were it not for NEB support of the firm; and one can reasonably predict that in the future it will export considerable amounts of this product. Though Zelda's predecessor might well have continued to manage health care facilities overseas, one major hospital management contract falling its way was successful only because the state agency backed its performance.

Finally, Hydraroll (real name), a small company in Wales that makes vehicle loading equipment, received a Queen's Award for Exports in 1985. This company was subsidised by the NEB as venture capitalist; but I did not include it in the case studies because I did not interview its officers. In all, five concerns that had received NEB aid were among the slightly over 100 enterprises receiving such an award in 1985 either for Exports or for Technology. This is a statistic of which those who have worked for the NEB in the past can be extremely proud!

NOTES

1. *NEB: a case for euthanasia,* pp. 13-16.

2. This is due to the fact that non-executive directors have equal status with executive (i.e. full-time) directors. '...[T]here can be no distinction between the position of executive and non-executive directors...' Philip Mitchell, *Directors' duties and insider dealing* (Butterworths, London, 1982), p. 17. See also ibid., pp. 222-23 for a discussion of the role of non-executive directors.

3. One person who has written about the NEB believes that 'it was most certainly the activity of the NEB [in investing in high tech firms] which created an interest in software companies, which previously the City had not thought good investments'. David Sainsbury, *Government and industry: a new partnership* (Fabian Society, London, 1981), p. 17. If Sainsbury is correct, we could include in our group of undertakings that would not exist (or would be smaller) but for the NEB concerns such as Fred, Olga and Velma. We could also add at least some of their employees to our sum of the jobs created by the NEB acting as a venture capitalist. However, because the men I spoke to at these firms said when I interviewed them in the mid-1980s that they would have obtained private help if the NEB had not been available to assist them, I shall not add their names or the numbers of jobs at their various sites to the lists that we have just completed.

8

Inmos

Inmos, the microchip maker, was one of the most ambitious NEB attempts at venture capitalism. (I shall use the firm's real name here because it is one of a kind and well known; and so it would be futile to try to veil it behind a cloak of anonymity.) At a conference in Montreal in September 1977 of persons interested in computer software, an English computer scientist, Iann Barron, met an American microelectronic venture capitalist, Dr Richard Petritz. Barron suggested that they form a company to manufacture advanced semiconductor devices (which we shall also refer to as 'integrated circuits'. The entire circuit is placed on one chip, called a 'microchip'. The sophisticated chips produced by Inmos contain at least 100,000 components.) They later conferred at a Chicago airport and discussed the matter further. Barron had been a consultant for the NEB and so knew that it would be interested in adding to its portfolio a concern such as he and Petritz had in mind. Barron sounded out Board officials and talked with them later that year. In the meantime, Dr. Paul Schroeder, a microchip designer and a partner with Petritz in the setting up of American high tech company Mostek in 1969, agreed to become one of the founders of the new enterprise.[1] Presentations were made to the Board in March 1978; and a 'shell' company was established by Barron, Petritz and Schroeder that very month. In July 1978, the NEB agreed to take an equity share of £25 million and to acquire a further £25 million stake if the firm seemed to be doing well.[2] Barron and his colleagues maintained that though other UK companies manufactured integrated circuits, these were designed for limited application while the Inmos semiconductors would be for more general use.[3] The NEB was quite intrigued by the expectation that the project would by the mid-1980s generate 4000 jobs in the UK as well as 1000 in the US.[4]

Though Inmos was conceived by Barron, Petritz and Schroeder, it is another concern that would not have come into being without the aid of the NEB. Though America is the 'birthplace' of the venture capital movement, Petritz was well aware that even US venture capitalists did not have enough cash in 1978 to found a big new semiconductor firm. Only governments, oil companies and banks had the funds needed; and there was no reason to believe that any agency of the US government or any oil company wanted to pour millions into another semiconductor undertaking. (Even US banks generally eschew the venture capital business.) So the NEB was the logical place for the organisers of Inmos to go; and they might have ended up there even if Barron had not had previous contact with it.

In our discussion of the relationship between the UK press and the NEB we saw that certain newspapers and segments of the business community were very sceptical about the prospects for Inmos when the NEB announced its support for it in July of 1978. They felt that established US and Japanese companies were about to start producing the chips Inmos planned to manufacture; and pointed out that it would not be fabricating anything at all for at least a couple of years since it was still a gleam in the eyes of its founders and the NEB rather than an existing complex of machinery, buildings and employees. These doubts were shared by some in the Department of Industry and also by the National Economic Development Office. NEDO felt that the NEB was participating in the project without having consulted enough knowledgeable people and that the development costs for 'standard' chips were high, which meant that Inmos would cost the taxpayers a great deal of money if it failed.[5] General Electric Corporation, the electronics giant, worried that the new venture would deprive it and other UK electronics firms of key staff and resources.[6] An officer of the American microprocessor company Intel declared, while Inmos was waiting for its second tranche of £25 million from the government, that even the most ingenious newcomer can break into the extremely competitive high technology market only when there is a complete change in the technology -- such as that which occurred when large-scale integrated circuits replaced transistors.[7]

Nevertheless, these caveats did not convince either Inmos' fathers or the Board to change their minds. In January 1979 Inmos said that its US factory would be located at Colorado Springs, Colorado.[8] Manufacturing was to be done in the US originally because that is where the engineers who knew how to put together sophisticated semiconductor devices then lived. (There is a distinction between designing and making chips.) To move the needed staff to the UK at that time simply would have cost too much in salary payments. One trouble the company ran into immediately was a lawsuit brought by Mostek, the old concern of Petritz and Schroeder, alleging that Inmos had lured away several key employees in order to obtain trade secrets and that it intended to entice more Mostek employees for the same purpose.[9] However, in August 1979 the action was dismissed.[10] In May 1979 there occurred an event as threatening to Inmos as the Mostek court action, i.e. the Tory victory. It was not that the organisers of Inmos were liberals or radicals: I have no idea at all what their political party preferences were or are. But not only had the Conservatives, as seen, threatened to severely curtail the scope of the NEB's activities; but, when the Inmos funding was announced, they had also proclaimed a bit ambiguously that they would honour any commitments to Inmos already made but that they would not provide any extra cash for the operation.[11] Thus it seemed quite possible, when Mrs Thatcher took office, that the firm would not be getting the second £25 million that it desperately needed.

However, the first sounds from the Tory government were quite reassuring. Secretary of State for Industry Sir Keith Joseph told the House of Commons that the NEB was contractually committed to spend that £25 million on Inmos.[12] Even Michael Grylls seemed to admit that the Board was bound by contract to give Inmos this bounty, though he added that the government should break the agreement and pay a penalty for breach.[13] (On 15 November 1979 Undersecretary of State for Industry Michael Marshall told Grylls that the contract between the NEB and Inmos was confidential and could not be made public by placing it in the House of Commons library.[14] A mere change of government could not break the UK state's

132

habit of keeping some of the Board's operations hidden from the light of publicity!) On the 21st of November 1979 Sir Keith informed the House again that high technology would be one of the areas in which the Board would be permitted to continue to venture.[15] And in July 1980 Prime Minister Thatcher announced the decision to give Inmos the second £25 million. The Board under Sir Arthur Knight had reviewed and approved the investment;[16] and the Government went along with that decision. By the end of 1980 the Board's equity investment was about £30 million and by the end of 1981 it had reached the £50 million mark. During 1983 a further slice of £15 million was added, making the Board's total equity holding £65.09 million.[17] This extra sum was forthcoming though the Government had insisted during all of 1982 that Inmos would get no more.[18] When grants and loans from other public sources are taken into account, the firm received a total of about £100 million from the British government before it was privatised.[19]

The Conservatives' complaisance in giving Inmos the extra £25 million needs more discussion. Late in 1979 the company announced that its first UK factory would be built in the Bristol area[20] -- and all hell broke loose. Just about every town and hamlet in the country wanted that plant with its possible 4000 jobs: no community was so prosperous that it could afford to turn up its nose at such an opportunity. Thus though Bristol was happy with the judgement that the facility should be sited there, nowhere else in the UK was. Areas of especially high unemployment were, of course, extremely vociferous in demanding that Inmos come to them; but even London desired it.[21] No one was placated by the NEB's suggestion[22] that Bristol be the locale of Inmos' technical operations and that the chips actually be produced in four regions suffering from severe joblessness. The founders of the firm clearly wanted Bristol: it was and is a pleasant city with an equable climate and good schools and universities. It is also easily accessible from London and Heathrow Airport. Not only would the undertaking's UK officials enjoy living there; but so would the bright young scientists and engineers whom they hoped to attract. Moreover, a consulting firm had recommended that the Inmos plant be constructed in Bristol, with nearby South Wales as a second choice.

The pages of the quality press indicate the extent to which the Inmos resolve to build its first factory in Bristol aroused anger in certain parts of the country. The leader of the Tyne and Wear (Newcastle area) County Council referred to the step as

> 'nothing less than a severe kick in the teeth, not only for Tyne and Wear, but also for every assisted [i.e. high unemployment] area in the United Kingdom. There will be a tremendous outcry from all local authorities and trades unions in the northeast at this betrayal by the Inmos directors, which appears to flout all authority.'[23]

Tyne and Wear had offered a £100,000 package to the firm to locate its first facility at Washington Newtown.[24] Alan Williams, MP for Swansea West in South Wales and a Minister in the Labour Government that had been in power when Inmos was first funded, claimed that the corporation had promised to set up its first two factories in assisted areas. He contended that when he had been Minister he had thrice refused to issue Inmos the Industrial Development Certificate necessary to allow its research and development centre to be constructed in Bristol. He continued that he had granted the permission in 1978 only after Inmos had consented to put its first two production units in regions suffering economic distress. He pointed to the NEB's 1978 Annual Report which said that 'The firm intention is that the UK production facilities will be located in Assisted Areas'.[25] To this the Inmos directors retorted that that was the Board's view, not theirs. They emphasised again that the Bristol location had been singled out by a consulting firm and added that that group had surveyed over 200 potential spots. They asserted that they wanted a 'prestige' location; not one 'in the midst of a run-down industrial estate'. (This phraseology was hardly likely to cool tempers.) Finally, they contended, the research and production facilities should be placed near one another so that those working on R and D would mix with those developing techniques of fabrication and each group would learn something from the other.[26]

Perusing the Parliamentary debates on the NEB of 12 March 1980 will give one an idea of the 'intellectual' level of the discussions about the location of Inmos.[27] The nature of the squabble was such that party labels were ignored: Tories and Labourites from City A joined in praising their own area and, sometimes, in denigrating City B. Michael Colvin from Bristol, a Conservative, said that the first of the Inmos production units should be erected in that municipality. He emphasised that Bristol area MPs of all parties favoured this. He admitted that the assisted areas were clamouring for the company; but the decision on siting was one for it alone and it wanted Bristol. (One wonders whether he would have made a similar comment to the effect that the choice was up to the firm had Messers Petritz, Barron and Schroeder selected, e.g., Cambridge!) Delay in funding the factory would mean simply that because of inflation, the costs of assembling it would rise. Moreover, his city had a reservoir of skilled and intelligent workers. The above-mentioned Alan Williams from Swansea also wanted the second £25 million to go to Inmos but did not want Inmos to go to Bristol. He remarked again that the NEB had told him that only its technology centre would spring up in that municipality. He then asserted that the NEB's Guidelines included the promotion of regional employment whenever possible and that his constituency and its neighbours comprised a region with great universities as well as great unemployment.

Then it was the turn of Tory William Waldegrave of Bristol West. He said that one of the NEB's great strengths was that it protected its sponsored industries against MPs who wanted their political interests to be taken into account when it came to solving the problems of the economy. Microelectronic engineers are mobile, he declared, and there were only about 1000 in the entire UK. Inmos needed 300 to 400 of them; and they would never move to the valleys of Wales. Donald Thompson, a Conservative from Sowerby in Yorkshire, wanted Inmos in his bailiwick. Within 40 miles of its boundaries are the Universities of Leeds, Sheffield, Manchester and Bradford; theatrical and cultural activities; a beautiful countryside; and a civilised way of life. Bristol's Waldegrave retorted that the crucial Dr Schroeder would probably leave Inmos if he believed that it was being used as an instrument of social policy.

Manchester, a highly depressed town, was eager for Inmos. Charles Morris, one of its Labour MPs, averred that it should settle there or in its even more troubled twin city of Salford.

Manchester University, the University of Manchester Institute of Science and Technology, and Salford University are all producing graduates skilled in computers; while Bristol University did not even have a chair in microelectronics. He added that Schroeder had never been in Britain before; so how could he possibly know that Bristol was the best site. Also, computer firms should be located near industry; and 50% of British industry was located within 75 miles of Manchester. Arthur Palmer, a Labourite from Bristol, interrupted to say that Bristol was the hub of the aerospace industry and that the Concorde supersonic aircraft had been developed there. Morris' comeback was that Bristol University does not produce nearly as many technologists as do the universities he had mentioned.

Williams from Swansea then claimed that he was not trying to obtain the site for his constituents but that he did want Inmos to benefit an assisted area. Palmer referred to the ancient rivalry between the Saxon and Celtic sides of the Severn (Bristol is of course on the Saxon side), and said that the Tories want state intervention when pleading for their constituents. The firm, he believed, should make the final decision. An MP from Sunderland in the Northeast insisted that Inmos should end up in the depressed Northwest or Northeast, which are losing industry. He referred to a letter about the Northeast from Barron that made made derogatory references to the region.

In any event, the Board and Inmos sometime around June 1980 decided to build its first factory near Newport in South Wales, though the UK headquarters of the enterprise was to be in Bristol. The costs of erecting the plant had increased while the debate about siting was raging. Inmos thus needed development grants from the government above and beyond the second £25 million to construct the works and these were forthcoming only to firms locating in the assisted areas. It must have been some consolation to Barron and his friends that Newport is not that far from Bristol. Moreover, an Inmos official I interviewed said that even the £25 million might not have been provided had the Board and Inmos not agreed that the firm should go to an area of high unemployment. At that time, he pointed out, the Thatcher Administration had only a small majority in Parliament and was seriously worried about the effects of high unemployment upon its political future. He also believes that Secretary of State for Industry Joseph (an individual who originally disliked Inmos intensely) had by February 1980 come to favour the grant to the company but that the rest of the Cabinet was still undecided then. He cautions, properly, that it is at present impossible to know exactly why the Government did come through with the second £25 million: Cabinet deliberations are secret and are supposed to remain so for 30 years. However, it is probable that the inability of private firms General Electric Corporation and Fairchild to co-operate in chip production and a government failure to get GEC involved with Inmos (as well as Inmos' job-generating potential) contributed to the consent to the funding.[28]

It was expected that Inmos would lose money for the first few years of its existence and, of course, it did. There was no way it could become profitable until it sold something. In 1978 it was about £500,000 in the red; in 1979 about £2 million; in 1980 about £5.7 million; in 1981, the first year it marketed anything, about £15 million on a turnover of £2.1 million; in 1982, about £19 million on a turnover of £13.7 million; and in 1983 £14 million on a turnover of almost £39 million.[29] The fourth quarter of 1983 saw its first profit.[30] The deficits in its five-and-one-half years of unprofitability (counting 1983 as a full year but 1978 as a half year since the company was only a shell until the NEB agreed to fund it in July 1978) came to over £56 million. It did turn a profit in 1984, making £14.4 million in pre-tax profits on sales of £110 million.[31] A small factory was opened in Colorado Springs in March 1980 but volume production was possible only after a larger plant was completed in the same town in 1981. Work on the Welsh facility began in January 1981 and production started there in 1983. Bristol has the administrative headquarters and design centre for new products; while Wales fashions the chips.

Up until recently, Inmos concentrated entirely on making complicated semiconductors that were not full computers but memory banks for a computer. These Inmos semiconductors were of two sorts. In the first place there were 16K static, random-access memory (16K ram) chips. (These possess 16 x 1024 (16,384) 'bytes' or 16 x 1024 x 8 (131,072) 'bits'. A bit is a unit of computer storage space. A letter or number occupies seven or eight bits.) And in the second place, there were the more common 64K dynamic ram chips. (The static 16Ks store less but, unlike the dynamic 64Ks, do not continually have to be refreshed.[32]) The company offered for sale various versions of the l6K static rams and the 64K dynamic rams.

By 1984 Inmos was doing so well that the government disposed of its stake in it to Thorn-EMI for about £95 million.[33] They might have been able to get a better price from a foreign company had they waited a few months.[34] But the UK's leaders did not want it transferred to a non-British concern such as the US American Telephone and Telegraph Co.[35] However, 1985 proved a disastrous year for it, witnessing a loss of £25 million. It also lost money in 1986.[36] The culprit was not Inmos itself but a serious world-wide slump in the semiconductor market. This recession led to an oversupply that caused a radical drop in price. The 64K dynamic ram chips that at the end of 1984 went for $3.00 sold in July 1985 for $0.50. The fall was greatest for standard chips, such as those fabricated by Inmos, as opposed to those tailored for the needs of specific companies.[37] As early as November 1984 it had to reduce the price of its 64K dynamic ram chips by one-third to meet Japanese competition.[38] As a consequence, it very reluctantly decided to stop their manufacture;[39] and plans to recruit workers for another factory were postponed.[40] In mid-1986 Thorn decided that no more Inmos chips would be made at Colorado Springs.[41] (Major semiconductor firms in other nations have also had to cut their workforces.[42])

In addition to this market glut Inmos found that almost one-third of its static memory chips were flawed due to difficulties at its Colorado plant: all these defective chips had to be thrown out.[43] On the whole, though, its static chips are an excellent product and by 1983 the firm had over 50% of the world market for them.[44] Unfortunately, that market is very small and the price is down;[45] and so Inmos' dominance in this area cannot in and of itself make it profitable. Its 1985-86 problems adversely affected its new parent. Thorn-EMI shares declined in value then, and the group is thinking of selling Inmos.[46]

Before continuing with Inmos' fortunes, let us look at the relationship that prevailed between the NEB and the company. The Board usually had at least one or two nominees on the Inmos Board of Directors. One of these spent 70% of his time on Inmos matters and now holds a full-time position with the company. After 1981 the NEB representative was not a member of the Board's staff. The director who devoted himself to Inmos' problems became very supportive of it and presented its case to the NEB. For obvious reasons, the Board spent more time on Inmos than on its average venture capital investment. There was constant communication between the public agency and its subsidiary, especially on the politically-sensitive issue of the locale of the Inmos UK plants. Though the Board did not tell Inmos how to make or market its chips, it did suggest to it how it could borrow money at lower rates. It also discussed with it its long-term goals and problems of unionisation.

To return to the state of Inmos' health, the overwhelming majority of its chips are sold outside the UK. It employs about 850 persons in Britain. This figure of 850 is, of course, a far cry from the 4000 predicted when Inmos was set up; but it is nothing to snicker at in a country plagued by very high unemployment. Thus our running total of jobs created by the NEB can be upped to about 5850. To the extent that UK firms buy its sophisticated semiconductors, it is an import saver. If national prestige requires that a country have a microchip maker, then Inmos preserves the UK's national prestige. And in the event that the UK were to become embroiled in a protracted conventional war and not be able to purchase semiconductors from the US, the Common Market countries or Japan, Inmos would supply its military forces and its defence industries with the integrated circuits they need.

One could argue that the future of Inmos looks extremely gloomy and that therefore those sceptics who opposed its creation in 1978 were right. As we saw, it has had to stop manufacturing 64K chips. As also noted, the total world market for 16K static rams is small and the price is low; and so Inmos cannot stay in business just through producing these even if it retains its strength in this market. Though it boasts of being the largest semi-conductor manufacturer in the UK and one of the biggest in Europe, it is really a small blip when viewed on a world-wide scale. In the multibillion dollar chip market, its £110 million (about $160 million) of sales in 1984, its best year, is minuscule potatoes. For example, during that year the Japanese NEC Corporation, No. 2 in world chip sales after the

American Texas Instruments, had sales of $2.2 billion.[47] Even worse, the large Japanese and US chip makers are now producing integrated circuits with memory capacities of 256K and 1000K. These may not only make serious inroads into the market for other chips, but also be too expensive for a relatively small concern like Inmos to produce.[48]

None the less, the founders of Inmos and their supporters may have the last laugh. It now has a office in Japan. It could re-enter the dynamic ram market, as its version of the 64K dynamic ram chip was technically a fine one. Though it had only a tiny share of the world-wide $2.8 billion commerce in this chip, it at times obtained as much as 18% of the market for the best-performing and more expensive ones. In 1987 IBM decided to use am Inmos good in the colour screens of its new personal computers; and the Britsh company thus expects to turn a profit very soon.[49]

However, Inmos' best hope for the future is a product which may be marketed in significant amounts in the very near future. This is its computer-on-a-chip or 'transputer'. The 16K and 64K chips Inmos has been relying on are memory devices only: they do not compute, i.e. they do not perform arithmetical or logical operations. The transputer is able to compute. Of course there are quite a few other companies (e.g., Intel and Motorola) that also make 'computers on a chip'. Thus, sold as isolated units Inmos' transputers would have extremely strong competition, to put it mildly.[50] To indicate how the transputer has an advantage over the single-chip computers made by other concerns, some background is necessary.

Large, mainframe computers are often shared by many users. Though the customer has the impression that he/she is the only person on the machine, it actually is splitting its time between the many tasks it has been given to perform. A program is run for a while and then is put at the back of the line and the next one worked on. As I found out through bitter experience when I took a programming course in which the students utilised the university's central computer, this often meant delays of hours before one's program could be printed out. It is possible to build computer systems with more than one large computer where different tasks are given to different computers. In fact, such systems are in existence.[51] However, there is 'a limit to the performance increase that can be obtained' this way.[52] Trouble also arises in getting the machines to communicate with and interrupt each other.[53] Moreover, at the 'software level, programs have to be written in a form which allows them to be split between machines'.[54] Problems have arisen in developing programs where communication is needed between the parts of the program used by the one machine and the parts used by the other.[55]

The transputer, which, remember, is itself a computer, can be joined to other transputers (i.e. to other computers) much more easily than large computers can be mutually linked. They are designed so that they can without difficulty be plugged into each other and then participate in 'parallel processing', i.e. each doing one task while the others are carrying out related tasks. This should overcome the performance problems with which systems of large computers are plagued. Three or four interconnected transputers make a high-powered personal computer: thousands of interconnected transputers form a supercomputer.[56] Moreover, a simple programming language called occam has been devised by Inmos to facilitate communication between the parts of the program run on transputer No. 1 and those run on the transputers with which it has been hooked up. This should take care of the software problems that bedevil multi-computer systems.

Technologically, the transputer is marvellous: it won a British Design Award in 1987.[57] Inmos hopes that it will be used in the much-publicised fifth generation of computers that the Japanese are seeking to develop.[58] Frankly, though, it is not certain as of my writing this that it will have the success it deserves. Inmos lacks the funds to aggressively point out its advantages to potential buyers;[59] though its parent Thorn-EMI may help it out here. Moreover, consumers may be deterred from buying it because they are afraid they will not be able to learn how to use it.[60] *Fortune* quotes an executive from one of the major microchip companies as saying about the transputer: 'It's a good piece of engineering from a little rinky-dink company. This is [however] a brutal market, and the best mousetrap doesn't always win.'[61]

If this particular mousetrap proves a financial dud, Inmos may well have to shut its doors and the critics of the NEB will then have another deadly arrow to add to their quiver. If it does take off, Inmos should prosper and 'pay off', even from a narrow 'pounds and pence' perspective. In fact, it is hard to believe that the transputer will *never* obtain popularity. If it does not do so under the Inmos logo, it may under the aegis of the corporation to which the assets of a bankrupt Inmos are transferred. If this be a UK concern, the country will still have benefited from the NEB's gamble. If it be a foreign firm, at least humankind as a whole will be better off. (It should be noted that even the conservative *Financial Times* now feels that despite the present problems of the company, it was not unreasonable for the NEB to participate in the founding of Inmos.[62])

NOTES

1. See Redwood, *Going for broke...,* pp. 74-5.

2. Ibid., p. 74.

3. Inmos 1978 Annual Report (Inmos, Bristol), p. 2.

4. Redwood, *Going for broke...,* p. 74.

5. Ibid., p. 75; *Daily Telegraph,* 22 July 1978, p. 15.

6. *Daily Telegraph,* 27 May 1978, p. 2.

7. *London Times,* 8 Jan. 1980, p. 13.

8. Inmos 1978 Annual Report, p. 2.

9. Ibid., p. 7.

10. Inmos 1979 Annual Report (Inmos, Bristol), p. 9.

11. *Daily Telegraph,* 22 July 1978, p. 15.

12. HC Debates, 19 July 1979, col. 2008.

13. HC Debates, 23 July 1979, col. 5. (Oral Answers.)

14. HC Debates, 15 Nov. 1979, col. 693. (Written Answers.)

15. HC Debates, 21 Nov. 1979, col. 397.

16. NEB 1980 Annual Report, p. 3.

17. Ibid., pp. 44-5; NEB 1981 Annual Report, pp. 38-9; 1983 Annual Report, pp. 28-9.

18. *London Sunday Times,* 2 Jan. 1983, p. 15.

19. *London Times,* 5 July 1983, p. 21.

20. *London Times,* 28 Dec. 1979, p. 11.

21. Redwood, *Going for broke...,* p. 75.

22. Ibid., p. 76.

23. *London Times,* 28 Dec. 1979, p. 11.

24. Ibid.

25. NEB 1978 Annual Report, p. 20.

26. Much of this paragraph is based on *London Times,* 7 Jan. 1980, p. 15.

27. The following comments by MPs who wanted Inmos to locate in their respective regions are taken from HC Debates, 12 Mar. 1980, cols. 1425ff.

28. Redwood, *Going for broke...,* p. 77.

29. See NEB 1978 Annual Report, pp. 40-1; 1979 Annual Report, pp. 32-3; 1980 Annual Report, pp. 24-5; 1981 Annual Report, pp. 30-1; 1982 Annual Report, pp. 30-1; 1983 Annual Report, pp. 20-1.

30. *Economist,* 30 July 1984, p. 108.

31. *London Times,* 26 Mar. 1985, p. 23.

32. *Business Week,* 30 July 1984, p. 108.

33. *London Times,* 6 Nov. 1984, p. 19.

34. An Inmos official made this point in an interview with me.

35. *Business Week,* 30 July 1984, p. 108.

36. *London Sunday Times,* 12 Ap. 1987, p. 64; *London Times,* 11 July 1986, p. 21.

37. *Financial Times,* 8 July 1985, p. 42.

38. *London Times,* 6 Nov. 1984, p. 19.

39. Thorn-EMI 1987 Annual Report, p. 35.

40. *Guardian,* 17 July 1985, p. 22.

41. *London Sunday Times,* 31 Mar. 1985, p. 57.

42. *London Times,* 11 July 1986, p. 21.

43. *Business Week,* 2 Sept. 1985, p. 21.

44. *Financial Times,* 12 Ap. 1983, p. 8.

45. *London Sunday Times,* 2 Jan. 1983, p. 15; *London Times,* 11 Dec. 1987, p. 20.

46. *Economist,* 12 Dec. 1987, p. 76.

47. *Guardian,* 17 Jan. 1985, p. 21.

48. *Financial Times,* 8 July 1985, p. 42.

49. *Business Week,* 30 July 1984, p. 108; *London Sunday Times,* 12 Ap. 1987, p. 64.

50. *International Herald Tribune,* 1 Feb. 1985, p. 11.

51. Inmos, *Writing parallel programs in occam* (Inmos, Bristol, nd), pp. 1-2.

52. Ibid., p. 2.

53. Ibid.

54. Ibid.

55. Ibid.

56. *London Times,* 13 Jan. 1987, p. 24. *New York Times,* 24 Dec. 1987, p. A1 has an informative article on the technique of parallel processing.

57. *Fortune,* 14 May 1984, p. 114; *London Times,* 13 Jan. 1987, p. 24.

58. Iann Barron *et. al., Transputer does 10 or more MIPS even when not used in parallel* (Inmos, Bristol, nd), p. 109.

59. *Fortune,* 14 May 1984, p. 114.

60. *International Herald Tribune,* 1 Feb. 1985, p. 11.

61. 14 May 1984, p. 114. In 1986 Japanese and American companies did show interest in the transputer as a possible component of the super computers they hope to build. *London Sunday Times,* 30 Mar. 1986, p. 57. Moreover, it appeals to many different types of customer. *London Times,* 19 Jan. 1988, p. 31. However, Inmos' transputer has competitors. See *Economist,* 28 Mar. 1987, pp. 91-2.

62. 8 July 1985, p. 42.

9

The Insac Debacle

The case studies in this chapter and the next cover bright NEB ideas that resulted in big losses to the agency. The inspiration behind Insac was to improve exports and reduce import dependence by setting up a joint venture to improve UK software and sell it abroad.[1] And that is what Insac was: a partnership among five companies producing computer software whose aim was to develop new software collections and push these overseas, especially in the US. Insac was to fund the refinement and foreign marketing of this software: money from the private sector was at the time not available for these purposes. It was also felt that these firms working together would be in a better bargaining position and have a more attractive portfolio to offer potential customers than any one of them acting solo. Moreover, bigger markets would mean that the partners would have on hand more money for research and development. The NEB was aware that the UK was not going to be the world's leader in the development of mainframe computers. But its staff, and others, felt that UK software was a superior article and that, properly improved and packaged, the country could be one of the globe's most important vendors of this commodity. Likewise, it was believed that co-operation rather than competition among the Insac partners would eliminate unnecessary duplication in R and D and product development.[2]

Five concerns were induced to participate in Insac: Fred, Olga, Velma, a company later taken over by Velma, and William. The NEB acquired less than 30% of the voting equity in all these companies except the one later purchased by Velma. All of Insac itself was owned by the Board; and each of the five members of Insac had a representative (its own

Managing Director) on its Board of Directors. The NEB had hoped to attract twelve participants, assuming that the grander clusters of software made possible by the presence of so many concerns would be the ones most likely to attract a large number of buyers. However, for a couple of reasons, the Board was never able to persuade more than the above-mentioned quintet to join. In the first place, as seen, the Tory leadership was threatening to cripple the NEB once their Party took power. This understandably scared some high tech firms away from Insac. Second, some of the potential joint venturers remained aloof for political reasons: they viewed the Board as the nose in the tent of the camel of nationalisation of the microelectronics sector. And not only did they refuse to co-operate with Insac; but they also had enough political clout to prevent it from marketing its products in the UK. (Here is an excellent example of how business hostility to the NEB presented an obstacle to its success not facing a private venture capitalist!)

Insac never operated at a profit. In 1977 it lost £180,000; in 1978 £1.3 million; in 1979 about £2 million; in 1980 about £1.45 million and in 1981 about £550,000 for a cumulative deficit of about £5.5 million.[3] In March 1982 its US operating arm was sold to an American company, Britton Lee, at a loss of £6.86 million and a bit later the rest of it was disposed of at a loss of £320,000.[4] At the time of the deal with Britton Lee, the NEB took a 10% share of that firm.[5] Britton Lee put $300,000 more into Insac's US branch but liquidated it soon afterward.

The reasons for this shipwreck (other than the above-noted private sector enmity) are several. First, Insac was not responsible for developing the software projects it was funding: its members were. Second, the NEB had too small a percentage of the stock in most of these concerns to force them to work with Insac and with each other. Third, these enterprises were basically competitors and their strong, brilliant and ambitious Managing Directors did not gladly co-operate among themselves or with their NEB-sponsored joint venture. Both the literature[6] and the persons connected with Insac and the NEB whom I interviewed are unanimous on this point. According to one of my respondents, they did not even talk over together their ideas about software. That is, they refused to get their companies to sit down jointly to, e.g., create new software collections or computer systems but, rather, concentrated on bettering their individual wares and marketing them overseas through their own offices. They felt that the funding from Insac should be used for their own rather than for co-operative projects.

Very few of its members' products were ever endorsed by Insac. This was due in part to the above-noted rivalry: remember that each had a nominee on Insac's Board of Directors. Moreover, the NEB's creation did look very closely at the projects for product refinement that they submitted to it, asking hard questions about the technological interest of the article and the market research that had been done with respect to it.[7]

The reluctance of Insac's members to act as genuine partners in polishing and advertising common software packages was compounded by bitter clashes between the NEB staff member who originally headed Insac and the officials of some of the member companies. The trouble arose when some connected with the joint venture, including its Managing Director, successfully marketed in the US and elsewhere a 'videotex' ('viewdata') system under a valuable licence for videotex software from the UK Post Office.[8] (A 'videotex' ('viewdata') service is one which links a tv set in a home, office or public place to central data banks via a phone line.[9] The shopping centre I frequented when I lived in England doing the research for this book featured several television receivers located along its malls. One had only to press a button on the set and s/he would be presented with up-to-date information about weather, news, etc.) Selling this system proved the most successful aspect of the Insac experiment.[10] In 1979 Insac was split into two companies. One was called Insac Products Limited, which I shall refer to as Insac since it was basically a continuation of the original Insac the Board had created; and the other was known as Aregon (its real name). Insac was supposed to keep on carrying out its original functions, i.e. to act as the vehicle through which the five members jointly compiled and marketed software abroad. Aregon took over the viewdata business; continued to purvey videotex software; and began writing new software of this genre.

This split greatly incensed Insac's constituent firms because only one of them was actively involved in working with videotex. The NEB had originally declared that it would ultimately spend about £20 million for Insac. By the end of 1979 only £6.1 million had been forthcoming; and the agency made it clear that whatever portion of the remaining £14 million it would grant would go not to Insac alone but would be split between Insac and Aregon.[11] (In fact, Aregon got £5 million during 1980 and Insac only £3.07 million.[12] Neither concern received more in subsequent years. Incidentally, the loss figures given a few pages ago are for Insac alone and do not include Aregon's deficits.) The hiving off of Aregon angered the partners not only because it deprived them of some government aid, but also because the leading figure in the new undertaking was the man who had been the Managing Director of Insac. They felt that his becoming the guiding spirit of the new concern meant that he was using his position as Insac chief to benefit himself by diverting government money to aid a new and probably ultimately-profitable corporation that he himself would be running. They feared, moreover, that the upstart would probably end up as a competitor of theirs. The partner firms complained loudly to the Department of Industry and the NEB about the Aregon arrangements, but to no avail. They even went so far as to ask Members of Parliament to put questions about the incident; and some actually leaked confidential minutes to the press. However, the government did not change its mind and Aregon continued to live: we shall describe its fortunes shortly below. But the companies were so disgusted with the Aregon affair that they wanted even less to do with Insac than before the divorce. (Insac's ex-head justified his departure by asserting that its continuing with its original goal of refining and developing UK software on a large-scale basis was futile as long as it had only five members.)

One incident illustrates how strained the relations were between Insac and its members. It set up an office in New York and encouraged one of these concerns to join it there, saying that it would give it leads about Americans who would be interested in doing business with it. But when that concern's employees arrived in that city, they discovered that the Insac staff who promised to furnish this information about customers were no longer working for it. Moreover, Insac wanted the firm to be promoted as part of Insac, not under its own name. The upshot was that the partner decided to open its own US office and to market its software on its own there.

A good way of looking at how Insac's members neglected to work together under its auspices is to compare its sales against those of its member firms. (We are speaking of Insac alone, not Aregon.) 1979 was the first year Insac sold anything -- £1 million worth of software.[13] In the same year the sales of the five firms totalled £47 million. In 1980 it recorded the same turnover,[14] while one of its members had takings of £7 million and another of £15 million. In 1981, the last year in which it did any marketing, its receipts were only £100,000:[15] one of its constituents had a turnover of £8 million while the NEB's share alone of the profits from two of the others came to £800,000. It is true that Insac operated mainly in the US while its member firms were active in the UK and all over the world. Yet if they had been serious about working with Insac and each other the difference between their gross earnings and those of this NEB creation would surely have been less. (The only products it sold in the US under its own label were German and Canadian software.[16])

The Insac experiment was not a total loss, however. The venture did fund various software innovations of its participants.[17] Also, Aregon, the viewdata software writer and vendor whose spin-off from Insac greatly annoyed the joint venturers, is alive and well as of this writing. Though it is not yet profitable, it is marching down the road to that goal. Half of its business involves exports; and it has signed agreements with US giant AT and T and Japanese multinational Mitsubishi under which these two companies are to market an Aregon product in their respective countries.[18] It employs 85 people; and so we can make our total of the jobs created by the NEB as venture capitalist about 5900. (It is highly unlikely that it could have received funding from private sources as opposed to the government.) In 1984 the NEB shareholding in it (more accurately, in the private company that owns it) was reduced from 91% to 44%. (When the NEB held the majority of its stock, it had two representatives on its Board of Directors. These people were competent but played a passive role. Aregon had to submit to the Board an annual plan and a budget. These were studied by knowledgeable people but they never raised much of an objection to what the company planned to do. This loose monitoring was, as seen, typical of the connection between the Board and all its venture capital investments.)

It can be seen that Insac, with its £5.5 million of total operating losses and with the loss of about £7 million sustained when it was wound down, was an important factor in making the NEB's record as a venture capitalist seem unimpressive. For example, we saw earlier that its total net loss on the disposal of its investments was about £28.2 million, which means that the deficit arising from the demolition of Insac accounted for about 25% of this figure.[19] The sad part about this is that Insac could have been healthier had a bit more thinking been done about its structure and purposes both before and after it was incorporated. Let us explore for a bit the weaknesses in the way Insac was organised. (Few argue that the concept behind Insac, i.e. that a group of small but talented UK software companies should pool their efforts and abilities to develop their products and market them abroad, was inherently flawed. In fact, the *laissez-faire* orientated *Economist* refers to it as an 'admirable' one.[20])

It should have been evident to the NEB before the Insac ship was launched that the individualists who ran its components would be leery of working with each other or with Insac. Accordingly, and most importantly, the Board should if possible have taken a larger share than it did in the member firms: this would have given it more leverage to induce them to co-operate. Second, steps should have been taken to ensure that some of the members' software would be marketed outside the UK under the Insac name. For example, a clause to that effect could have been inserted into the NEB contract with the five firms. Third, the London offices of the Board and Insac should have monitored the latter's US staff more closely (1) to make sure that they were being helpful to the representatives of the participant firms and (2) to see to it that they operated more efficiently. Some members of Insac's American sales force were mediocre. They were paid fancy salaries and given big company automobiles. In return, they showed up in the office only two or three days a week and did not strain themselves to popularise Insac's wares. Fourth, it was probably an error to have the busy, driven Managing Directors of the member firms represent these enterprises on Insac's Board. Had that body been composed of perhaps less preoccupied 'middle' as opposed to 'top' management, the firm that it led might have been a triumph rather than a flop.

NOTES

1. *London Times,* 4 Jan. 1980, p. 15.
2. See *Economist,* 22 Dec. 1979, p. 61.
3. NEB 1978 Annual Report, pp. 40-1; 1979 Annual Report, pp. 32-3; 1980 Annual Report, pp. 24-5; 1981 Annual Report, pp. 30-1.
4. NEB 1982 Annual Report, p. 8, 22; 1983 Annual Report, p. 12.
5. NEB 1982 Annual Report, pp. 44-5.
6. *Economist,* 22 Dec. 1979, p. 61; *London Times,* 4 Jan. 1980, p. 15.
7. *London Times,* 4 Jan. 1980, p. 15.
8. Ibid.; *Guardian,* 28 Jan. 1980, p. 15; *London Times,* 22 Nov. 1979, p. 19.
9. *Guardian,* 28 Nov. 1984, p. 24.
10. *Guardian,* 28 Jan. 1980, p. 15.
11. Ibid.; NEB 1979 Annual Report, pp. 48-9.
12. NEB 1980 Annual Report, pp. 42-5.
13. Ibid., pp. 24-5.
14. Ibid.
15. NEB 1981 Annual Report, pp. 30-1.
16. *Guardian,* 6 Nov. 1981, p. 18.
17. *London Times,* 29 Dec. 1979, p. 17; 4 Jan. 1980, p. 15.
18. Pearce Technology Limited, *Corporate profile* (Pearce Technology, London, 1985), p. 8.
19. The NEB's purchase of Britton Lee's shares, which was part of the transaction in which it disposed of Insac's American operations, proved surprisingly profitable for the Board. It purchased 875,000 shares of this US high tech firm's common stock at a total cost of £1.96 million (NEB 1982 Annual Report, pp. 44-5); and several years later sold these shares for a profit of £2.76 million. See NEB 1984-85 Annual Report, p. 12; 1985-86 Annual Report, p. 13.
20. Dec. 22, 1979, p. 61.

10
The Nexos Disaster

Nexos' Birth and Wares

The NEB staff who believed that it should spearhead the burgeoning of a UK high technology sector that would be competitive with those of the US and Japan felt that the market for automated office systems would grow rapidly during the 1980s. They perceived that UK companies were not doing much to meet this projected demand and that were this situation to continue, the country would suffer in export markets and have to import the ingredients of these systems. They also saw that there were a few British firms that were making or could build some of these components. They thus decided to set up a company, Nexos, that would impel these concerns to improve and interrelate their electronic office equipment products and that would then market these products either singly or, even more desirably, as a package.

Nexos was born in January 1979 (several months before the Tories ousted Labour from office) and was initially promised £15 million by the NEB.[1] It established handsome headquarters in London and Bristol[2] in preparation for a drive to sell the office machines that it anticipated would be shortly coming into its warehouses. Salesmen and marketing executives were enticed from other companies and were promised excellent retirement benefits. Some were even provided chauffeur-driven cars.[3]

Nexos placed its hopes for selling the system that came to be known as the 'office of the future' on three types of device. One was equipment that scanned and recorded graphic materials and business documents and also transmitted them in facsimile form. This item was to be supplied by a British company called

Muirhead plc. The Board and Muirhead formed a firm called Muirhead Office Systems Limited (real name), which we shall refer to as MOSL. MOSL agreed to develop and manufacture this 'facsimile' equipment with NEB funding while Nexos agreed to market it -- either as a separate unit or as a segment of a totally automated office. MOSL was 75% owned by Muirhead and 25% by the Board. Though Muirhead did make a facsimile machine, about two-thirds of the facsimile apparatuses that MOSL eventually transferred to Nexos were made by Oki Electric Co. of Tokyo, Japan.[4] As even a thorough and very critical Report on Nexos emanating from a study recently carried out by the Department of Industry[5] seemed to admit, there was nothing venal or inept about this substitution of Japanese for British products even though one of the purposes behind Nexos in particular and the NEB in general was to conserve imports and increase exports. Muirhead simply realised that the office facsimile machine it itself was assembling and selling in September 1979 when the agreement between it and Nexos was signed was technologically obsolete and that it was unable to quickly come up with a substitute that would meet Nexos' needs. This is why it furnished the NEB subsidiary with the Japanese equipment.[6]

The second ingredient of the computerised office was to be a new word processor. This is the main reason that the Board took a stake in the concern that we are calling Olga (which, remember, was also a member of Insac). The Board supplied Olga with over £2.5 million in funding for this processor[7]: at that time Olga could not have developed it on its own. The NEB and Olga formed a jointly owned subsidiary (that we shall call Olga, Jr) to effectuate the actual development and manufacture of the product.[8] The contract between Olga and the Board and another document passing between the two gave rise to some serious problems that we shall turn to in a few pages. The processor Olga was to build was to have a full-sized screen: Nexos also decided to market a processor made by the Ricoh Company of Japan that displayed just a single line.[9] This Japanese article was distributed by a British office equipment sales and maintenance firm called UDS. Nexos at the time desired more salespeople but did not want to hire them without having any wares at all to market. It therefore acquired UDS thus giving it both additional personnel and a workable product to tout.[10]

The capstone of the 'office of the future' -- the device that was to integrate the separate components and make the office fully automatic -- was to be a computer that would substitute for a telephone answering system and that would not only recognise the 'boss's' voice but would also be able to then give instructions to a word processor or facsimile machine. That is, this computer would not only receive the message but also store it in digital form and transmit it to another device that, in turn, would reproduce it.[11] In order to get this so-called 'communications management computer' into operation the NEB again reached overseas -- this time not to Japan but to the US. It entered into a contract with Delphi, the computer subsidiary of oil company Exxon. Under this licence agreement, Nexos received the exclusive right to make in the UK and market for office systems use in Europe a still on-the-drawing-boards computer referred to as Delta II. Nexos agreed to pay Delphi an initial royalty of £2 million plus additional royalties over the next ten years. Because it turned out that the product was not as finished as Nexos had believed when the licence contract was executed in 1979, it recruited in 1980 several UK software engineers to travel to California to expedite its development. Nexos bore the cost of these moves without compensation from Delphi. (The reason it chose to do business with this Exxon holding was that the latter had exhibited in 1977 an automated telephone answering system involving speech recognition.)[12]

Nexos' Financial Woes

In 1979 Nexos lost £2.7 million on a turnover of £400,000.[13] There was nothing alarming about this: this was its first year and no one could have expected that this period would be devoted to anything more exciting than getting organised. It was assumed, anyway, that it was a high-risk investment.[14] Real trouble arose during 1980. It had been hoped that Olga, Jr's word processor would be ready by summer of 1980,[15] and that 2000 of these machines would be sold by the end of 1981.[16] However, Olga, Jr could not complete the product as quickly as had been anticipated, which means that the NEB subsidiary was stuck with a highly paid sales force that had little to ballyhoo. By the end of 1981, in fact, only 600 had been disposed of.[17]

One may wonder why, when Nexos saw that the word processors that it had to get on time and that had to be of the highest quality were late and (as we shall see) defective, it did not attempt to get a comparable article from another manufacturer. The answer is that the agreement between Olga, Jr and Nexos bound the parties very closely to one another. Nexos was granted the sole and exclusive right to sell and service the device world-wide while Olga, Jr was to be its sole supplier.[18] In other words, under the contract Nexos probably could not have turned to another concern until the period of time for which the agreement was to run (50 years) had elapsed. If Nexos had tried to get it somewhere else, all rights to the Nexos-funded article would most likely have reverted to Olga.[19] Moreover, Nexos could not apply much pressure to Olga, Jr to move more rapidly to have a satisfactory machine available. Under the agreement, Nexos could not directly participate in the enhancement of the processor. Nor could it exercise much control over its cost, since the compact with Olga, Jr was for practical purposes a cost-plus one.[20] In short, that agreement was unfavourable for Nexos, placing it at the good faith, skill and luck of Olga, Jr.

The reader should not infer from the last sentence that Olga, Jr was guilty of either bad faith or lack of ability. We shall see that the processor was ultimately a good one. Moreover, the people at Olga, Jr and its parent were themselves unhappy about the delay. One of Olga's leading officials said that for its directors and senior staff, '...these were the most painful periods of their business life, I suspect, that they have [ever] lived through. We would never ever want to live through that again for any upside gain, for any eldorado.'[21] Relations between Olga and Nexos soon turned extremely sour. When the agreement was signed, the two felt warmly toward each other. However, after holdups in delivering the processor, '[M]utual trust soon gave way to mutual recrimination' and Nexos and Olga 'simply didn't get on'.[22] As a result and a symbol of this two-way suspicion, there was built up an 'enormous pile of correspondence which floated around at the time between

Nexos, [Olga] and the NEB'.[23] Thus a letter from a Nexos senior official to an Olga, Jr counterpart says that

'[Olga, Jr's] letter to me of 6 August is unacceptable. I can only assume it went out without your knowledge and approval and if you read it, you will see why I object to the tone and content. It reads like an attempt to set up an alibi in advance for late delivery by a group, supposedly expertly professional in software development, and also like an attempt to shift the blame for being late on to Nexos.'[24]

The 1980 nightmare over Olga, Jr's word processor was compounded by the fact that Nexos had no chairperson during that year. If it had had such an officer then, it would have been able to put more pressure on Olga and to get the NEB to push the firm as well.[25] When Nexos was inaugurated in January of 1979, Sir Leslie Murphy had selected David Dunbar, the head of NEB's computers and electronics division, to be Nexos' first chairman. When he left the NEB in 1979, the NEB Deputy Chairman, Richard Morris, was picked to run Nexos.[26] Then, as seen, Morris together with Murphy and the rest of the NEB Board quit in 1979. This resignation did not automatically mean that Morris was also out as Nexos' captain. However, one of my informants, a man who knew the NEB inside and out, told me that Murphy's successor Sir Arthur Knight disliked Morris from pre-NEB days and forced him out as Nexos' skipper. Knight never appointed a successor to Morris. When asked why he had not done so, he replied that at first he could not find anyone of quality to take the position and, later on in the year, when it became conceivable that Nexos would be phased out, no one would assume the helm.[27] (Another important post that was vacant too long was that of director of sales and marketing, empty until almost a year after Nexos' birth.[28])

Let us turn in more detail to the financial woes that were plaguing Nexos during this crucial year of 1980 when it was headless. It sold only £5.2 million worth of wares during the period and had an operating loss of £10 million.[29] By the middle of the year, its initial stake of £15.8 million had been fully committed.[30] At this juncture the NEB temporarily halted all further funding, subject to a review of Nexos' prospects by independent consultants commissioned by the Board and including a former British Telecom official and the consulting firm of Arthur Andersen.[31] While awaiting the verdict of the experts, Sir Keith Joseph, the Secretary of State for Industry, authorised what was referred to as a 'drip feed' operation, the drops totalling a mere £800,000. The consultants reported in October 1980 and said that Nexos' corporate plan was high-risk and ambitious but sensible; and recommended that the strategy in that scheme be carried out and that the government give Nexos additional cash to make the total investment in it £35 million, including the £15.8 million that had already been handed out.[32] Convinced by this seal of approval, the NEB decided to ask for the additional £18-£19 million. The DOI of course received a copy of the consultants' report and also approved the additional assistance.[33] The Secretary of State, however, showed himself rather reluctant to go along with the review team, the Board and his Department on this matter. In December 1980 he did allow an investment of £5.3 million and in January 1981 one of £1 million more in order to enable the company to meet its cash requirements.[34] He acted slowly in the hope that Nexos would be able to supply the rest of its financial needs (£13 million) from the private sector by February 1981. However, it could not do so and, in fact, the 'drip feeding' impaired its ability to get private investors to take an interest in it.[35]

So in February 1981 the Tories were faced with an issue relating to an NEB high tech start-up investment similar to the one they were confronted with with respect to Inmos in the summer of 1980. That is, should they give it another large tranche of money or let it go down the drain. By this time, Sir Frederick Wood was NEB Chairman; and he and the NEB Chief Executive, Mr. Brian Willott, wanted Nexos to get the additional £13 million.[36] The decision was to be made on 19 February. On 18 February three of the four executive directors of Nexos sent 'an extraordinary letter...by messenger to the House of Commons'.[37] It was delivered to Secretary of State Joseph and asked him not to give the venture the slice of funding it was asking for[38] -- unless it were merged with Olga, Jr to give it more control over the development and manufacture of the word processor that it planned to sell.[39]

157

(The Chairman of Olga and an officer of Muirhead were non-executive directors of Nexos throughout its existence.[40]) The executive directors felt that without this change in the Olga-Nexos connection, private investment, which had been made a condition of further government aid, could not be attracted.[41]

On the 19th Wood and Willott went to the DOI to ask for the money -- and they received it. Willott then went back to NEB headquarters to reveal what he thought would be taken as good news but was met by the rebel Nexos directors who told him about their attempt to temporarily spike the funding. Needless to say, he was annoyed and told them that their answers were 'improper and impertinent'.[42] It is uncertain whether the matters brought up in their letter were discussed at the February 19 meeting of Wood, Willott and Joseph. Wood says that as far as he remembers the issues were not mentioned; and Willott, now a very high-level civil servant, was not available for comment on this matter. However, Nexos did receive a letter of acknowledgement from Sir Keith's Private Secretary, which asserted that the questions raised by the directors' note had been mentioned at the Wood-Willott-Joseph conclave. Why Sir Keith went along with the NEB Chairman rather than with the Nexos executive directors is still unclear.[43]

Despite the receipt of the £13 million, things went from bad to worse for Nexos in 1981. Its staff had expected sales of over £25 million during the year. In the first three months, it looked at least slightly possible that this prediction would be on the mark: during this quarter, monthly sales did increase from £722,000 to £1,107,000. By the end of the year, though, the subsidiary's turnover was only £8.93 million and its losses totalled about £13 million.[44] By October of 1981 the NEB realised that Nexos never would secure private sector angels and that it could never become self-supporting with the funds available from the government. So it was decided then to put it into receivership.[45]

The Termination of Nexos

In November of 1981 the winding down began. In that month, Nexos ended its licensing agreement with Delphi. The termination of the licence plus the payment of one month's extra salary to the Nexos employees who had relocated in California cost it over £300,000.[46] Delphi and Nexos had devoutly wished the integrating 'communications management computer' to materialise; but had not as of this time designed one that would satisfactorily tie together the executive's voice with the word processor and the facsimile machine.[47] In fact, the Delphi answering system that had so impressed some Nexos officials had not even solved the voice recognition problem and had to be staffed by human operators.[48]

In January 1982, three years after it first saw the light of day, the rest of Nexos' activities came to a halt and many of its staff were made redundant. However, a liquidator was not appointed until May 1983.[49] Olga, Jr's word processor was to be marketed by ICL, though Olga could sell it as well.[50] Muirhead Office Systems Ltd took over the vending and servicing of the facsimile equipment that it had been supplying to Nexos.[51] As a result of its assumption of the selling end of the facsimile equipment business, MOSL was handed about 875 Japanese and UK-made facsimile machines which it had earlier disposed of to Nexos for more than £1.8 million. To get the devices back, it paid Nexos the princely sum of £1. It also agreed to give Nexos the same 'overwhelming' amount for 590 machines ordered from Japan and then in transit.[52]

The NEB defended this deal using the following arguments.

(1) MOSL had to assume the significant costs of refurbishing, installing and maintaining the machines for which it paid the £1, as well as of establishing a marketing operation for them, and

(2) Under the transfer agreement, MOSL waived its right to potentially large damages arising from breach of contract.[53] None the less, Tory MP Phillip Oppenheim, the co-editor of an office equipment magazine, was not at all satisfied by these assertions and demanded that the DOI inquire into the £1 affair in particular and the Nexos operation in general, which he charged on the floor of the House was run by the NEB with 'an abandon that verged on the fraudulent'.[54] This study (whose Report of 1985 we have already cited and which we shall turn to in more detail shortly) was on the whole bitterly critical of the Nexos operation. Nevertheless, it accepted much of the NEB's contentions concerning the £1 issue.[55]

We remarked in Chapter 2 that the winding down of Nexos contributed -£34 million to the NEB's total loss of about £28.2 on the disposal of the investments it made in its role as venture capitalist. (Actually, by 1985 the tax benefits accruing to the NEB from Nexos' failures reduced the red ink on its termination to 'only' £24.5 million[56] and thus the total deficit from the marketing of the NEB's venture capital holdings to £18.7 million.) However, the country ultimately gained one good product as a result of the Nexos gamble: the 2200 word processor eventually (and tardily, from the vantage point of Nexos) developed by Olga, Jr and now sold by ICL. A spokesperson for ICL whom I interviewed referred to it as an 'excellent' machine. Moreover, it won a 1983 Queen's Award for technological achievement and obtained about 20% of the UK market.[57] *The Financial Times* too considers it a fine instrument; though it points out that one reason that Nexos could not market many was that IBM entered the word-processing field with low-price equipment.[58] (Other, more crucial reasons why the 2200 did not become popular when it wore the Nexos label will be indicated shortly.)

Why Nexos Failed: The 1985 DOI Analysis

As with Insac's, much of the Nexos wreckage was avoidable. If the NEB, Nexos' management or the DOI had taken certain steps, or refrained from taking others, at certain points of time, the venture would have come to much less grief. In other words, those connected with the affair were quite shortsighted in certain respects, which we shall turn to now.

The 1985 Report springing from the DOI study of Nexos that was sparked by the sale of the 1465 facsimile machines to MOSL for £2 concluded that Nexos' failure resulted primarily from the creation by its management of

'a much larger organisation, with higher outgoings, than was justified by either the actual level of sales or by the amount of funding approved by the NEB...It appears to me [the individual hired as a DOI consultant who was the person most responsible for the Report] that Nexos failed essentially because its management tried to do too much too quickly, having regard to the amount of NEB funding committed to it. In particular a large organisation was built up, and Nexos effectively committed to a level of expenditure which was out of proportion to the gross profits being earned...'[59]

By the end of 1979, Nexos had a staff of 144. This was actually not unreasonable: about 100 of these persons had worked for the company (UDS) that had sold and maintained Japanese word processors; and, as seen, taking it over gave Nexos an item to sell and a sales force to work with it and future products.[60] It was in 1980 that Nexos hired a host of men and women. By the end of April it had 273 employees; of July, 323; of September, 363; of December, 405; and of January 1981, 410 -- its high point.[61] This build-up of staff, including the expansion during the last half of 1980, took place despite the following events, among others.

(1) Under an Olga, Jr 'Development Plan' for Nexos, the first 2200 machines should have been ready for trading in summer of 1980. However, by early April of that year Nexos' development department was aware that the apparatus was delayed and could not be 'launched' (i.e. a publicity and sales campaign started) until the first week in September 1980; and that the 'First Customer Sales' could not take place until the first week in November 1980. Olga, Jr started assembling the hardware during July but the necessary software was not yet in place. Because it was missing, the 'launch' had to be moved back again to mid-October;[62] and the first product could not be shipped to buyers until January 1981.[63] Despite Nexos' management's knowledge that the machine would not appear as scheduled, it refused to postpone the accretion of its sales force on the ground that a large marketing organisation was needed from the start. Only in this way, it was believed, could a new outfit get the large custom that would enable it to compete with giants like IBM and ICL.[64] For example, a Nexos document of April 24, 1980 said that 'The [Olga, Jr 2200 word processor] will not now be available for supply to customers until September 1980, a slippage of 3 months', but added that 'The delay in...[its] availability obviously affects our staff requirements but senior marketing management has decided not to defer the recruitment programme decided upon at the start of the year'.[65]

(2) Nexos assumed that it would sell about £2.4 million worth of MOSL's domestic and Japanese facsimile machines during the fourth quarter of 1979 and the first half of 1980. As things turned out, it purveyed only £328,000 worth of these during this period. For the second half of 1980, it predicted that it would dispose of £2.1 million worth of this equipment; but it in fact grossed only £1.2 million from its sale.[66]

(3) The NEB's initial allocation of funds to Nexos was, as seen, £15.8 million. However, from the beginning Nexos operated on the theory that it would get £20 million from its parent even though it knew that the extra money could not be granted to it in the absence of the nod of the Secretary of State for Industry. Finally, in July 1980 it was told that it would have to live with the £15.8 million, even though this sum had been totally committed, subject to the already-discussed review of its financial prospects by independent consultants. None the less, though it knew that this study was underway, that it might be closed down, and that in any event it had already obligated all its cash on hand or promised to it, it 'continued to increase its overall staff numbers...from 307 at the end of June, 1980 to 405 by the end of December 1980'.[67] (The Report points out that the NEB knew or could easily have discovered this rapid build-up in personnel.[68] However, it seems to accord weight to the Board's defence that it should not be blamed for allowing this snowballing to continue because it itself had lost many employees, because it had to worry about divesting itself of many of its holdings, and because its membership and Chairperson during most of 1980 were new to the job.[69])

Why Nexos Failed: Other Contributing Factors

I have no doubt that the 1985 DOI Report is correct in its view that Nexos hired too many people too quickly. However, I disagree with its assertion that this was *the* major reason for its failure. It was one important cause, but not the only significant one, as I shall shortly attempt to demonstrate. Before doing this, I should mention another aspect of this document that is annoying, i.e. that the Department of Industry itself seems to be absolved from all blame for the shipwreck.[70] This conclusion just does not make sense. The DOI approved all the investments in Nexos, including, as we have seen, the final tranche of £13 million in February 1981.[71] If the management of Nexos were as inept as the 1985 Report claimed, it was surely the duty of the Department to have recommended against further funding until it mended its ways!

In fact, a 1983-84 Report of the Public Accounts Committee that we have already cited in this chapter did place some of the blame for Nexos' foundering on the Department's shoulders. The Department at this time (1983-84) was claiming that the main reason for the collapse was the nature of the agreement with Olga, Jr for the new word processor;[72] it made no mention about sloppy administration on the part of those in control of Nexos. But, as the Committee pointed out, the Department should be faulted for not having recognised the flaws in this agreement much sooner than it did. Though the Department realised as early as autumn of 1980 that Nexos was not getting the processors from Olga, Jr as quickly as it should have been, it was not until the NEB began negotiations with various concerns to take over Nexos' assets and contractual rights (i.e. late in 1981) that it dawned upon it that one of the major snags was the contract.[73] The DOI was also mistaken, the Committee said, in approving the initial investment in Nexos simply on the basis of an assurance by the Board that the company would earn an adequate return on capital employed. It did not even question the Board's sales and profit forecasts or have before it a Board estimate of what the total funding would have to be.[74] The Committee, while not absolving the NEB of responsibility for the mess,[75] also contended that the Department erred in not quantifying the odds involved when it realised that Nexos was high-risk.[76] (The Department said that it accepted the NEB's assertions because it thought the UK needed a company of the Nexos type and because in early 1979 the atmosphere for NEB investment was favourable.[77])

To return to this section's main theme, we find that the 1985 DOI Report refused to admit that delays in the production, or chinks in the quality, of Olga, Jr's word processor were significant factors in Nexos' collapse.[78] Yet the data it itself provides indicate that this time lag and these flaws were important reasons why the NEB subsidiary flopped. Had the 2200 been ready by summer 1980, as the Olga, Jr Development

Plan had promised,[79] sales might have commenced in August. In this event, revenues from the machine would have started entering Nexos' cash registers five months earlier than they did and its sales force would then have been able to earn a bit of their keep.

However, promptness in the delivery of adequate quantities of this device would not have sufficed by itself. During 1981 sales proved very disappointing. It was hoped, for example, that these would total 100 a month in June 1981 but the figure for that period reached only 50.[80] The main reason was that the processor lacked both 'communications facilities' (devices for, e.g., allowing 2200 machines to pass data to other 2200s, to act as a teletype terminal[81] or to communicate with computers) and an 'automatic correspondence' (AC) characteristic (a software characteristic that 'allows the automatic generation by the machine of a number of individual documents...').[82] In July 1981 an acceptable AC feature was finally made available;[83] but by then it was too late to keep Nexos alive. The original 1979 specification for the 2200 required the AC but not the communications features.[84] It was not until the end of 1980 that Nexos realised that its failure to demand the communications parts and the delay in producing the AC software seriously threatened the competitiveness of the processor.[85] The Report does fault Nexos' marketing department for not including the communications items in the original product specification.[86] What I object to is not the laying of blame on Nexos for this example of shortsightedness but, on the contrary, the failure to emphasise how dangerous it was for Nexos *not* to have insisted on this at the start. This omission was a more fundamental cause of its tumble than the 'overstaffing' -- which would not have been an extravagance had the initial version of the processor been on time and commercially satisfactory! Additionally, the engineers and computer scientists working at Olga and Olga, Jr should have been lambasted in the report as much as Nexos' management was. They, too, should have recognised how necessary the communications components would be -- and should have produced a workable AC software segment by the time the bulk of the 2200 finally was ready.[87] (Nexos decided to launch the machine in mid-October 1980 rather than wait for the AC device because it expected it to be ready soon. However the version of the AC that was initially delivered to it in March 1981 contained a 'bug'.[88])

Next, as we have seen from the DOI report, the domestic and Japanese facsimile machines provided to Nexos by Muirhead Office Systems Limited (MOSL) moved very poorly -- total sales for 1981 were only £1 million, even less than the low level for 1980.[89] This lack of buyer interest was due to several factors.

(1) The facsimile machines fabricated by MOSL itself were late going into production and needed frequent repairs.[90] (As noted, at the time Muirhead signed the agreement with Nexos its main product was a less sophisticated apparatus; but it was working on the one it eventually transferred to this NEB holding.[91])

(2) The Japanese facsimile machines MOSL distributed to Nexos and which the latter marketed were 'not immune from problems, and...proved to be oversensitive to the quality of the telephone link'.[92]

(3) Unforeseen, low-priced Japanese competition raised its head in 1981.[93] The disappointing turnover in facsimile equipment was certainly another important reason that Nexos became awash in an ocean of red ink -- perhaps as important as the overstaffing; but probably not as crucial as the holdups and technical deficiencies of the 2200.

The word processor contract ('Supply and Marketing Agreement', or 'S & MA' for short) between Olga, Jr and Nexos was another example of the shortsightedness of the Nexos management (and of the NEB) that played an important role in the venture's demise -- once again, as least as significant a role as the free and easy recruitment of staff. As seen, the Department of Industry stressed in 1983-84 the weaknesses in this contract;[94] and it is hard to see why in 1985 it accorded this factor little if any importance.[95] It is true that by the latter date its consultant had unearthed good evidence about the unwarranted size of the staff; but it does not follow from the fact that the swollen workforce played a significant part that the S & MA's negative impact was minimal!

Let us explain in more detail the snags in this contract and how they affected Nexos. First, a point made by the Committee of Public Accounts,[96] how Nexos and the NEB could have been convinced to concur in the contract's provision making Olga, Jr the sole supplier of the processor is almost impossible to understand. At the time the agreement was concluded this particular device was not in existence. It should have been obvious to the Board that a product that was *in posse* rather than *in esse* might not be available when Nexos needed it, or, at least, that it might contain significant flaws as of that date. The NEB and Nexos staffs were all experienced business people; and should have known that there is many a slip in moving a ware from the drawing board to the production room; that the attempt to convert a stroke of genius into a marketable good might run into difficulties that could not have been anticipated when the device was a mere sketch on an inventor's pad. (These difficulties could, of course, be caused by errors in the product design itself or by the inability of suppliers of component parts because of strikes or natural disasters to deliver these anywhere near on time.) Thus the compact should have clearly stated that if for any reason the word processor's hardware or software would not be available from Olga, Jr on such and such a date; or were completed by then but contained significant flaws; Nexos would have the right to turn to another undertaking for the purchase of a marketable word processor until Olga, Jr had a satisfactory apparatus all set for delivery. For a buyer not to have left itself such an out is hard to excuse, whether it be state-owned or private. It is true that Olga might have been the only UK company that then had the talent to construct a good word processor. However, Nexos did not hesitate on other occasions to contract for good non-British products when there was no domestic firm that showed promise of manufacturing what it needed. The reader will remember the selection of US company Delphi to develop the communications management computer and of the Japanese Ricoh Corporation to supply a single-line-display processor. Moreover, a sentence allowing Nexos to purchase from others than Olga, Jr in case its processor became bogged down would have adequately protected the latter since it would have committed Nexos to buy from it as soon as its machine was up to snuff.

It was also a mistake for the NEB and Nexos not to have insisted on an arbitration clause in case conflict developed between it and Olga, Jr.[97] Surely they could have foreseen that some disputes between Nexos and that company would arise for, it cannot be mentioned too often, the simple reason that Nexos was asking for a new product made to order. In this situation, the Board, Nexos (and Olga, of course) should have realised that delays were almost inevitable; that the customer would, at least initially, have some serious qualms about what came off the assembly line; and that an arbiter empowered by contract to act in the event of misunderstandings between buyer and seller might be able to frame interim solutions that met the needs of both. For instance, he/she might have permitted Nexos, when it found itself confronted with the tardiness in the arrival of the 2200 word processor and the automatic correspondence software, to allow it to acquire workable, saleable machines from another supplier for, e.g., a maximum of twelve months. Another quarrel that he/she could have resolved was whether the salaries of the staff lent Olga, Jr by Olga but paid by Olga were among the 'development costs' of the processor to Olga, Jr for which Nexos should have reimbursed it. This wrangling was yet one additional detail souring the relations between Olga and Nexos.[98] (A high NEB official admitted to me that the NEB did not vet the Nexos supply contracts rigorously enough. He asserted, as well, that it was a mistake to have the contract for the processor a cost-plus agreement. The market constrained Nexos to sell for no more than a certain price; and this was less than the cost of the item to it.)

Even bitter critics of the NEB feel that the concept behind Nexos was a sensible one. John Redwood, for example, asserts that

'These developments [e.g., word processing, electronic mail, linking of phones to computers] were likely to proceed quickly, and the potential market for the correct products was enormous. It was difficult to see who would exploit them most effectively. The NEB was correct in its view that there was a great business opportunity for those who would exploit it. Nor was it necessarily rash to assume that the market could be exploited by new companies...After all, IBM and Xerox had started only some thirty or forty years before as quite small ventures...'[99]

It is not surprising, therefore, that NEB officialdom and the Department of Industry viewed Nexos' establishment quite positively.[100] It is the bitterest irony in the Board's history that this promising progeny played a significant role in its downfall!

NOTES

1. NEB 1979 Annual Report, p. 17.

2. Transcript of BBC-2 programme of 27 January 1985, 'The money programme', at pp. 2-3.

3. Ibid., p. 3.

4. HC Committee of Public Accounts, *Nexos: minutes of evidence,* p. 51, 92, 94.

5. This study was cited in the preceding footnote. Henceforth in this book it will be cited as 'CPA 1985'.

6. CPA 1985, pp. 51-2, 75.

7. Ibid., p. 67.

8. Ibid., p. 17.

9. Ibid., p. 21.

10. Ibid.

11. *London Times,* 30 Nov. 1979, p. 23.

12. See Redwood, *Going for broke...,* pp. 82-4; *London Times,* 30 Nov. 1979, p. 23; CPA 1985, pp. 39-41.

13. NEB 1979 Annual Report, pp. 32-3.

14. HC Committee of Public Accounts, *Reports 1983-84, No. 15: DTI monitoring of British Technology Group* (HMSO, London, 1984), p. xi. Henceforth in this book this report will be cited as 'CPA 1983-84'.

15. CPA 1983-84, p. 35.

16. *Financial Times,* 11 Dec. 1981, p. 14.

17. Ibid.

18. CPA 1983-84, p. 34.

19. Ibid., p. 35.

20. Ibid.

21. 'Money programme', p. 7.

22. Ibid., p. 3.

23. Ibid.

24. CPA 1985, p. 48.

25. 'Money programme', p. 4.

26. CPA 1985, p. 59.

27. 'Money programme', p. 4.

28. *Economist,* 22 Dec. 1979, p. 61.

29. NEB 1980 Annual Report, pp. 24-5.

30. CPA 1983-84, p. 35.

31. Ibid., p. 24.

32. Ibid.

33. Ibid., p. 7.

34. Ibid.

35. Ibid.

36. 'Money programme', p. 5.

37. Ibid., p. 1. Actually two letters were sent together, one from one executive director alone. CPA 1985, p. 55.

38. 'Money programme', p. 1.

39. CPA 1985, p. 83.

40. Ibid., p. 9, 24.

41. See ibid., pp. 33-5, 83-7.

42. 'Money programme', p. 5.

43. Paragraph based on ibid., p. 1, 5, 6.

44. NEB 1981 Annual Report, pp. 30-1; CPA 1983-84, p. 34.

45. See NEB 1981 Annual Report, p. 8 and CPA 1983-84, p. 7.

46. CPA 1985, p. 69, 91.

47. Redwood, *Going for broke...,* p. 85.

48. CPA 1985, p. 40.

49. CPA 1983-84, p. 34.

50. *Guardian,* 12 Jan. 1982, p. 18.

51. Ibid.; also CPA 1985, pp. 93-4.

52. CPA 1985, p. 93.

53. CPA 1983-84, p. 32.

54. HC Debates, 6 June 1984, col. 297.

55. See CPA 1985, p. 94, 103-04.

56. Ibid., p. 65.

57. 'Money programme', pp. 6-7.

58. 11 Dec. 1981, p. 14.

59. CPA 1985, p. 7.

60. Ibid., p. 21, 63.

61. Ibid., pp. 63-4.

62. Ibid., pp. 42-4.

63. Ibid., p. 44.

64. Ibid., p. 27.

65. Ibid.
66. Ibid., p. 52.
67. Ibid., p. 30.
68. Ibid., p. 60.
69. Ibid., p. 6, 61-2.
70. See ibid., p. 7.
71. CPA 1983-84, pp. 6-7.
72. Ibid., p. xii.
73. Ibid., p. 35.
74. Ibid., p. xiii, 24-5.
75. Ibid., p. xiii.
76. Ibid., p. xi.
77. Ibid., pp. 24-5.
78. CPA 1985, pp. 6-7.
79. Ibid., p. 42.
80. Ibid., p. 36.
81. Ibid., p. 45.
82. Ibid.
83. Ibid., p. 46.
84. Ibid., p. 45, 46.
85. Ibid., pp. 44-5.
86. Ibid.
87. Ibid., p. 46.
88. Ibid.
89. Ibid., p. 52.
90. Ibid., p. 53.
91. Ibid., p. 51.
92. Ibid., p. 53.
93. Ibid.
94. CPA 1983-84, p. 27.
95. See CPA 1985, p. 100.
96. CPA 1983-84, p. xii.
97. See ibid.
98. Ibid., p. 19.
99. *Going for broke...*, pp. 81-2.
100. CPA 1983-84, p. 25.

11
Alfred Herbert

We now turn to the NEB's life as a saviour of various large corporations. In only one of these instances (Fairey) can it reasonably be considered a venture capitalist, as the other concerns were (as seen) given to it by the government without its having an option to reject them.

At one time, Alfred Herbert was one of the glories of UK industry. Essentially a family firm and named after its founder, its machine tools, especially its No. 4 capstan lathe, were known all over the world. Up until World War II it never bothered to acquire any subsidiaries and eschewed fabricating articles other than machine tools. Mr Herbert kept production steady: in times of slack he built for stock. Moreover, he lived over a company shop and ploughed his profits back into the enterprise. He lived until after the War, dying at 93.

In certain ways, the management that succeeded the founder was more 'up to date'. It purchased other firms and expanded by diversification. However, it lacked the intelligence and dynamism of the 'old man'. During the 1960s Herbert did not shrink when it should have and, in fact, expanded more than demand justified. It did not, however, invest much money to improve its own range of machine tools. Nor, even worse, did it anticipate that many machine tools soon would be operated by computers rather than directly by people, i.e. that the microchip would revolutionise the machine tool industry. Thus by the 1970s its products were out of date.[1] Between 1965 and 1970 the company earned only £8.7 million in profits but paid out £9.2 million in dividends. In the decade 1965-1974 experts were hired to improve productivity and profits but though some

171

workers were fired, the company's economic position went from bad to worse.[2]

In addition to its own lack of perceptiveness, Herbert's management was in the early 1970s confronted with forces beyond its control. World War II had created too much capacity in the machine tool trade and foreign competition, especially from Japan and the Germanies, began to make inroads into its markets. Everything went haywire in 1974, the year Labour took over from the Tories and Wilson became Prime Minister with Benn his Secretary of State for Industry. The firm's Chairman resigned, seven senior executives suffered heart attacks, and it went bankrupt.[3] A group of businessmen who were advising the Government on aid requests made under the 1972 Industry Act recommended that the company be dismantled.[4] However, it then had almost 7000 employees and the unions representing the workforce wanted to see it saved. Moreover, it still had a prestigious name and was continuing to sell some of its wares abroad. Some shop stewards proposed that it should be owned by its employees or the NEB and that its production should be coordinated with that of the entire UK machine tool industry.[5] None the less, more 'traditional' socialist views won out and it was nationalised in 1975.[6] Sir John Buckley, a person with a background in production engineering, was asked to become the non-executive (part-time) Chairman; and remained in this capacity until close to the time that the undertaking was wound up. It was transferred to the NEB in 1976, much to the relief of the Department of Industry. As soon as he took over, Buckley surveyed the situation and declared that Herbert should go out of business then and there; but the Government refused to accede to this drastic step. Some persons high in the ranks of the Board agreed with his analysis; but he, it and the full-time Herbert management had to soldier on.

At the beginning of 1977 the government's equity and loan investment in the company was over £29 million (£25 million of which was given at the time of the rescue[7]): in that year the NEB put in £2.5 million more by way of loans.[8] In 1978 it took £10 million more in equity shares;[9] while in 1979 the outstanding loans were converted into equity and it purchased about £3 million in stock above and beyond the sums represented by this conversion. This made its total shareholding in Herbert about £44 million;[10] and, as seen in Chapter 2, the government's total loss upon the tool-maker's liquidation was £57 million.[11] Sir Leslie Murphy himself said before he left the NEB that the firm would not get any more state funding. This decision was made final by the new Board in June 1980 and Herbert went into liquidation in October 1980.[12] Throughout the period of government ownership, Herbert either was in the red or made very little. For example, it did have small profits before taxation of £880,000 in 1976 and £130,000 in 1977[13] but lost £3.22 million in 1978[14] and £15.63 million in 1979.[15]

One might think that the 1978 and 1979 deficits and the loss upon disposal would have brought the wrath of God, or at least of the Tory and journalistic right, upon the NEB; but, in fact, there was remarkably little criticism from these quarters of its dealings with Herbert. The bitterness in this situation came from left wing trade unionists who were angered at the discharges of personnel that were initiated by management and backed by the Board after the company had been handed to it.[16] The workforce shrunk to 4200 in 1980 and was down to about 1000 in 1981, while the firm was being wound up.[17] The unions at Herbert objected to the redundancies, of course, and strikes erupted; but ultimately the union leaders became convinced that they had no course other than to go along. Some of the shop stewards and others on the left of the British trade union movement were furious not only because the NEB accepted the loss of the workers but also because Murphy adamantly rejected their requests that the employees should be allowed a share in the running of the firm.[18]

Ironically, the discharge of a great many staff did not, at least in the short run, help Herbert financially. The fired men and women received high levels of redundancy pay, which absorbed a good deal of the cash the concern was getting from the NEB. There were, as well, other 'unproductive' uses to which the Board's funding had to be put. It had to be employed to pay overdrafts, customs, interest, back taxes and compulsory wage hikes.[19] As a result, the undertaking did not have as much money as it needed for research and development. Yet it did manage to fashion new and technologically-excellent types of lathe.

None the less, even this improvement in the quality of its product offerings failed to save it. There were several reasons for this. First, a world-wide recession hit the machine tool industry in 1977.[20] Second, the firm's product range was still too wide then; and as a result it was stuck with mounds of unsold inventory.[21] Third, a rise in the pound made it hard to export any UK-made machine tools. Fourth, Herbert had difficulty convincing UK companies to manufacture the electronic components for its new tools: one major British electronics firm complained, for example, that the Herbert order was too small. (It may well have been that the company felt that it would not have paid its bills.) Fifth, American firms investing in the UK did not buy their machine tools from Herbert but from US factories. A person who had been high in the ranks of the British labour movement told me that he suspects that there may have existed an agreement among US firms to purchase from American plants; but, once again, it might have been that the Americans believed that the shaky Herbert sites might be shut at any time and that they might thus be left without the machine tools that were an essential segment of their own operations. Finally, Herbert needed cash but could not raise prices due to strong competition.[22]

Given the unprepossessing state of Herbert's financial situation, relations between the Board and its management were not as bad as they could have been, though naturally tensions existed. The NEB made one of its own staff responsible for supervising the machine tool firm; but Buckley never had any trouble contacting Ryder and Murphy personally. The Board as a general rule did not try to take control of Herbert's day-to-day operations. As normal for a NEB subsidiary, it had to submit its corporate plans to the Board; but these were usually approved. As it was more concerned with British Leyland and Rolls Royce, the NEB did not appoint a director to Herbert's Board until 1979.[23]

Some NEB officials thought that the mid-1970s version of Herbert's management was weak and should have been even more aggressive in firing superfluous workers. (Management may have been 'soft' but 2400 jobs were lost between October 1975 and July 1978. A Herbert director who resigned received £67,000 in a payment labelled 'compensation'.[24]) The Board felt that the company's sales department needed improving. It wanted Herbert to move faster in developing new products but its managers felt that there were practical limitations upon the number of innovations it could refine or introduce. Buckley stood side-by-side with Sir Kenneth Keith of Rolls Royce and Sir Michael Edwardes of British Leyland in successfully contending against an NEB suggestion that one person be made an NEB 'personnel director' for the three subsidiaries. The plan was to have this individual involved in the labour relations of the companies. They opposed this idea because they felt that he or she would start controlling their personnel policies and thus tie their hands in their dealings with their unions.

A couple of men who participated in the Alfred Herbert saga argue quite plausibly that it did not turn out anywhere near as disastrously as the press and public thought. Bits and pieces of the company were purchased by various firms at its liquidation. These sell some of the new machine tools conceived after the 1975 nationalisation. To some extent, it was easier to push them in the 1980s than in the 1970s because their American competition was harmed by the rise in the value of the dollar that lasted until 1987. The fact remains, however, that they are fine products that would not be available to buyers had the UK government not tried to salvage Herbert.

NOTES

1. *Government and industry: a new partnership*, p. 19.
2. Coventry Trades Councils, *State intervention in industry,* pp. 60-1.
3. Ibid., p. 60.
4. Sainsbury, *Government and industry: a new partnership*, p. 18.
5. Coventry Trades Councils, *State intervention in industry,* pp. 60-1.
6. Sainsbury, *Government and industry: a new partnership,* p. 18.
7. *Daily Telegraph,* 1 Ap. 1978, p. 19.
8. NEB 1977 Annual Report, pp. 38-9.
9. NEB 1978 Annual Report, pp. 46-7.
10. NEB 1979 Annual Report, pp. 48-9.
11. *London Times,* 18 Oct. 1980, p. 17.
12. NEB 1980 Annual Report, p. 7; 1981 Annual Report, p. 30.
13. NEB 1977 Annual Report, pp. 32-3.
14. NEB 1979 Annual Report, p. 13.
15. NEB 1980 Annual Report, pp. 24-5.
16. See, e.g., Coventry Trades Councils, *State intervention in industry,* pp. 94-8.

17. Ibid., p. 170.
18. Ibid., p. 95.
19. *Daily Telegraph,* 9 Sept. 1978, p. 17.
20. *London Times,* 21 Oct. 1977, p. 19.
21. Ibid.
22. *London Times,* 1 Ap. 1977, p. 19.
23. *Financial Times,* 7 Dec. 1979, p. 7.
24. Coventry Trades Councils, *State intervention in industry,* p. 96.

12
Fairey and Ferranti

Fairey Holdings is a group of engineering companies. Its constituent firms manufacture controls and stabilisation systems for planes and helicopters; robots for factory use; control and monitoring systems for mines; filtration devices for defence, aeronautical and manufacturing plants; ceramic cores for the casting of components of aircraft and jet engines; military bridges and military loading vehicles; equipment for nuclear power reactors; generating equipment; patrol boats for military, police, fire, customs, coastguard and commercial use; and insulators for electricity-generating stations. In 1978 it employed about 3000 persons[1] and had a turnover of £50 million: in 1984 it had a UK workforce of over 5000 and sales of £150 million. In 1977 it ran into serious financial difficulties because a Belgian subsidiary that manufactured aircraft ran out of money: its planes were not sophisticated enough for modern needs. During the summer of 1977 it became apparent to investors that this holding was suffering from an overstock of aircraft and the price of Fairey shares fell during a two week period from 85 pence to 47 pence.[2] Big orders for these planes from Africa, the Far East and North America failed to materialise.[3] When the Belgian government refused to rescue the subsidiary, Fairey asked its bankers to put the whole conglomerate into receivership and a receiver was appointed.[4]

A private concern, Trafalgar House, asked the receiver if they could buy it. However, lo and behold, the NEB came in with a higher bid -- £2.5 million more -- and completed its purchase of the firm for £18 million in January 1978.[5] The initiative for this bid came from the Board itself, which justified the purchase to the press and public in general terms as fitting in with the government's industrial strategy.[6] One can sensibly assume that the more concrete reason behind the acquisition was the desire to save a concern that employed large numbers of people, that was important to the defence forces, and that was active in exports.

Needless to say, this transaction was strongly denounced by the Conservative Party and the more conservative elements of the press. Why was it necessary for the NEB to carry out this rescue, they said, when a reputable private firm had shown itself ready and willing to step in. We have already discussed, for example, an article in the *Daily Express*[7] entitled 'Let's Destroy This Monster Before It Destroys Us'. This story appeared just after the transfer of Fairey to the NEB and was in fact precipitated by this event, which the author refers to as an attempt at 'back-door nationalisation'. He admitted that Trafalgar House controlled the *Express* but denied that it controlled him. The *Financial Times* said that it was a bad purchase because it was a hodgepodge of companies linked only by common ownership and was not vital to the health of the UK economy.[8] Grylls and Redwood moaned that it made no industrial sense for the NEB to buy both tiny lockmaker Thwaites and Reed and the 16-subsidiary Fairey Group.[9] Actually, those who accused the Board of 'imperialism' in outbidding Trafalgar neglected to inform their readers that the Board, unlike its rival, was willing to take all the Fairey subsidiaries except the troubled aircraft manufacturer while Trafalgar wanted only ten of these concerns. Unlike Trafalgar, it had done a fine job of researching Fairey's prospects. It obtained good advice from a merchant bank; and concluded, quite accurately as things turned out, that most of the group's non-aircraft holdings would continue to be or soon become profitable.[10]

After the Board's purchase of Fairey, Sir Leslie Murphy recruited new management for it. Also, the fact that almost all its units had been saved improved morale. The Board let the new leadership function autonomously. It had to approve the company's main appointments, its profit plan, and its large capital expenditures; but never turned any of these down. It facilitated Fairey's getting a bank loan and did not object to the closure of its Tress subsidiary which made stainless steel valves. Not surprisingly, though, this shrinkage did not sit well with many in the UK labour movement. They argued vehemently that Tress had been profitable as recently as 1975 and 1976; that it was located in Tyneside, an area of high unemployment; that it could become successful again were Fairey to replace the existing old machinery there; and that the past profits of this subsidiary should have been invested in its modernising and diversification rather than being siphoned off to the head office. Yet Fairey remained adamant; the NEB did not pressure it to change its mind; and Tress was eliminated.[11]

In addition to pushing this controversial closure, the NEB-appointed managers introduced a tighter system of financial planning and controls. The company made over £5 million in 1978 and 1979.[12] After the Conservative Party won the 1979 election, it decided that there was no further purpose served by Fairey's remaining in public ownership; and it was sold in June 1980 for £22 million.[13] In January 1987 it bought itself out from the UK firm of S. Pearson and Son. Almost half of its business is export and it has acquired subsidiaries in the US. Fairey is arguably one of the NEB's triumphs; and it is not unreasonable to term it a success resulting from its role of venture capitalist as it was very shaky indeed when the Board took it over. Perhaps one-third (about 1500) of the 5000 workers it employed in the UK as of 1984 can be added to the number of positions the Board saved acting as venture capitalist. It is true that Trafalgar House bid for Fairey at the same time as did the NEB; but it was uninterested in about a third of the group's UK units. Thus the cumulative total of jobs that the Board generated in its role as venture capitalist should be increased to about 7400.

Ferranti is another important British electronics and engineering group. It manufactures computers, computer peripherals, computer systems, radar, lasers, navigation display systems, communication systems for offshore oil fields, semiconductor products, microwave equipment, domestic and industrial meters, instruments for submarines and planes, telecommunications devices including domestic telephones, container handling items, high speed resistors and agricultural products. More than 50% of its stock used to be owned by the Ferranti family, which very much wanted to remain in control of it. It was a very innovative enterprise that never garnered big profits. One reason why it was not much of a money-maker between 1964 and 1974 was a heap of losses suffered by its

179

transformer department, which it had expanded in the 1950s to meet government forecasts of demand for electricity that never materialised. For sentimental reasons the family did not want to dispose of this part of their business. In 1974 the company faced collapse and needed to secure additional financing in the form of loan or equity -- in the past, the Ferrantis had been unwilling to seek new equity out of a fear of having their shareholdings reduced below the magic 50% figure. It required this funding in order to compensate for the troubles of the transformer division and to help finance the development of its semi-conductor unit.

Its bankers at this time said that they could not afford to lend Ferranti any more money and urged it to approach the government for assistance. By this time (1974) Labour was in power and had many reasons for wishing Ferranti saved. The Ministry of Defence was one of its important customers; it then had 16,000 employees; and many of these were located in Manchester and Scotland, areas of high unemployment and strong Labour support. In 1975 the Government consented to lend it £6.33 million and purchase £8.67 million worth of its stock, giving the state control of 62.5% of its equity. As part of the government's agreement with the Ferranti brothers, it was to reduce its shareholding to 50% if the company was listed on the stock exchange by 1 October 1978.[14] The Department of Industry transferred its Ferranti holdings to the NEB in February 1976. It is a matter of dispute whether Ferranti could have received private sector financing when it was nationalised. David Sainsbury says that this was unavailable.[15] John Redwood claims that it is unlikely the company 'would have been put into liquidation and nothing salvaged...' then; but even he confesses that private enterprise let Ferranti down.[16]

The Board brought in as Managing Director Mr. J. D. Alun Jones, a dynamic, imaginative and hardworking man. He reorganised the company, tightened financial controls, developed a planning system that formulated objectives for each division, and produced detailed budgets for achieving these goals.[17] In 1976 matters started breaking the right way for Ferranti. Alun Jones admitted he had a bit of luck that year. A Canadian subsidiary that Ferranti had been trying to sell in 1974 made an amazing profit of £3.6 million in 1976 because some profitable transformer contracts had been bunched into that twelvemonth period. Because of this transatlantic windfall and of inflation, Ferranti netted £4 million, its highest profit ever. This turnaround helped things for the future by putting paid to the atmosphere of panic that was pervading it. It was this increase in morale that enabled Alun Jones to initiate his reforms.[18]

In the fiscal year ending 31 March 1978 Ferranti made a before-tax gain of over £9 million.[19] Before the government takeover it always had had trouble raising cash; but with the increased capitalisation provided by the NEB's equity stake it found this chore much simpler to accomplish. In 1977 it was able to obtain loans totalling £15 million from Chase Manhattan, some of which it used to pay off the sums it had borrowed from the government as well as its own overdrafts.[20] The NEB funding was used as a bait to get new loans and to develop new products. The defence business picked up in 1977 as did the electronics industry, all of which contributed to the above £9 million figure and to a profit of almost £10 million in the year ending 31 March 1979.[21] The troublesome transformer department was shed during 1978 and 1979;[22] and Ferranti continues to be very profitable. In September 1978 it was officially listed on the stock exchange; and the NEB honoured its compact with the Ferranti brothers and sold some of its stock, reducing its holdings to 50% of the equity.[23] In 1980 the Board marketed the remainder of its equity under circumstances we have already described -- circumstances which did not permit the Board to receive as much as it would have obtained in the open market. (As will be remembered, the purchasers of the shares were 300 individuals and institutions, as opposed to a single undertaking. Also, the 300 had to agree not to dispose of their purchases for two years. The idea behind this latter limitation was that Ferranti might prove very profitable during the 24 months and thus be in a better position to defend itself against a takeover bid by an outfit that might close its Scottish operations.[24])

Relations between the NEB and Ferranti while the former was a shareholder were not at all bad, though they had their moments of unpleasantness. The NEB appointed two voting members of Ferranti's Board of Directors. These were not NEB staff but were supposed to, and did, represent the NEB's views and interests. They participated actively in Ferranti Board discussions and remained with it even after privatisation. One NEB staff member was made responsible for monitoring Ferranti. In the early days, he met frequently with members of its management, who resented him because they felt that he represented a wedge to open up the firm for greater NEB control. The Board required it to submit both short-term and three year plans: before the government takeover it had never drafted long-range plans. The Board was not always happy with the documents it received; and at times what a Ferranti official has called 'healthy debates' erupted between the Board and the company over the latter's proposed policies. There was, for example, a conflict over whether the firm was doing enough to sell its products. Moreover, the NEB did not want it to close one of its plants: the factory's gates were locked, but only after some delay. And yet, that Ferranti staff member told me, the disagreements that did break out between the NEB and Ferranti's management were similar to those that arise between any parent company and its subsidiaries. In fact, because the group went into the black in 1976 and thereafter, and because its management was wont to counter NEB proposals by saying that the Ferranti Board had to protect the interests of the minority shareholders, the NEB did not intervene much in its day-to-day management. After it reduced its shareholding to 50%, it bothered with Ferranti even less.

The almost unanimous opinion is that the NEB did an excellent job in handling Ferranti. It appointed first-rate management and did not thwart the efforts of these new leaders to improve the company. As noted, Ferranti's prosperity continues until the present day: 35-40% of its business is in exports and in March 1983 it had over 18,000 employees,[25] about 2000 more than on the day when it was nationalised. Even bitter critics of the NEB have little to say that denigrates the way it treated Ferranti. John Redwood declares that though many felt in 1974 that the private sector would have saved the enterprise, 'the Government must be given credit for seeing the opportunity, backing the venture with cash and seeing it through to a successful conclusion'.[26] The *Daily Mail* admitted, as seen, that Ferranti was the NEB's 'biggest success story'.[27] And the *Daily Express* employed similar language in confessing that Ferranti was a felicitous example of the government's support of private enterprise.[28]

NOTES

1. Coventry Trades Councils, *State intervention in industry*, p. 173.

2. *Daily Mail*, 21 July 1977, p. 25.

3. *Daily Telegraph*, 21 July 1977, p. 19.

4. *Daily Telegraph*, 12 Oct. 1977, p. 21.

5. *Daily Telegraph*, 6 Dec. 1977, p. 21; NEB 1977 Annual Report, p. 22; 1978 Annual Report, pp. 46-7.

6. *Daily Telegraph*, 6 Dec. 1977, p. 21.

7. 13 Jan. 1978, p. 10.

8. 6 Dec. 1977, p. 34. However, the same newspaper said in its issue of 19 Dec. 1978 at p. 11 that the purchase may have been justified!

9. *NEB: a case for euthanasia*, p. 4.

10. These last couple of sentences are based upon an interview with an ex-NEB official; an interview with an official of Fairey; *Daily Telegraph*, 6 Dec. 1977, p. 21; and Sir Leslie Murphy's testimony before the Committee of Public Accounts. See HC Committee of Public Accounts, *Reports 1977-78*, No. 8, p. 113.

11. Coventry Trades Councils, *State intervention in industry*, pp. 82-5.

12. NEB 1979 Annual Report, pp. 32-3.

13. NEB 1980 Annual Report, p. 7.

14. See Sainsbury, *Government and industry: a new partnership*, p. 18; Grylls and Redwood, *NEB: a case for euthanasia*, p. 31; J. D. Alun-Jones, 'My business experience at Burmah Oil and Ferranti: 1973-82', pp. 9-10. (Mimeographed speech delivered by Ferranti's Managing Director, nd.)

15. *Government and industry: a new partnership*, p. 18.

16. *Going for broke...*, p. 141.

17. Alun-Jones, 'My business experience', p. 13; *Daily Mail*, 7 Feb. 1978, p. 29.

18. Alun-Jones, 'My business experience', pp. 12-3.

19. NEB 1978 Annual Report, p. 19.

20. Redwood, *Going for broke...*, p. 97.

21. NEB 1979 Annual Report, p. 12.

22. Ibid.; NEB 1978 Annual Report, p. 19.

23. NEB 1978 Annual Report, p. 20, 46-7.

24. This parenthetical note is based upon my interview of a Ferranti official plus Redwood, *Going for broke...*, p. 68, 97-8.

25. Ferranti 1983 Annual Report, p. 2.

26. *Going for broke...*, p. 98.

27. 7 Feb. 1978, p. 29.
28. 7 Sept. 1978, p. 31.

13
Rolls Royce

As noted in the first chapter, enough ink has been spilled discussing the relations between the NEB and its biggest lame ducks Rolls Royce and British Leyland to make it unnecessary for me to devote a great deal of room to these matters. This is especially true as in my outline of the Board's history I have already sketched something of the conflict between RR Chairman Sir Kenneth Keith and NEB head Sir Leslie Murphy that culminated in (1) the return of RR to the direct control of the Department of Industry and (2) the resignation of Sir Leslie and his entire Board. (As emphasised before, we are talking about RR the manufacturer of plane engines as opposed to Rolls Royce the manufacturer of automobiles. In 1971 the RR that fabricated both aircraft engines and expensive cars was split into two and the aero-engine unit alone nationalised.)

Some brief background to this state takeover will help the reader. In 1969 Minister of Technology Benn asked the Industrial Reorganisation Corporation to examine the viability of Rolls Royce's plans in the light of its cash requirements and profitability. The investigation showed that RR needed a substantial amount of capital to finance the development of its new plane engines.[1] In 1969 the government decided to give it £47 million to fund the development of the RB 211 engine for the US Lockheed Tristar.[2] By the middle of 1970, the company told the government, at that time headed by Heath, that the cost of this machinery would be £135 million. The state then agreed to provide another £42 million, subject to an inquiry. But even before the investigators produced a report, the firm informed the Cabinet that the terms of the Lockheed contract had proven so unfavourable that the losses from it would exceed the concern's assets. So a receiver was appointed for it.

The Administration decided that despite its anti-socialist principles, it had no choice but to nationalise the aircraft division of the company. It was an important supplier to the armed forces, a good earner of foreign exchange, and one of the two or three major aircraft engine manufacturers outside the Soviet bloc.[3] Moreover, it employed over 60,000 workers.[4]

In 1971 it made a small after-tax profit and in 1972, 1973 and 1974 a somewhat larger one (e.g., in 1974 of £12.2 million on a turnover of £469 million).[5] None the less, it continued to be the recipient of state assistance, getting over £40 million in 1974 to refine a more powerful version of the RB211.[6] (Under the Civil Aviation Act of 1949, the government may fund the development of aircraft engines by private and public firms: this assistance, as indicated at the start of Chapter 1, is termed 'launching aid'.[7]) In 1975, of course, the NEB was set up and RR was transferred to it in February 1976. One individual formerly connected with RR thought that this was done to add a bit of class to the new entity; while an ex-Cabinet Minister said to me that both BL and RR were added to the Board's portfolio because it was thought that the civil service was not equipped by background or role to manage concerns as large and as crucial to the nation's economy as these.

At the end of 1972 Prime Minister Heath appointed Sir Kenneth Keith, now Lord Keith of Castleacre, to chair RR. Keith is a Tory who had direct access to and good relations with Heath. When the Wilson Labour Government took office in 1974, Keith offered to resign but Wilson asked him to stay on. Actually, he and Wilson got along famously; and his relations with Wilson's successor James Callaghan were also good. Not so scintillating, however, was the impression one important figure in the Cabinet had of his managerial abilities. It is possible that this person's dim view of Keith's talent for administration was one reason the firm was put under the wings of the NEB and its first Chairman Sir Donald Ryder.

Immediately after the transfer of RR to the NEB, Ryder and Keith (as seen in Chapter 3) engaged in a feud that delighted the press and was fought out in its pages. The *Daily Mail* of 9 February 1976 reported[8] in its delightfully reactionary manner that the two were clashing about which one should be 'numero uno' at RR. Keith complained that he could not see what role the Board would play at RR. He said that he and his staff had gone a long way towards making it viable and that it would be highly unfortunate were the Board to barge in on RR's decision making. Two men couldn't run a company, he lamented. On the next day, the same paper reported that Keith was worried that the Board would be a 'back seat driver'.[9] The *Daily Telegraph* of 10 February 1976[10] featured a story saying that Keith desired greater freedom to run RR along commercial lines and continued direct access to Ministers. An editorial in the same issue said that Ryder's wings ought to be clipped since he wanted to be a sort of industrial generalissimo pushing the boards of all the lame ducks to act in accordance with his wishes.[11]

Keith lobbied hard with important political figures, including the Prime Minister himself; and soon a memorandum of agreement between RR and the NEB was signed that seemed to satisfy both contestants. Under this compact the Board agreed not to take over the day-to-day management of RR but accepted responsibility for insuring that it functioned successfully. It was, therefore, given the prerogative to select the company's Board of Directors and to determine their salaries. (RR had the right to veto the NEB's choices.) It was also accorded the power to approve the subsidiary's long-range and annual plans; and RR was placed under a duty to submit these to it. RR had to get NEB permission for its major investment programmes, certain purchases of subsidiaries, and capital expenditures of £15 million or more.[12] Furthermore, RR obtained the right to be present at the NEB's discussions with the government about the firm's plans and to explain these plans to the Cabinet. The RR Chairman was given the authority to have direct access to a Minister, if the NEB Chairman was consulted beforehand and accorded the privilege of attending if he wished. RR was also allowed to continue dealing directly with Departments such as Industry and Defence on day-to-day problems.[13] After this truce was signed, the relationship between Ryder and Keith (and thus RR and the NEB) took a significant turn for the better. Ryder never exercised, for example, his authority to accompany the RR head when the latter made use of his privilege to have an appointment with a Minister.

After Murphy became NEB Chairman, the detente between the Board and RR collapsed, especially during 1978 and 1979. There was no love lost between Keith and Murphy on a personal level. Both had a merchant banking background and one of my interviewees felt that Keith resented being told what to do by his fellow merchant banker. (At one of their meetings, Keith taunted his antagonist by saying he had been Chairman of Hill Samuel while Murphy had only been Deputy Chairman of Schroder Wagg.[14]) The same individual, however, gave me what I believe is a better reason (above and beyond simple visceral repulsion) for the hostility between the two. Keith, despite his banking experience, had his heart in marketing: he wanted to sell RR engines and was not overly concerned with the cost of producing them or with the concessions made to purchasers in order to induce them to take the product. Murphy, despite his willingness to have the NEB sponsor sometimes-risky high tech investments, was more cautious and worried about keeping expenses down. Another person connected with the NEB while Murphy and Keith were slugging it out said that Keith realised that to sell engines he had to meet contractual delivery dates. Thus it was all-important to him to avoid strikes and, to achieve this goal, he on occasion refused to discharge employees who some believed were superfluous. NEB staff kept asking him why he was such a profligate spender, and this line of attack incensed him.

Had there been only minimal contact between RR and the NEB the tension between Murphy and Keith could have been ignored by their respective colleagues. But, of course, as the Board was responsible for putting RR on an even financial keel, in the nature of things this could not be. Not only did RR have to submit plans and financial data to the Board, but staff from both institutions had to meet on a regular basis. One member of the NEB staff was appointed to act as a liaison between the two. He managed to reduce friction to some extent, as he was a non-aggressive person who used to work for an aircraft manufacturer and therefore knew RR's business well.

One specific example of RR-NEB (i.e. Keith-Murphy) conflict erupted when RR signed a £250 million contract with American airline Pan American to have twelve RB211-524 engines for jumbo jets installed in Lockheed planes used by this carrier.[15]

In the first place, contrary to the NEB-RR memorandum of agreement as interpreted by Murphy, the contract was made without the Board's knowledge or approval. The firm proved unable to articulate the profit implications of the deal; and, in fact, its terms were such that it was highly unlikely to make money as a result of it. (Keith plausibly maintained that this contract and its terms were necessary to prevent RR's permanent exclusion from a big share of the US market and that later spare parts sales ultimately would make it profitable.[16]) Murphy made it crystal clear to Keith that he was very dissatisfied with the Pan Am arrangement. He also refused to support an RR proposal to expand so as to significantly increase its capacity: this recommendation angered the NEB so much that it convinced them that Keith had to go, though Secretaries of State for Industry Eric Varley and Sir Keith Joseph refused to fire him.[17]

To continue with our examples of RR and NEB misunderstandings, both the DOI and the NEB rejected an RR plan for 1977-81. They also forced it to submit a plan for 1978-82 that was revised from the firm's original draft though it said it had been planning to make these changes anyway.[18] Keith turned down Murphy's suggestion that RR appoint a full-time chief executive to supervise the company's day-to-day management.[19] In November of 1979 Keith went to see the Secretary of State for Industry (still Joseph) without bothering to inform the NEB Chairman, which was a violation of the Ryder-Keith truce. At this meeting, Keith notified Joseph that he was going to resign as RR head.[20] This was shortly before Joseph took RR from the NEB and precipitated Murphy's departure. Another NEB-RR disagreement arose because the Board had the right to veto the appointment of an RR finance director. Keith wanted for this position a man who had worked in a Scottish brewing company but Murphy thought that beer was different enough from aviation to make this person unsuitable for the job. Ultimately, Murphy bowed and Keith's candidate received the post.

In general Keith and RR managed to get away with ignoring the NEB's complaints about the (real or alleged) inefficiency of its operations. By November 1978 Keith had stopped replying to Murphy's letters (though Murphy was his 'boss') and told his staff not to co-operate with the Board in studying alternatives to RR's corporate plan.[21] Neither the DOI nor the Cabinet forced it to adopt some of the reforms for which the NEB was pressing. How was this 'insubordination' possible, given that the NEB owned 100% of RR's shares? The reasons for this virtual autonomy are interrelated. First Keith, though a Tory had, as noted, good personal relationships with Labour Prime Ministers Wilson and Callaghan. He also got along well with Labour Secretary of State for Industry Varley. The second factor making Keith feel free to disregard the wishes of his nominal masters was that (a situation not true for many of the Board's other subsidiaries) the NEB was not his major source of funding. What is important to an undertaking such as RR is that it receive government launching aid for its engines and government contracts for its products. And these came from the Department of Industry and the Ministry of Defence directly.[22] In other words, RR used to go straight to these Departments[23] (as it had a right to do for day-to-day matters under the agreement with the NEB[24]) -- as well as to the Ministers who headed them (as its Chairman had the power to do under that compact after notifying the NEB head) -- to ask for launching assistance and state contracts for its engines. In fact, he went right to the Prime Minister to have funding okayed for the improvement of the RB211-535 engine for 160-180 seat aircraft. Of course, when the PM or the head of a Department decided to succour RR in these ways, there was nothing the NEB could do to veto the aid even if it had wanted to.

The following may show even more concretely why RR could operate without worrying too much about what the NEB and Murphy thought and did. In March and April of 1979 the DOI and the Government announced that they were making available to the firm £250 million in 1978 prices over a three year period in launching aid for new engines in the RB211 series, including the RB 211-524 engines for jumbo jets.[25] And a letter from a former RR official informs me that between 1976 and 1979 the DOI provided the engine manufacturer with £167 million in funds while the Ministry of Defence gave it during that period an additional, confidential amount. On the other hand, the letter continues, the NEB disbursed to RR during these years only £185 million: £97 million in equity and £88 million in loans. (The money from the Board was employed for short-term funding.[26]) In other words, RR was more dependent on the DOI and the Ministry of Defence than on the NEB for meeting its cash needs.

Neither the government's 1971 nationalisation of RR nor the 1976 handing over of the company to the NEB nor its 1979 return to direct DOI supervision placed it on a straight path to profitability. Though, as seen, it made after-tax profits from 1971 through 1974, it suffered a big pre-tax loss in 1976.[27] In the black in 1977 and 1978,[28] it lost a whopping £58 million in 1979.[29] Even in 1977 and 1978 its return on capital employed was only 12% and 9% respectively.[30] (The reason for the 1979 collapse was that its civil aviation sales usually were priced in dollars; and, to everyone's surprise, the value of the pound increased from $1.80 to $2.30 that year, which meant that its dollars were not worth as much in pounds as the firm had expected them to be. The Public Accounts Committee gently chided the company, the NEB, the DOI and the Treasury for not taking sufficient steps ahead of time to prevent this fluctuation from having harmful effects.[31]) As recently as 1983 it lost a record £193 million. However, in 1984 it made £20 million and in 1985 a full £81 million; and so the Thatcher Administration privatised it in 1987.[32]

Fairness demands mention that not all the bonds between the NEB and RR were poisoned and destructive. We have already noted, for example, that Keith was satisfied with the NEB employee who acted as liaison between the two. In fact, RR respected the other full-time NEB staff who worked with it.[33] The Board asserted that the company should move forward with the RB211 series of engines and agreed with it that the US government provides its American competitors with considerable financial support.[34] Also, it favoured RR plans to construct plants in Atlanta and Miami in the US. To RR the Board was an irritant but not a major obstacle to the realisation of its plans.

This said, it must be admitted that placing the firm under the wings of the NEB was hardly a success. The Board was not a fertile source of ideas about new programmes for the company to work on. The accomplishments that Keith did have as Chairman cannot be credited to it, for it neither recruited him nor was able to push him in any particular direction. It failed in its attempt to make him and the company more cost-conscious. And it was one of the bodies that perhaps ought to have advised it to hedge more adequately in 1979 against a possible rise in value of the pound against the dollar, an increase, it will be remembered, that put it deeply in the red that year. In other words, it is hard to discern how making RR subject to the Board had any significant effect on the corporation's fortunes for better or for worse. Though the Board did not harm it; it did not help it much either.

Had the personalities or business philosophies of Sir Kenneth and Sir Leslie been more compatible, it is likely that the NEB would have had an impact upon RR. This probably would have helped the firm, since in some respects, as even Sir Keith Joseph confessed,[35] its management was weak. It was, for example, plagued with a shortage of aerospace engineers and had to subcontract some of its basic research to a US lab. It had trouble convincing engineers to stay because it paid them so little. It often had to rush its work and cut corners: as a consequence, it had to pay out considerable sums under penalty and warranty clauses in its contracts. Eastern Airlines, for instance, said that it had serious problems with the RB211-22B engine.[36] RR's engines took a very long time to build; it was a full two-and-one-half times less productive than its US counterparts; stock levels were high; and production was so poorly planned that many of its machines stood idle. The NEB diagnosed many of these problems;[37] but, for reasons several times reiterated, was unable to do much about them.

NOTES

1. Hague and Wilkinson, *The IRC*, pp. 297-98.
2. Ganz, *Government and industry*, p. 9.
3. Grylls and Redwood, *NEB: a case for euthanasia*, pp. 27-8.
4. Coventry Trades Councils, *State intervention in industry*, p. 170.
5. Grylls and Redwood, *NEB: a case for euthanasia*, p. 29.
6. Ganz, *Government and industry*, p. 9.
7. Ibid.
8. at p. 2.
9. 10 Feb. 1976, p. 9.
10. at p. 1.
11. *Daily Telegraph*, 10 Feb. 1976, p. 12.

12. Ganz, *Government and industry,* p. 65; HC Committee of Public Accounts, *Reports 1977-78,* No. 8, p. 155.

13. See Ganz, *Government and industry,* p. 66.

14. *New Statesman,* 30 Nov. 1979, pp. 837-38.

15. Ibid.; NEB 1977 Annual Report, p. 16.

16. *New Statesman,* 30 Nov. 1979, pp. 837-38.

17. Ibid.

18. HC Committee of Public Accounts, *Reports 1977-78, No. 8,* p. 114.

19. *New Statesman,* 30 Nov. 1979, pp. 837-38.

20. *Guardian,* 12 Nov. 1979, p. 17.

21. *New Statesman,* 30 Nov. 1979, pp. 837-38.

22. See ibid.; *Economist,* 11 Feb. 1978, p. 113.

23. See, e.g., *Financial Times,* 9 Nov. 1979, p. 20.

24. Ganz, *Government and industry,* p. 66.

25. *New Statesman,* 30 Nov. 1979, pp. 837-38; HC Committee of Public Accounts, *Reports 1979-80, No. 6: Departments of Energy and Industry* (HMSO, London, 1980), p. 42.

26. *Daily Telegraph,* 7 Aug. 1976, p. 13.

27. Grylls and Redwood, *NEB: a case for euthanasia,* p. 29.

28. Ibid.

29. HC Committee of Public Accounts, *Reports 1979-80, No. 30,* pp. xi-xii.

30. *Economist,* 17 Nov. 1979, p. 108.

31. HC Committee of Public Accounts, *Reports 1979-80, No. 30,* p. xiv. See also *Economist,* 29 Sept. 1979, p. 100.

32. *London Times,* 19 Ap. 1985, p. 21; 23 Ap. 1986, p. 21; 23 Jan. 1987, p. 25.

33. *New Statesman,* 30 Nov. 1979, pp. 837-38.

34. HC Committee of Public Accounts, *Reports 1977-78, No. 8,* p. xxi.

35. *New Statesman,* 30 Nov. 1979, pp. 837-38.

36. *New Statesman,* 19 Mar. 1979, p. 320.

37. *New Statesman,* 30 Nov. 1979, pp. 837-38.

14

British Leyland

Let us now turn to the ties between British Leyland (BL) and the NEB. (BL is now called the 'Rover Group'. However, we shall refer to it by its old name since it was known as British Leyland and then simply as BL while it was under the Board's jurisdiction.) BL was by far the largest ailing firm transferred by the government from the Department of Industry to the Board. In February 1976, when this move was consummated, it had 191,000 employees in comparison to RR's 'mere' 62,000, ICL's 24,000, Ferranti's almost 17,000 and Herbert's 6700.[1] It also absorbed more money by far than any other Board holding; and received, not astoundingly, more publicity than any of these other enterprises. As was the case when we dealt with RR, a brief historical sketch will help the reader understand the nature and magnitude of the difficulties the Board inherited when it took responsibility for BL.

During the 1920s and 1930s there was a bundle of UK firms making automobiles in Britain. By 1968 this number had shrunk to two. This duo, Leyland Motors Corporation and British Motor Holdings, were themselves the product of various mergers. BMH was a descendant of the separate concerns that developed such popular cars as the reliable Austin and Morris, the expensive Daimler, and the 'sporty' Jaguar. Leyland came from a series of marriages of companies assembling Standard, Rover, Leyland and Triumph cars.[2] In 1967 BMH had 30% of the UK motor car market and Leyland 7% -- just about all the other automobiles sold in the country were foreign imports or built by UK subsidiaries of foreign multinationals such as Ford (Ford UK), General Motors (Vauxhall) and Chrysler (Chrysler UK). However, BMH lost money during the 1967 financial year and the Wilson Labour Government was pressing for a union of

194

the two UK-owned undertakings.[3] This merger, which created BL, took place in 1968 and, as seen in Chapter 1, was facilitated with an Industrial Reorganisation Corporation loan of £25 million, the IRC having taken an active role in the talks leading to the fusion.[4]

The new entity (which manufactured trucks, buses and auto parts as well) remained in private hands and beset with serious problems. By 1974 its share of the UK car market declined from the 40% it had managed to attain in 1968 to 32%.[5] It was in the red and could not raise internally the £100 million it needed for investment purposes. Nor could it get this sum from private banks without a government guarantee for the loans; and so the Government (once again headed by Wilson) was approached to act as surety. It consented; but in return forced the company to agree that at least to some degree it would come under state ownership and that it would not undertake large capital expenditures, new borrowing, or sales of its subsidiaries without the consent of the state.[6] In 1975 it was nationalised.[7]

There is virtually no disagreement about why BL was doing so poorly in 1974. The concern was not able to effect enough investment.[8] 'Between 1970 and 1974 British Leyland had invested only about £250 in new capital equipment for every one of the workers it employed. The other major European owned corporations invested twice as much.'[9] Moreover, it had too many plants (59 in 1974): most of these were small and so unable to take advantage of economies of size.[10] It was still bringing out a great number of models and components. This meant that it was 'unable to spread the considerable costs of research and development and of the machine tools used to produce the components over a larger output';[11] and that it 'had to keep a host of different parts and different spares...'[12] Moreover, some of its vehicles (e.g., the Rover and the Triumph 2000) 'competed directly with one another...'[13] There were management failures: some managers were basically engineers who made a fine product but who were not vitally concerned about costs, net profits, or setting up procedures that would give them information about their expenditure levels.[14] Labour relations were poor, not only between management and workers generally but even between unions.[15] Labour productivity was low: 'Output per man in British plants was less than half that in continental plants'.[16] And lower tariff rates meant that BL faced greater competition from Japanese and European-made automobiles.[17]

In December 1974 the government had Donald Ryder do a study about the prospects of BL.[18] He was put in charge of this inquiry not in his capacity as future Chairman of the NEB but in his role as Industrial Adviser to the Prime Minister.[19] His report (known as the Ryder Report) suggested that BL should, by increasing car output and sales, avoid having to reduce its workforce. To achieve such growth, an investment of £2800 million between 1975 and 1982 was deemed necessary.

'Lord Ryder proposed, and the Government agreed, that public funds should provide up to half that sum, with £200 million to be made available immediately, followed by sums up to a total of £900 million in stages through to 1978, with the remainder of the Government's £1400 million to be provided in the form of either loan capital or equity capital after 1978.'[20]

For 1976 through 1981, the state was supposed to give the concern £1000 million.[21]

It is generally admitted that Ryder was over-optimistic.[22] He postulated, for example, that in 1977 BL would have 33% of the UK market for cars -- in that year it obtained 23% only.[23] None the less, the polity could not, and probably still cannot, tolerate its demise. It is still one of the nation's largest employers, even though by 1988 its workforce had been reduced to just over 50,000.[24] Furthermore BL's exports are not negligible; and British politicians of all political parties feel that an important nation ought to be the home of a major automobile manufacturer.[25]

The NEB's takeover certainly was not accompanied by any sudden BL recovery. The company's slice of the UK car market declined from 30.8% in 1975 to 27.6% in 1976.[26] Labour relations continued highly unpromising. Ryder visited BL plants personally and urged workers to help improve the company's situation, but with no tangible results.[27] A major, month-long unofficial strike by toolmakers to receive separate bargaining rights in February 1977 idled about 40,000 BL workers and was termed 'the most disastrous dispute ever faced by the company...'[28] The NEB and Secretary of State for Industry Varley said that they would cut off funding for the group unless the strike ended, rapid improvements in productivity were made, and production went from 6000 to 20,000 cars per week within 28 days. The work stoppage did end, partly because the firm threatened to sack the strikers; and for a few months conditions were better. So the NEB recommended, and the government agreed to, a resumption of assistance.[29]

It was a couple of months after the end of the strike that the *Daily Mail* printed its forged letter charging that BL, with Ryder's approval, was paying bribes to get overseas orders. This letter, mentioned in an earlier chapter, is of course irrelevant to any picture of the relationship between the Board and the company. Nonetheless, it was of importance in BL's history because it may have been one of the factors contributing to Ryder's resignation in July 1977.[30] Leslie Murphy, his successor, was naturally less committed to the *Ryder* plan and felt that the group had to be shrunk in order to be made manageable. (Ryder apparently took a 'protective attitude toward British Leyland at NEB Board Meetings...'[31]) Murphy told the leadership of BL to plan a different strategy in case it failed to improve its market share. The management disliked this ukase and prepared no plan. Moreover in September 1977 BL had to borrow £50 million from the Board just in order to meet its bills. It received this sustenance even though the NEB's money was supposed to be used for purposes of investment and even though it was nowhere near earning the £1.4 that it was supposed to make for every £1 of government assistance.[32]

Murphy at this time determined to get rid of BL head Sir Richard Dobson and his chief assistants. He thus offered the Chairmanship to NEB Board member Sir Michael Edwardes, Chairman of battery company Chloride.[33] Murphy thought the group was too big and too centralised: the chiefs at the individual plants had no delegated power and had to wade through too much red tape to change things. Luckily from the NEB Chairman's point of view, Dobson made a speech to a group of businessmen where he remarked that the *Mail* had accused BL of the 'perfectly respectable fact that it was bribing wogs'.[34] Sir Richard also said in the course of his discourse that he doubted that the average British worker was worried that a number of black people in north London were underpaid. Unknown to him, a young man in the audience secretly taped these assertions and gave them to a radical magazine. When they appeared in print Sir Richard resigned and Edwardes agreed to become BL Chairman. The public assumed that Dobson was forced out because his comments could be interpreted as racist; but the truth was that Murphy a few weeks earlier had taken the decision to replace him and Dobson's indiscretions simply made this resolve more politically feasible to enforce.[35]

Edwardes, like Murphy, believed that BL had to become less bloated if it were to survive. Before he consented to take the job, he demanded a free hand to manage it as he saw fit, including firing and redeploying managers, closing factories, and shrinking staff numbers.[36] Murphy gave him 'the necessary assurances without any reservation...':[37] the Ryder Report, with its assumption that the workforce need not be hit by any reduction in size, had to this extent been abandoned earlier in the year.[38] However, BL still remained rather hungry for state financial assistance.[39]

In 1978 Edwardes began his programme of scaling down the company by making a controversial decision to phase out the strike-plagued Speke plant near Liverpool.[40] This made the Triumph TR 7 and Edwardes felt that its production should be switched to the Canley site (near Coventry) where the other Triumph models were fashioned.[41] The closure cost 3500 jobs and was bitterly opposed by left-wing unionists.[42] (One volume refers to it as 'The murder of Speke'.[43]) The NEB backed the shutdown as 'regrettable' albeit 'commercially necessary...'[44] According to one ex-NEB member, the workers at Speke were given the option of having it remain open if they increased their productivity; but they refused to take the necessary steps to do so. In addition, BL plants in Scandinavia and South Africa were shut.[45]

In early 1978 Edwardes drafted his first plan for the future of BL, which was accepted by the NEB and DOI. He called for more decentralisation of management, cutting 12,500 jobs, and additional investment in new models. Also, the car division was to have three profit centres, one for luxury cars, one for volume cars, and one for bodies and parts.[46] One left wing MP feels deeply that one of the unarticulated cornerstones of

Edwardes' strategy was 'breaking union power'. However, the union members of the NEB themselves accepted this programme of curtailing the size of the workforce as otherwise the government would have ceased funding the company, especially after the Tories won power.

A second Edwardes plan, promulgated in September 1979 and called the Recovery Plan, called for the phasing out of 28,000 jobs and the closing of 13 plants: he convinced the workers over the strong opposition of the shop stewards to accept this blueprint.[47] The BL Corporate Plan for 1980, which included the Recovery Plan, asked the polity for over £500 million -- including £225 million still due under the Ryder Report. This document was approved by the NEB in November 1979 and by the government the next month.[48] The latter finally agreed to give BL £430 million of the £500 million requested (partly for the development of new models), though only £300 million was to be paid in 1980.[49]

Edwardes himself admits that he on the whole got along very well with Murphy and the NEB. His own words are the best testimony on this point.

'...I was saddened at the way Sir Leslie Murphy and his team were treated [in the Keith-Rolls Royce affair of November 1979]; they were right to resign. It would be an incomplete account if I did not emphasise what great support the NEB gave to me personally. Nothing was too much trouble - all the key people (including the union members) were accessible 24 hours a day and over weekends - and I had some very helpful advice, not least from the trade union representatives, whose counsel was usually in the direction of cooling situations which could otherwise have led to difficulties for BL and for its employees.'[50]

Another reason why BL, unlike RR, worked well with the Board was that, as an official of another firm that the NEB had aided pointed out to me, many even in the Labour Party were quite sceptical of BL and the possibility of its continued viability. The NEB was therefore needed by the company to argue for it in government circles. RR needed no such spokesperson, as both its civilian and military aero-engine accomplishments were respected by the members of the Government.

Furthermore, BL, unlike RR, did obtain most of its funding from the NEB until it was removed from its control. The initial grant of £200 million envisaged under the Ryder Plan came directly from the government; but the first tranche of the subsequent £1000 million that the Board was supposed to get from 1976 through 1981 under that proposal was received in 1977 from the Board. The amount totalled £150 million, the relative modesty of this sum being due to 'investment freezes during major strikes'.[51] Then in 1978 the Board purchased £449 million worth of new equity in the undertaking, which acquisition was the main reason the state agency's spending limit was raised from £700 million to £1000 million in April 1978.[52] In early 1979 BL asked for £300 million more of the Ryder Plan £1000 million. From this petition arose the one major conflict between BL under Edwardes and the NEB under Murphy: the Board recommended that only £150 million be granted. The compromise ultimately arrived at was that the NEB would give the group the £150 million and £50 more if the extra sum were needed (which it was not). Edwardes notes that he was irritated not only by the NEB's rejection of the full amount embodied in the BL request but also in the latter's public description of the BL Corporate Plan for 1979 as 'optimistic'.[53] (We showed in an earlier chapter that the struggle over whether to close the Scottish plants of BL refrigerator subsidiary Prestcold was really one between Edwardes and the Labour Government, not one between him and the NEB.)

After the Tory victory in May 1979, BL began seriously considering the possibility of leaving the NEB to return to the direct control of the DOI. The NEB's slash of BL's funding request in 1979 was one factor making some of its directors wanting to place it under DOI auspices, as they believed that the Department would be an 'easy touch'. Also, they were well aware that the Board occupied one of the new Government's many doghouses. The problem was solved when Sir Arthur Knight, Murphy's successor, indicated after his appointment in November 1979 that he wanted no part of the auto manufacturer. As a result, the responsibility of the NEB for BL for practical purposes ceased then and there; though, as noted earlier, the NEB shareholdings were not formally transferred back to the Department until March 1981.[54] Before the *de facto* end of the NEB's authority over BL the latter did, however, receive a total of about £750 million from that organisation -- the £150 million in 1977, the £449 million in 1978, and the £150 million in 1979. This amount is much more than the approximately £11 million coming to BL directly from the DOI between October 1975 and December 1979 under Sections 7 and 8 of the 1972 Industry Act and in Regional Development Grants.[55]

As indicated, the NEB had one division devoted entirely to the affairs of BL and RR; and both Ryder and Murphy personally gave a good deal of thought to the auto maker's problems. Some persons associated with the Board hold that it spent too much time on these giants and, accordingly, neglected a bit the other components of its multi-faceted mission. However, other former Board staffers strongly disagree with this point of view. As they emphasise, though NEB and BL executives met on a regular basis, the NEB division dealing with BL and RR matters consisted of only a handful of persons.[56] Moreover, as they and the earlier pages of this book attest, much NEB planning considered how the Board could make the UK an important factor in the developing world of high technology.

Whatever effects BL may have had on the Board's operations, there is no doubt that the Board had a considerable impact on BL. It was, after all, the instrument of Edwardes' recruitment, and it was he who began shrinking significantly the size of the company's workforce and abandoning some of its plants. Had it not been for these actions, the firm would have lost even more money than it did and the Thatcher Administration would in such a case probably have shut it down. Thus, in a very literal sense, the NEB saved its subsidiary's hide. Murphy on at least one occasion contributed directly to keeping the company's size in bounds. It wanted to modernise one of its foundries for £125 million. He informed it that this plan was too grandiose and that it could get its castings from outside. On another occasion he refused to let it spend £65 million to centralise its research and development operations. He told it that it was short of engineers anyway and that the £65 million could be better expended elsewhere. Furthermore, when the NEB took over BL the management was fuzzy about the costs and profits of its various divisions. NEB staff members, with the aid of people knowledgeable about the auto business, helped them ascertain this data and draft a plan based upon it.

We can say that the NEB made BL less of a loss-making outfit than it would otherwise have been; but we cannot conclude that it made it profitable. In 1974, before the government and the NEB took it over, it was £123 million in the red.[57] In the fifteen months ending 31 December 1976 it did earn a pre-tax profit of £71 million. In 1977 its pre-tax gain was announced as £3.2 million. However, as noted in Chapter 2, to get a true view of its financial picture during the year we have to subtract from this a loss arising from the closure of the Speke and South African assembly works and of certain operations in Sweden and Norway. This gives us a *deficit* for the year of about £37 million.[58] Likewise in 1978 BL showed a tiny profit of £1.7 million before taxation. However, when we deduct from that a drain of £20.7 million arising from various shut-downs, we get a reverse of about £19 million for that year.[59] And in 1979 it lost about £120 million.[60]

However, those who denigrate the NEB cannot take much comfort from BL's financial performance after it was in all but legal form returned to the Department of Industry at the end of 1979. In 1980 it suffered a deficit of almost £400 million and in 1981 one of somewhat more than £300 million.[61] It lost £126 million in 1982, £67 million in 1983, £73 million in 1984 and £110 million in 1985.[62] In 1987 its total car and truck production was only 468,000.[63] This should be contrasted with 1968 when its total car-truck output was about 950,000 and with 1976 when that figure exceeded 800,000.[64] Its profitable Jaguar unit was privatised in 1984.[65] Its well-known MG sports car has been phased out;[66] and its bus section was hived off via a management buyout.[67] BL also continued to swallow up public funds after the NEB bowed out of its picture: by early 1986 government grants and guarantees committed to it totalled £3.8 billion.[68] Nevertheless, it made an operating profit in 1987;[69] and this success is enabling the UK government to unload what is left of it.

NOTES

1. Coventry Trades Councils, *State intervention in industry,* pp. 169-70.

2. Andy Pollard and Rosalind Levačić, 'The British Leyland case study'. This is Part six of Block five of the Open University course *Decision making in Britain* (Open U. Press, Milton Keynes, 1983).

3. Pollard and Levačić, 'British Leyland', pp. 132-33.

4. Hague and Wilkinson, *The IRC,* p. 271.

5. Pollard and Levačić, 'British Leyland', p. 138.

6. Coates, *Labour in Power,* p. 121.

7. Pollard and Levačić, 'British Leyland', p. 155.

8. Ibid., p. 142.

9. Coventry Trades Councils, *State intervention in industry,* p. 58.

10. Pollard and Levačić, 'British Leyland', p. 143.

11. Ibid., p. 144.

12. Redwood, *Going for broke...,* p. 27.

13. Edwardes, *Back from the brink,* p. 33.

14. Pollard and Levačić, 'British Leyland', pp. 139-40.

15. Ibid., pp. 144-45.

16. Ibid., p. 145.

17. Ibid.

18. Coates, *Labour in power,* p. 121.

19. Edwardes, *Back from the brink,* p. 34.

20. Coates, *Labour in power,* p. 121.

21. Edwardes, *Back from the brink,* p. 211.

22. Pollard and Levačić, 'British Leyland', p. 156.

23. Redwood, *Going for broke...,* p. 30.

24. *Economist,* 16 Jan. 1988, p. 67.

25. See Coates, *Labour in power,* p. 122; Pollard and Levačić, 'British Leyland', p. 137.

26. Pollard and Levačić, 'British Leyland', p. 157.

27. Edwardes, *Back from the brink,* p. 37.

28. Ibid.

29. Ibid., pp. 37-8; *Daily Mail,* 3 Mar. 1977, p. 9; 7 Mar. 1977, p. 13; *Daily Telegraph,* 3 Mar. 1977, p. 1.

30. See also Edwardes, *Back from the brink,* p. 39.

31. Ibid., p. 40.

32. *Daily Mail,* 30 Sept. 1977, p. 1.

33. Edwardes, *Back from the brink,* pp. 39-43.

34. *Daily Mail,* 22 Oct. 1977, p. 1.

35. See Edwardes, *Back from the brink,* pp. 40-5; *Daily Express,* 26 Oct. 1977, p. 2; *Daily Mail,* 21 Oct. 1977, p. 1; 22 Oct. 1977, p. 1.

36. See his *Back from the brink,* p. 44.

37. Ibid.

38. Pollard and Levačić, 'British Leyland', p. 157.

39. See ibid., p. 158.

40. Redwood, *Going for broke...,* p. 32.

41. *Back from the brink,* p. 70.

42. Coventry Trades Councils, *State intervention in industry,* pp. 85-8.

43. Ibid., p. 85.

44. Edwardes, *Back from the brink,* p. 210.

45. *Daily Express,* 5 May 1978, p. 22.

46. Pollard and Levačić, 'British Leyland', p. 157; *Economist,* 4 Feb. 1978, p. 108.

47. This sentence is based on my interview with a former NEB member and Redwood, *Going for broke...,* pp. 34-5.

48. Edwardes, *Back from the brink,* pp. 199-200, 225-26, 233; *Economist,* 3 Nov. 1979, p. 78.

49. *Economist,* 22 Dec. 1979, p. 59.

50. *Back from the brink,* p. 217.

51. Ibid., pp. 211-12; NEB 1977 Annual Report, pp. 38-9.

52. NEB 1977 Annual Report, p. 12, 22; 1978 Annual Report, pp. 46-7.

53. *Back from the brink,* p. 213.

54. Ibid., pp. 216-17; *Guardian,* 10 Nov. 1979, p. 1.

55. NEB 1979 Annual Report, p. 56.

56. HC Committee of Public Accounts, *Reports 1977-78, No. 8,* p. 108; HC Committee of Public Accounts, *Reports 1976-77, No. 8,* p. 377.

57. *Economist,* 25 Mar. 1978, p. 98.

58. NEB 1977 Annual Report, pp. 32-3; HC Committee of Public Accounts, *Reports 1979-80, No. 6,* p. xxv.

59. NEB 1978 Annual Report, pp. 40-1, 45. We noted these closures when in Chapter 2 we analysed the NEB's profit and loss statements.

60. *London Times,* 15 Mar. 1980, p. 1.

61. Pollard and Levačić, 'British Leyland', p. 158.

62. *Guardian,* 20 Mar. 1985, p. 24; *London Times,* 19 Mar. 1983, p. 11; 8 July 1986, p. 17.

63. *New York Times,* 31 Dec. 1987, p. D14.

64. Pollard and Levačić, 'British Leyland', p. 158.

65. *London Times,* 26 July 1984, p. 15; 31 July 1984, p. 15.

66. *Business Week,* 7 Nov. 1983, p. 62.
67. *London Times,* 25 July 1986, p. 17.
68. *Economist,* 29 Mar. 1986, p. 14.
69. *New York Times,* 31 Dec. 1987, p. D14.

15
The NEB and
The Ministry of Defence

To recapitulate what has been discussed in the last few chapters, the NEB had some scintillating successes and some gloomy failures with several of its big subsidiaries. The three 'victories' are Rolls Royce, Fairey and Ferranti: the two 'routs' are British Leyland and Alfred Herbert. Fairey and Ferranti have been hived off by the government and are making good profits. After many years of alternating between peaks and valleys, RR is staying in the black and has been privatised. In contrast, Herbert is no longer in existence and until 1987 BL lost money hand over fist.

The perceptive reader may have noted one major difference between BL and Herbert on the one hand and RR, Fairey and Ferranti on the other. The first two received little or nothing in the way of *defence* contracts while the latter trio have the military as one of their most important clients. It will be remembered, for example, that Rolls sells engines for military aircraft to the Ministry of Defence (MOD). Fairey manufactures parts for military planes, military bridges and military vehicles. It also assembles small combat support boats for which the UK, US and Greek armies are customers, as well as fast patrol boats which the Royal Navy purchases. Ferranti's 1983 report confesses that

'Defence equipment is an important component of our activity and the conflict in the South Atlantic [with Argentina, arising when the latter invaded the UK-owned Falkland Islands] emphasised the responsibilities we bear as a major supplier to the armed forces. Much exceptional activity was occasioned by the urgency of the requirement and the excellent performance of our naval computer systems, avionics, radar and laser equipment in action has been widely reported.'[1]

The group makes sales of defence material to other European countries[2] and 'The defence field remains the most important part of the [Ferranti] Scottish Group activity, accounting for almost three-quarters of the turnover...'[3] Increased defence spending was an important reason for its rebound in the late 1970s. In general, without large military contracts, it would still be in serious financial trouble.[4]

Several of the NEB's other healthy children benefited and continue to profit from military contracts. Olga, as seen, is one of the UK's major developers of software. Despite its having become embroiled with the NEB and Nexos in the development of the 2200 word processor, it is a highly promising company that will almost certainly continue to be one of the country's most innovative high tech firms. Once again, however, the military is a major customer for its products. It is so strong in aerospace and defence that it recently formed a subsidiary to deal with these fields. It does work for the UK Army, Navy and Air Force as well as for products made by private firms that vend these to the military. It has entered into contracts with the Danish armed forces and with NATO. Velma is another UK high tech firm that is expanding and profitable. Once again, it has not neglected the defence segment of the market. One of its four profitable UK trading divisions is dedicated to this area. It designs communications systems for the UK Army and Navy and provides software to the Navy and Air Force.

Fred Company is another UK software and systems design concern that the NEB once aided and that is now flourishing. 29% of its sales come from what it calls the 'science and defence' markets. It has, for example, developed systems for minesweeping vessels and is working on advanced technology for submarines and ships. It is also refining microprocessor-based systems for helicopters to measure the weight of a payload suspended below a chopper's bottom. Inmos, the microchip manufacturer that was created by NEB funding, does not directly cater for the military but does sell to companies that deal with the armed forces. Thus indirectly military business accounts for a significant percentage of its turnover. Bruce Company, created by an NEB-funded management buyout, is now in the black: its main product is a special type of battery that it sells to the armed forces, and it also performs research and development work for them.

Various other Board-formed or aided undertakings beside BL and Herbert that had a considerable amount of financial trouble had few dealings with the military. David teetered on the edge of bankruptcy for the first five years it operated under NEB auspices: were it making electric motors not for a device in common civilian use but for tanks or submarines, it might have sailed out of the doldrums much earlier. If Elspeth were to service and repair Royal Navy battleships and destroyers in addition to the offshore oil rigs that it keeps in good shape, its profit record might have been more impressive and its long-term future would certainly be brighter. (The UK will have a fleet even after the last drop of oil has been extracted from its offshore waters.) Were Krumpet to fabricate its large storage tanks for warehousing poison chemicals the army feels it might have to use in a life or death war, it might well be making an enormous rather than a minuscule annual increment. If Ulysses develops a blood derivative that will treat bullet wounds rather than haemophiliacs, it will accumulate pounds sterling very rapidly. And if Xerxes or Yolanda discovers a method of using computer-aided-design for guns and bombers, these young concerns will be on easy street. To sum up the thoughts of this and the previous paragraphs in another way, a transfusion from the state *was* in fact helpful or essential to the good health of a good number of NEB-aided firms; but a noteworthy percentage of the life-giving cash came from the Ministry of Defence (or its counterparts in other countries) rather than from the Board itself. Moreover, some of the shakier ventures in which the Board was involved could have used military contracts to bolster their fortunes -- and some still could.

Let us be clear what I am not contending here. I am not saying that the NEB assistance and good counsel was irrelevant for all its vigorous firms. The new management it inserted into Fairey and Ferranti was certainly one factor in turning these groups around. That 2200 word processor the NEB through Nexos helped develop is selling well for ICL. And, if the NEB had not given it tens of millions of pounds to get off the ground, there would not be an Inmos today despite its indirect sales to the military.

Furthermore, I am not asserting that all the NEB-subsidised firms that are hale and hearty do all or even a majority of their work for the MOD. For most of them, a significant part of their turnover does come from the civilian sector. Thus electronic photo-typesetting machine manufacturer Pet does little business with the armed forces. RR derives a considerable percentage of its revenues from the sale of civilian aircraft engines. As for Fred, industry accounts for almost 50% of its sales and providing financial services about 20%. Velma markets software to banking, insurance and brokerage firms, telecommunications companies, and industry. Of Olga's total sales in 1983-84, only 9% involved defence work as opposed to, e.g., 16% for banking and finance; 27% for office automation; 12% for post, telecommunications and broadcasting; and about 10% for manufacturing, retail and transportation. Fairey supplies robot and robot parts for industry; control systems for underground mining; superfine filtration systems for, e.g., the chemical, petrochemical, pharmaceutical and other areas; ceramic water filters; and components for nuclear power reactors. And Ferranti offers computers and data-handling systems for business as well as freight-container handling equipment including cranes. Only the small Bruce company sells almost exclusively to the military, though the armed services appear to be the largest customer for both Fairey and Ferranti.

Yet one must stick with the conclusion that *some* of the credit for the NEB's successes should go to the UK (and certain foreign) armed forces. The best reason for holding this position is the fact that, as seen, a number of NEB-succoured concerns that did not enter the defence market struggled for a long time, or are continuing to struggle, to achieve profitability -- or went out of business. If all NEB firms had had dealings with the military, one could possibly argue that those of these that flourished would have done as well had the MOD never given them a shot in the arm. But it is difficult to support this thesis given the tribulations of certain Board-supported undertakings that had no defence contracts.

None of this should come as any surprise. The contribution of defence spending to the (at least short-run) prosperity of industry in the western world is immense. There was absolutely no reason to predict that NEB-subsidised enterprises would remain more aloof from army, navy and air force riches than would their counterparts that were never blessed by the Board. The industrialists, bankers (and even the union chiefs) who managed and staffed the Board were not drawn from the wing of the Labour Party that is committed to spending much more on butter and much less on guns. Therefore no one should have expected that they would pressure their subsidiaries and associated companies to eschew lucrative agreements from the MOD. This is especially true as the Board, as seen, was under a duty to obtain a reasonable rate of return on capital employed. Given the fact that transactions with the military tend to be such plums for the civilian half of the arrangement, it would have taken the nobility of saints for the NEB heads to urge their companies not to do business with the armed forces even if (as clearly was not the case) they thought there was something inherently 'tainted' about the defence spending arena. In any event, it would have been sheer political suicide for them to preach to the agency's holdings in this way!

NOTES

1. Ferranti 1983 Annual Report (Ferranti, London), p. 5.
2. Ibid.
3. Ibid, p. 10.
4. *London Times,* 6 Dec. 1983, p. 23.

16
Is an NEB Now Needed in
the United Kingdom?

As a preliminary to deciding whether the United Kingdom should revitalise the NEB or create a new agency with powers similar to those possessed by the Board in its glory days, we must, first of all, review this body's record as a state venture capitalist to see whether it had real achievements. Then we must ascertain whether the country needs an institution of this sort now, even assuming that in the past it had important triumphs to its credit. And, in the next chapter, we shall ask whether the US would benefit from creating a similar organisation. (We shall ignore the frequently-discussed question of whether a public body should be established to 'bail out' the BLs and the RRs of the next decade.)

In previous chapters we described some significant accomplishments the Board effected wearing its venture capitalist hat. Most obviously, it provided capital to firms which could not get money from private banks and which are now flourishing or promise to bloom in the near future. However, the NEB not only directly added to the quantity of venture capital in the UK, but also did so indirectly by inducing private venture capital to come forth. It acted as a magnet for private venture capital in two ways. First, on occasion private venture capitalists would invest in a firm only when the Board was going to take a share in it as well. For example, the Board convinced a private bank to participate in the rescue of Pet and persuaded private entrepreneur Industrial and Commercial Finance Corporation (ICFC) to help it nurture Carol, the small but profitable manufacturer of rubber sheets. Likewise the NEB said that it would not invest in promising high tech concern Morton unless its bank increased its loan to it. More crucially, the NEB educated the cautious, conservative

211

British private sector on the need to provide venture capital: it will be remembered that before the Board graced the scene in the mid-1970s, ICFC was just about the only UK private venture capital concern. Whatever the failings of the Board, it thus served as a catalyst stimulating the private sector to make available some venture capital funding: it showed the City that there was a real need for this in the UK and that it could be invested creatively and patiently without leading to financial disaster. Some former NEB staff members feel that its greatest victory was its overcoming of this traditional reluctance of UK finance to bolster firms temporarily in hot water or small enterprises with good ideas but not much of a cash flow.

There are several other trophies that the NEB can display. Whether or not management buyouts of small subsidiary firms whose large owners want to close them down were totally foreign to the UK prior to the NEB's creation, they certainly were not the fashion. The NEB's financing of Powerdrive's management buyout helped make private funds less reluctant to buttress this genre of transaction. It often replaced poor with competent leadership -- Pet, Ferranti, British Leyland and Fairey are the best examples. It forced others of its firms to better their management techniques. Remember, for instance, that the firm that was Zelda's ancestor had never bothered to draw up a budget but that the Board made Zelda take this step. As also seen, oil-rig maintenance firm Elspeth is an import saver; while Harlan sells about 90% of its biotechnology products abroad. Various articles manufactured in firms that the Board once succoured are technically excellent: Inmos' high-quality static microchips, its transputer, and Olga, Jr's 2200 word processor are examples.

We have calculated that the NEB's efforts as venture capitalist saved or created about 7400 jobs. Of course, 7400 jobs barely dent the surface of the current unemployment figure of over two-and-one-half million; but then the Board as venture capitalist did not have billions of pounds to work with. Incidentally, as stressed earlier, some of these 7400 places are in promising firms. Thus it is possible that within a few years we shall be able to attribute a significant number of additional positions to the NEB.

We also showed that in some respects, the NEB's financial record as a venture capitalist was not all that sickly. For political reasons, it had to sell some of its holdings for less than the highest price that they could have commanded. The percentage of its venture capital companies that became total failures was about the same as that of the venture capitalists analysed in American studies. Some of its firms saw sizeable increases in the value of their stock while they were in its hands. And these results -- and its other accomplishments -- were effectuated in an economy that was basically weaker than the American and with enemies (many business people, segments of the press, quite a few adherents of a major political party) that would not have confronted a private venture capitalist. One argument to demean the NEB's achievements as venture capitalist can be drawn from the thesis of the last Chapter: i.e. that some of its success stories were due to their getting a significant number of defence contracts, that these companies owe their present robustness as much to the Ministry of Defence as to the NEB. Fairey and high tech firms Fred, Velma and Olga all fall into this mould. Nonetheless, the advocates of undiluted 'free enterprise' are estopped from using this fact of its member firms' participation in the arms race to show that the NEB was a dud. The reason they are foreclosed from bringing up this argument is obvious, i.e. that so many of the important concerns in the 'pure' private sector that they worship are indebted for much of their prosperity to this very contest. To put this in another way, a thesis that the victories of a government venture capitalist are mirages because many of its subsidiaries owe their vitality to the war machine can be turned about to demonstrate the incompetence of quite a few bell-wethers of the 'pure' private sector, as these are just as dependent on arms production.

The Board can thus boast of substantial achievements, some of which are discoverable only through an in-depth analysis of *prima facie* unfavourable statistics. Real failures it did have. However, the fact that the two most glaring (the Insac and Nexos entanglements) sprang, as seen, from wholly-avoidable sins of omission and commission is an argument that, paradoxically, can buoy those who would like to see the Board reborn in the UK. That is, these disasters were easily preventable and thus cannot be used to demonstrate that public corporations supplying venture capital to private businesses are intrinsically flawed -- especially as the errors that gave birth to these fiascos also can and do plague the private sector.

Naturally, it does not follow from the fact that the NEB took actions as a venture capitalist that benefited the UK and that some of its serious mistakes could easily have been averted that a body similar to it is needed now. We must, therefore, directly confront the following two issues. (1) Is there currently an important task for a state venture capitalist to perform in the UK? (I define a state venture capitalist as a public agency whose purpose it is to subsidise small and medium-sized firms in new areas of technology, as well as concerns of this dimension that make more traditional products and that are in temporary financial difficulties and/or having trouble getting cash from the private sector.) (2) If the answer to (1) is 'yes', should that state venture capitalist resemble an NEB with the power to take shares in, as well as lend to, private undertakings?

One can make a weighty argument to the effect that the UK needs no state venture capitalist at present. As seen, when the NEB came into being in 1975, Finance For Industry (FFI, now called 3i), acting through its Industrial and Commercial Finance Corporation (ICFC) division, was the only British private sector venture capitalist that would provide help to firms that for one reason or another could not raise money elsewhere. In 1976 Equity Capital for Industry (ECI) was founded for more or less the same purpose. Still, as of early 1977 the NEB, FFI and ECI were (aside from a few institutions serving a particular industry such as films or agriculture and regional development agencies in Scotland, Northern Ireland and Wales) the only 'venture capitalists' in the UK in the sense of organisations that would aid established but temporarily-troubled small and medium-sized companies with good products or most concerns that were dubbed 'high tech'.[1] However, by 1984 there were (thanks to a considerable extent to the NEB's pioneering example!) over 100 venture capital firms operating in the country with a total of £500 million to invest. During that year, they aided over 250 undertakings.[2] Moreover, there are now in existence 'conurbation' enterprise boards, which are in a real sense venture capitalists. For example, in 1984 the Greater London Enterprise Board (GLEB) bought from a liquidator a plant employing over 30 highly-skilled precision engineering workers that made parts for IBM, Xerox, London Transport and other major corporations. It had been highly profitable until the recession of the early 1980s subjected it to a cash flow crisis. GLEB by purchasing it saved all its jobs; and expects that it will employ 50 persons.[3]

Nevertheless, (putting to one side the theoretical objections to such an agency that Chapters 18 and 19 will cover) there is still a spot for a body sponsored by the national government to act as a venture capitalist (as defined above) in the UK. We have noted earlier that ECI has become less willing to succour ailing enterprises.[4] As of mid-1985 it was investing in 65 undertakings; but said that only 41 of these were venture capital situations.[5] It admits that it is very reluctant to invest in the very small company, though it will aid funds set up to support such organisations.[6] Moreover, some promising high tech companies will take quite a few years before reaching profitability. These firms may well be rebuffed by private venture capitalists who, if they are like their counterparts in the US,[7] often like to see their investments become profitable within five years at most. As seen, Harlan, the UK's largest biotechnology undertaking, was founded in 1980 and is still not in the black as of my writing this. As a result, ICFC, one of the original sponsors of the firm, no longer has an interest in it.

Also, private venture capitalists in the UK testify that they are ploughing a lot of their resources into projects in which they already have invested.[8] They argue that this is due to the fact that few British business people develop sound, exciting projects. They contend that there are not enough entrepreneurs coming forward from industry and universities who want to try to make a commercial success of their ideas.[9] They confess, though, that they get many more applications for support than they approve; and a 1986 study shows that *'Small and seedcorn or start-up projects, mostly involving investments of less than £250,000, are still being starved of resources'*[10] (emphasis supplied). Only about 50% of UK venture capitalists will put their cash into any sort of 'start-up'; and this type of operation accounted for just 16% of all UK venture capital investments in 1986.[11] Even a Minister in the Thatcher Administration notes that Britain's multibillion pound pension funds and insurance companies refuse to invest in small businesses.[12] Surely not all the rejected petitioners and all the hungry fledgling and modest-sized companies are unworthy of assistance. Certainly, some of them should be bolstered by a venture capitalist and since the private sector will not do the job, the public sector should via the NEB or another state venture capitalist. One could argue that the conurbation enterprise and the regional (e.g., Scottish, Welsh) development boards should be the ones to fill the cracks, but there are many areas of the UK that are not within the jurisdiction of any one of these bodies, which in any event have limited resources. (For example, the funds available to the Greater London Enterprise Board have been severely reduced.[13])

In sum, a new or resuscitated NEB could aid start-ups and small or modest-sized concerns that make goods or supply useful services of high quality, but that are not profitable now and/or lack good prospects of ever becoming glittering moneymakers. Many of these ventures still cannot obtain private sector backing; and one or two of them might even turn out to be an IBM or Sony! Not only will the processes of manufacturing their articles and providing their services create jobs; but these wares and services will make life more comfortable for the average person. And this is certainly the major purpose of economic activity! (I personally would prefer that NEB-assisted firms accept few military contracts.)

Finally, ought a UK (and a US, if we find the creation of one desirable) state venture capitalist to have the NEB's power to aid firms via the equity in addition to the loan route? The answer to this question is clearly 'yes'. In the first place, equity may be more helpful to the assisted undertaking. Big loans mean that a good deal of the subsidised concern's revenues must go for interest payments rather than for expansion.[14] In fact, there will be situations where debt servicing will drive an undertaking bankrupt.[15] Secondly, where the state has a reasonably high percentage of the shares it can, if it is willing, push its subsidiary in a direction that it believes is socially valuable. For example, it can pressure the company not to shed jobs as quickly as the latter would like. (As seen, the NEB rarely took this step.) Moreover, it can push its companies to work together in a way that would benefit the nation as a whole. If the NEB had owned more stock in the members of Insac, the concern it set up to market British software abroad, it might, as mentioned in Chapter 9, have insisted that these firms be less reluctant to co-operate in product refinement and selling in the US. Partnership of this sort might have made the UK share of the US software market more impressive than it is today. It is true, of course, that even providing a loan to an undertaking can enable the government to twist its arm to strive for a good other than the maximum possible profit. But once the last of the money has been transferred to the recipient, the state will no longer have any trump card available to enable its wishes to prevail over those of the firm. (The leverage that its equity participation in a concern can give the polity will be alluded to further in Chapter 19.)

NOTES

1. See Committee to Review the Functioning of Financial Institutions, *Evidence on financing of industry,* vol. 1, p. 10, 26-30.

2. C. Spray, 'The capital adventure', *Management Today,* Aug. 1984, p. 72.

3. Greater London Council, *Working for jobs in London* (Greater London Council, London, 1984), p. 4.

4. *London Times,* 21 June 1983, p. 13.

5. ECI 1985 Annual Report, p. 8.

6. *London Times,* 10 May 1985, p. 16.

7. US General Accounting Office, *Government-industry cooperation,* p. 19.

8. *London Times,* 10 May 1985, p. 16.

9. Ibid.

10. Ibid. and *London Times,* 6 Oct. 1986, p. 21.

11. *Economist,* 19 Dec. 1987, p. 67.

12. *London Times,* 2 Feb. 1987, p. 1.

13. *New Statesman,* 5 Dec. 1986, p. 11.

14. A Business Department colleague emphasised this point in a conversation with me.

15. Committee to Review the Functioning of Financial Institutions, *Evidence on financing of industry,* vol. 4, p. 30. (Murphy testimony.)

17

Does the US Need an NEB?

An opponent of a suggestion to set up an NEB-type of state venture capitalist in the US would vehemently retort that there is no want of venture capital in that country, whatever might be the case in the UK. But venture capitalists in the US receive many, many more proposals than they are able to help:[1] surely some of the rejectees ought to be able to get subventions somewhere. In fact, despite the increased availability of venture capital, the shortfall in this 'commodity' increased significantly during the 1970s.[2] The American economist John Kenneth Galbraith laments the lack of funding for innovation in industries 'where the firms are numerous and small' -- e.g., home construction, clothing manufacture, the service industries.[3] Remember, moreover, that the source for the proposition made in the last chapter that private venture capitalists want to see their firms become 'winners' within a five year period is an American publication.[4] Consequently, undertakings refining an article that is socially useful but unlikely to soon become a big money-maker may well cry in vain for private funding in the US as well as in the UK. This is especially true as the late 1980s are witnessing a tendency for US venture capitalists to prefer investments promising short-term profits over high tech companies that will stay in the red for many years.[5]

Were the US economy essentially robust it would not greatly matter that a bundle of enterprises that could provide jobs and place on the domestic and export markets high quality goods and services are condemned to wither on the vine -- all because they cannot get from public or private sources the cash they need for research and development, plant and equipment modernisation, or marketing. However, millions of

Americans are unemployed and millions more are poor. Moreover, many sectors of US industry, both 'traditional' and 'high tech', have been losing customers to foreign competition during the past decade and a half. Among the areas hit are machine tools, video recorders, semiconductor chips, industrial robots, fibre optics, cameras, electronic equipment, drugs and medicines and professional and scientific instruments.[6] As democratic socialists Barry Bluestone and Bennett Harrison colourfully put the matter in their book *The Deindustrialization of America*:

'It is disturbing to learn...that the 1980 trade deficit with Japan reached over $10 billion...In terms of dollar value, the number one Japanese product sold to America was passenger motor vehicles, followed by iron and steel plates, truck and tractor chassis, radios, motorbikes, and audio and video tape recorders. In contrast, America's top seven exports to Japan, in order of dollar value, were soybeans, corn, fir logs, hemlock logs, coal, wheat, and cotton. The trade deficit hides the disconcerting fact that, at least with respect to our most important competitor, the United States has been reduced to an agricultural nation trying desperately to compete with the manufacturer of the world's most sophisticated capital and consumer goods.'[7]

The massive US trade deficit continues despite a significant 1987 drop in the value of the dollar. One reason is that imported products are sometimes of a higher quality than their US-made counterparts: for example, American integrated circuits and computer chips are deteriorating in excellence relative to Japanese. Another is that the country no longer manufactures certain components of various products: for example, all Goodyear-made radial tyres assembled in the US contain steel wire from Belgium and Japan because American suppliers no longer fabricate the appropriate wire.[8]

Thus because even in the US there is now in some respects a deficiency of venture capital, and also because those who cannot get such funding might well be able, if assisted financially, to furnish services or assemble goods that would contribute to reinvigorating an export and job-weak American economy, it would make sense to set up a public venture capitalist to aid small and medium-sized firms. Also, for reasons noted in the previous chapter, this agency should be an NEB-type body with the power to grant equity as well as make loans. It should, first of all, invest in traditional industries that make high quality, possibly import-saving products but that are having difficulty raising funds. It should also bolster industries that would like to again assemble a good for which a demand has re-emerged. And it should aid high tech firms (including start-ups) that are having trouble getting financing from the private sector.

Many of the writers who have diagnosed the ills of the US economy favour some sort of government assistance to specific undertakings. Authors Ira Magaziner and Robert Reich (liberal Democrats) certainly agree with me on the final proposition of the above paragraph. They note that 'Outside the defense and energy areas, the US has no such programs [e.g., serving as a direct source of venture capital] to stimulate investment in high risk ventures. A government-subsidized lending institution should be established to fill this need for high risk capital.'[9] (They appear, admittedly, to prefer that this body operate by making loans.) They would also like to see government fund non-military R and D for selected small and medium as well as large concerns.[10]

Bluestone and Harrison are in accord with me on the view that the polity should provide funds for certain private firms as well as on the loan versus equity matter, contending that when the government gives more than a specified amount of aid to a private company, it should 'insist upon acquiring at least a minor equity position...'[11] Even wealthy investment banker Felix Rohatyn (a moderate Democrat) suggests the formation of a governmental corporation to extend credit to, and aid the exporting activities of, companies that have the potential to become more productive and competitive.[12]

So an 'NEB of some sort' for the US is an idea backed by respectable authority of diverse ideological viewpoints. And quite a few subnational US jurisdictions have taken steps to put this concept into practice. As the level of unemployment and underemployment in the US remains high despite the passage of several years of the so-called Reagan recovery, some states are finding that equity assistance to specific private concerns is a possible route for expanding or maintaining the level of employment in the face of a national polity that seems to care only about war-related industries. Michigan's state pension fund takes equity shares in high-risk enterprises that promise a good rate of return. For example, it purchased $6 million worth of stock in a dynamic corporation that makes computerised controls to monitor operations in manufacturing plants. 5% of that fund has been set aside for this type of investment. Between 1982 and 1986 it placed $48 million in 23 companies and thus created 3000 jobs. It has another $80 million to put into industries such as automobile suppliers, forestry, food processing and tourism.[13]

Likewise, Ohio's Industrial Technology and Enterprise Board has funds that support the growth of high technology firms through taking equity in them and/or extending them credit.[14] New York's Corporation for Innovation Development Program, which began operations in 1982, had by 1985 provided start-up capital for 14 modest-sized, high tech companies in the state. One of them, for example, produces a system that transmits medical images such as X-rays over telephone lines. Another has invented a network to link home computers all over the country. All in all, about twelve states have enacted schemes for public investment in private companies.[15] Probably many of the legislators in these states had never heard of the NEB when they passed the legislation enabling the government to grant these subsidies; but what these men and women did in essence is to set up little NEBs in a land whose basic philosophy is supposed to be 'government: keep your hands off business'.

It is, however, unlikely that the existence of these 'state NEBs' makes a national NEB unnecessary. First, state pension funds cannot be invested in companies that bear too much of a risk. The pension fund systems cannot jeopardise the retirement prospects of those whose have contributed to the oceans of dollars that they manage. Second, the states, if American history is any guide, will be reluctant to tap ordinary tax revenues to a significant extent in order to directly subsidise private concerns. This would mean hiking state and local taxes; and states are reluctant to do this for fear of driving private firms and middle class individuals to other states. And, third, the eagerness with which private firms are accepting state venture capital is the best possible evidence that even in the

US, there is a shortage of private venture capital. Thus the success of the 'state NEBs' strongly albeit paradoxically supports my view that the US as a whole needs a public venture capitalist!

To recapitulate this and the previous chapter, the UK should breathe new life into its NEB and the US should create one. Both agencies should have the power to take an equity interest in temporarily financially-troubled or marginally-profitable small or medium-sized concerns in 'standard' industries that make superior articles for domestic or foreign consumption; as well as in firms that intend to again fabricate goods once out-of-fashion but now in demand. They should have similar authority *vis-à-vis* start-up and other high technology ventures. They should be most willing to step in when a company finds that private financing is either unavailable or carries too high a price. In the US such a Board could have a budget of perhaps $18 billion; in the UK of about £4 billion. These seem like large amounts but really are not. The sum can be raised in the US simply by building one less nuclear-powered aircraft carrier with its team of support ships and the planes it would ferry.[16] In the UK the cash could be found simply by the government's refraining from purchasing £4 billion worth of US Trident submarine missiles.[17] The carrier and the missiles are icing on an already big defence cake and do the ordinary person little good; but the firms that the UK and US NEBs would assist would fabricate a wide range of quality articles; provide multifarious services; create *in toto* many jobs; and in these ways enhance the pleasures the ordinary woman and man encounter in their daily lives.

NOTES

1. Wilson, *The new venturers*, p. 7.

2. US General Accounting Office, *Government-industry cooperation*, pp. 34-5.

3. *The affluent society*, 4th edn revised and updated (North American Library, New York, 1984), pp. 100-01.

4. US General Accounting Office, *Government-industry cooperation*, p. 19.

5. *New York Times,* 6 Feb. 1987, p. A1.

6. Bruce Scott, 'National strategy for stronger U.S. competitiveness', *Harvard Business Rev.,* Mar.-Ap. 1984, p. 77, 80; Lester Thurow, 'Revitalizing American industry', *California Management Rev.,* Fall, 1984, pp. 9-12.

7. Basic Books, New York, 1982, p. 5.

8. *New York Times,* 13 Feb. 1987, p. A1; 14 Jan. 1988, p. D1.

9. See p. 353 of their *Minding America's business* (Harcourt Brace Jovanovich, New York, 1982).

10. Ibid., pp. 350-51.

11. *The deindustrialization of America,* p. 246.

12. 'Time for a change', *New York Rev. of Books,* 18 Aug. 1983, p. 46, 49.

13. *New York Times,* 30 Nov. 1975, p. 8; 23 June 1986, p. A1.

14. US Congress, Office of Technology Assessment, *Technology, innovation and regional economic development* (US Congress, Office of Technology Assessment, Washington, 1983), p. 59.

15. *New York Times,* 23 June 1986, p. A1; New York State Science and Technology Foundation, *Corporation for innovation development program* (New York State Science and Technology Foundation, Albany, 1985), p. 1, 4, 11. In addition, some US cities are taking equity shares in hotel and shopping mall corporations. *New York Times,* 4 Ap. 1987, p. 33.

16. This figure is taken from David Stockman, *The triumph of politics* (Harper and Row, New York, 1986), p. 280.

17. *New York Times,* 30 Nov. 1986, Sec. 1, p. 20 notes that the Thatcher Administration plans to acquire Tridents from the US for $13 billion (about £9 billion).

18

Government Subsidies to Specific Firms: An Evaluation of the Conservative Critique

As the previous paragraph noted, there seems to be a need for state venture capitalists in the UK and US with the NEB's power to take equity in the firms they bolster. However, both conservatives and radicals offer some serious theoretical arguments against the notion of a public institution with power to funnel public aid to specific private firms. This chapter deals with contentions of this sort coming from the right -- the next with their counterparts from the left. Among the most common arguments against state assistance to particular undertakings that have been propounded by conservatives are the following.

(1) State subsidies designed to keep alive well-established companies that are experiencing financial difficulties will take away from these concerns the incentive to reorganise or in other ways reduce expenses. The workforce will, for example, forget about the necessity for moderating wage demands while management will not bother to insist that the employees accept lower wage hikes.[1]

(2) Such subventions impose costs on other areas of the economy. If, for example, they are financed through taxes, they reduce consumer demand and thus adversely affect those companies from whom the public would have purchased goods were it not for the tax.[2] If they are financed via public borrowing, they will raise interest rates.[3]

(3) Such subsidies can lead to the continued production of goods no one now wants or needs.[4]

(4) Furthermore, they divert resources from industries that would produce commodities that are or will shortly be in great demand.[5]

(5) They will reduce the incentives of the aided firm to take risks to develop more useful products.[6]

(6) The bankruptcy of such a company does not necessarily mean the end of its assets and/or an increase in unemployment. Its land and capital and the skills of its workforce may be purchased from the trustee in bankruptcy by another firm and set to work again.[7]

So far, we have been talking about government aid to particular businesses that make established products. The UK government's rescues of British Leyland, Alfred Herbert and Rolls Royce are classic examples of such support. The NEB's financing of concerns such as Able, Charlie, Fred, Graham, Ivy and Olga show the state fostering high tech ('sunrise') enterprises making goods such as computers, computer peripherals and biotechnology products. The demand for these goods and services is increasing, both domestically and abroad. Clearly, arguments (1), (3), (4) and (5) above cannot be used to attack public subventions to this kind of enterprise. However, the practice of according them to these firms is not immune from points (2) and (6). Moreover:

(7) If a company is or promises in the near future to be profitable, it will probably be able to raise capital from the private sector.[8]

(8) Private entrepreneurs are more likely to be successful in predicting what 'sunrise' enterprises are likely to flourish. This is because the hopeful entrepreneur has more incentive to acquire a detailed knowledge of the market into which he/she will be plunging and of the potential of the firm in which she/he is interested. This is so because he/she, unlike the bureaucrat, will personally suffer an economic loss if it turns out to be a dud.[9]

(9) It will be almost impossible for a government to intelligently guess in which 'new' sectors its nation is likely to be successful. History shows that to a considerable extent a country's dominance in a particular area is due to unpredictable factors, e.g., one firm's establishment of a niche in a market due to imagination, energy and hard work. The capture of this nook will then be followed by, e.g., economies of scale for the firm and the acquisition of special skills and know-how by it and related enterprises in the land.[10]

Two arguments that can be interposed against any system of subsidies to particular companies, whether located in advancing or declining sectors, are:

(10) There is never enough government money available to satisfy all the ventures that want government assistance. Consequently, each of these enterprises will have to spend time and effort lobbying for such help; and this time and effort could be better spent contemplating how to improve markets, productivity, etc.[11]

(11) In a democracy, the undertakings that would probably get the bulk of government aid are the largest and most inefficient.[12]

However, the defenders of the practice of government aid to specific firms (i.e. of what was termed in Chapter 1 'selective' assistance) can do a good job of countering many of these points. Contrary to conservative point (7), the NEB experience certainly reveals that not all potentially successful companies can procure private financing. Remember, for instance, computer-peripheral assembler Ivy and electronic photo-typesetting machine manufacturer Pet. Additional points that the backers of the public subsidisation of particular concerns may make include the following.

(1) Conservative critique (1) above forgets that the polity may condition its subsidy on the appointment of more efficient management for the firm. Remember that NEB aid to Fairey, Ferranti and Pet was followed by the agency's selection of top-notch leadership for these enterprises.

(2) With respect to conservative critique (8) above, surely public servants can operate under a system of rewards under which they will personally benefit (through, e.g., promotion, bonuses) if their agency, acting upon their suggestions, selects a company to assist that soon starts to thrive. Moreover, private employers might well hire at a high salary public agency workers who display foresight.

(3) The next argument involves conservative critique (9), i.e. that government cannot tell what 'sunrise' economic sectors will be successful because this depends on the 'unpredictable' fact that a particular firm will establish a niche in a market due to hard work, etc. To the extent this assertion is true, private venture capitalists will also find it impossible to intelligently guess what fields of business will 'take off'. Their

misjudgements here will be as wasteful of resources as similar blunders by civil servants.

(4) A grant from the government may make a firm large enough to take advantage of economies of scale.[13]

(5) Certain important industrial projects are so large that private enterprise cannot summon up the wherewithal to invest in them.[14]

(6) Other countries grant subventions to their industries and thus, e.g., the UK had better do so too if it wants to maintain reasonably full employment and avoid a monstrous balance of payments deficit. For example, the Japanese government has subsidised that nation's phenomenal growth first in heavy industry and then in electronics.[15]

(7) The next pro-subsidy argument is not aimed at demonstrating that government assistance to specific firms is beneficial but is, rather, directed at an assumption underlying the oft-heard anti-subsidy contention that pure competition tends to produce the most efficient allocation of resources. Those making this contention emphasise that under pure competition, at the point where the quantity of a good produced by a firm will give it maximum total profit and thus where the rational firm will cease additional production, the marginal cost of producing that article, i.e. the money cost of producing the last unit of it, will equal its price.[16] (The sentence is complex but part of the idea behind it is not. Assume that you have made four word processors, the first costing you £65, the second £75, the third £85 and the fourth £100 to assemble; and you have sold them for £100 each. It would normally be silly to fabricate a fifth one, also priced at £100, that would cost £105 to put together.) They continue that it is most efficient from the point of view of society as a whole for production to stop at the point where price equals marginal cost because they assume (in the words of a typical textbook on microeconomics) that 'price is a measure of the marginal social benefit of the last unit of the good that is produced [more accurately, the last unit that is produced assuming free competition], and...marginal cost truly represents the social cost of that last unit in terms of resource use'.[17] The trouble with subsidies given to producers, many of the pure-competition advocates would argue, is that because of the following reasons they put an end to this happy harmony of

Production By Rational Firm Stopping Where Price Equals Marginal Cost and thus Where Social Benefit from Last Unit Equals Social Cost of Producing Last Unit.

(a) They enable the purchaser to charge a sum for that last unit that is lower than the 'free enterprise' price. This causes additional demand that will result in more production of the article. This extra production will hurt society as a whole because its real social benefits (which usually will decline per unit as more are produced) will be less than its real social costs (which usually will increase per unit as more are produced).

(b) They reduce the money cost to the firm of the last unit below its real social cost; and this, in turn, encourages the enterprise to produce additional units since the cost to it (as opposed to society) will be less than the revenues from these new units. Of course the real social costs of these new units will probably swell far above their real benefits.

There are, however, holes in this assumption (underlying, as seen, the view that free competition will give rise to the most efficient allocation of resources) that the price of a good equals the social benefit from the last unit of the good that is produced under free competition and that the money cost of that last unit equals its cost to society. These weaknesses are so severe that the assumption, and the edifices built on it, should be discarded. It cannot be overemphasised that it is just an assumption, and a rather dubious one at that. First, I see no realistic way of demonstrating the truth of the proposition (which is part of the assumption mentioned in the first sentence of this paragraph) that price (which is defined as the average revenue from the sale of the product[18]) will be equivalent to the social benefit derived from the last unit of the good that is produced under free competition. In fact, examples can be given that create great doubt that it is generally valid. Assume, for instance, that reasonably free competition prevails and that the total revenue from ten Rolls Royces is £1 million and that from ten Ford Fiestas is £100,000. The average revenue (price) of the Rolls is thus £100,000; that of the Fiesta is only £10,000. It is very unlikely, however, that the social benefit from the last Fiesta is only one-tenth as much as the social benefit from the last Rolls. The former gets you from one place to another almost as well and its owners have fewer parking and theft worries. Under free competition, price may equal social benefit of last unit in some cases; but there are quite possibly so few of these cases that one should rest upon this equation neither a theory of society nor any critique of the workings of a particular institution! (By the way, this equation is simply an example of the confusion of the exchange value of an object with its use value that Karl Marx and Adam Smith warned us against![19] And when we realise that use and exchange value are separate phenomena, we have to admit that it is reasonable to speak, as we did in, e.g., Chapter 16, of the possibility that a good may simultaneously be useful and lacking in significant profit potential.)

Next, the proposition (part two of the assumption mentioned in the first sentence of the last paragraph) that the (money) cost of the last unit produced (assuming free competition) is equivalent to the real social cost of producing that unit is just as unprovable as the proposition that under pure competition the price of the good will be an indication of the social benefit of that unit. Therefore we must be quite dubious about any social theory or any attack on social policy that employs it (instead of or together with the Price Equals Social Benefit of Last Unit theory). As many economists themselves emphasise, the main reason that we must be sceptical about the proposition that the money cost of the last item that would be produced under free competition reflects the social cost of that item is that the real social cost must in part be measured by the 'negative externalities' (e.g., air or water pollution) arising from the processes of its production.[20] The money cost, however, will not include these detrimental by-products of assembling the good. Even if a sincere attempt is made to up money cost to reflect social cost, this may well be a futile effort, as the assessment of the money cost of these unhappy side-effects can under the best of circumstances be little more than a guess. Can we meaningfully slap a cash figure upon, for example, the harm to the family of a worker resulting from the tensions created in her while the good is being manufactured?

To sum what has preceded, since there is no way to prove that under pure competition price equals the social benefit from the last-produced unit or that the real cost to society of that unit equals the (money) cost to the firm of that unit (i.e. marginal cost), it is silly to jettison the idea of subsidies simply on the ground that they make it unlikely that the production of the assisted good will stop at the point where its price (defined, it will be remembered, as the average revenue from the sale of the product) equals its marginal cost. The price of a good might diverge from the social benefit from the last unit of that good that would be produced under free competition; as could the social cost and money cost of that unit. Ergo, that unit's social benefit and social cost might well differ from each other even when the good's price equalled such unit's money cost (i.e. the good's marginal cost). And if in fact that unit's social benefit *exceeds* its social cost, we should subsidise additional production of the article. I am certainly not arguing that every government subsidy given to a firm for the fabrication of a ware will be socially beneficial; but do assert that whether a particular such grant is on balance useful must be determined by looking at the real world and not automatically answered in the negative by deductive reasoning from questionable premises.

NOTES

1. John Burton, *Picking losers* (Institute of Economic Affairs, London, 1983), pp. 44-5.

2. Ibid.

3. Ibid.

4. Victoria Curzon-Price, *Industrial policies in the European Community* (Macmillan, London, 1981), p. 120.

5. Ibid., p. 123.

6. Alan Peacock, *Structural economic policies in West Germany and the United Kingdom*, p. 125.

7. Burton, *Picking losers*, p. 43.

8. Grylls and Redwood, *NEB: a case for euthanasia*, Ch. IV.

9. See Burton, *Picking losers*, pp. 37-40.

10. Charles Schultze, 'Industrial policy: a dissent', *Brookings Rev.*, Fall, 1983, p. 3, 8.

11. Burton, *Picking losers*, p. 56.

12. See Schultze, 'Industrial policy: a dissent', p. 10.

13. T. Cripps, 'Economics of labour subsidies' at p. 105, 107 of Whiting (ed.), *The economics of industrial subsidies*.

14. John Burton, *The job support machine* (Centre for Policy Studies, London, 1979), p. 29. Burton himself dislikes this argument.

15. *Business Week*, 30 June 1980, p. 139.

16. Edwin Mansfield, *Micro-economics: theory and applications*, 2nd edn (W. W. Norton, New York, 1975), pp. 199-200.

17. J. Holton Wilson, *Microeconomics: concepts and applications* (Harper and Row, New York, 1981), p. 202.

18. Ibid., p. 81.

19. See Marx's *Capital*, (International Publishers, New York, 1967), vol. 1, p. 36 and Smith's *Wealth of nations*, (Modern Library, New York, 1937), p. 42.

20. Dominick Salvatore, *Microeconomics: theory and applications* (Macmillan, New York, 1986), pp. 613-15.

19
Government Subsidies to Specific Firms: An Evaluation of the Radical Critique

Having dealt with the probable attacks from the right against a suggestion to revitalise the NEB or create an agency similar to it, let us wrestle with the various criticisms that the Marxist and socialist left would direct at such a proposal. One of these arguments would certainly be that a policy of government subsidies filtered through an agency such as the NEB would not effect any genuine transfer of power in society. Surely there is much merit in this thesis. Those who will receive the subvention and decide how it should be employed are the managers of the firms getting the largesse. These persons dominate the economy now: parcelling out government cash to them will not reduce and may even increase the pile of chips they can deal out and the number of lives they can influence. The argument articulated in this paragraph is analogous to David Coates's complaint about what happened following the nationalisation of British Leyland. 'Far from achieving a "fundamental and irreversible shift in the balance of power and wealth in favour of working people and their families", public ownership in the car industry completed the alliance of management and the State *against* any such shift...'[1](emphasis in original). And Samuel Bowles, David Gordon and Thomas Weisskopf contend that 'industrial policy' (of which NEB-type assistance is an example) might even 'transfer resources to the wealthiest and the largest corporations'.[2]

No totally satisfactory answer can be given to the position that subsidies are undesirable because they do not hand power to an exploited class. One partial reply would be that a revived or new NEB should be compelled (as the prototype was not) to promote workers' control of the enterprises in which it had

232

holdings. Moreover, as Bluestone and Harrison point out, a body such as the Board ought to use its equity stakes to achieve not only industrial democracy but also affirmative action in hiring and fair treatment of the workforce in plant relocations.[3] Following this line of reasoning, one can point out to the left wing critics of the NEB-type institution that it could use its leverage to force its holdings to grant their workers more freedom on and off the job. It could, for example, prohibit the use by the concerns it aids of unreasonable employee dress and residency requirements; and of mandatory lie detector, genetic-defect and (in most cases) drug testing. Likewise, it could act to shield the cadres of the firms it supports from being fired for protesting the way the office or the factory is managed or the performance of an inept or tyrannical supervisor. Of course, these several steps would effect no radical swing of authority from managers to workers; but they would grant employees some economic power and make it somewhat more difficult for employers to treat their hired hands in an arbitrary fashion.

Another major criticism that the left, especially the Marxist left, would make about a plan to reinvigorate or create an NEB would be that such an institution would do nothing to remove the essential contradictions that plague even a welfare state when the bulk of the means of production is privately owned. Most late twentieth-century democratic Marxists agree that welfare state capitalism is rent with fundamental contradictions that, in the long run, will lead to its collapse. Thus Alan Wolfe contends that a liberal democratic capitalist state suffers from the 'inherent and necessary contradiction' that it will have to help private parties 'accumulate' on the one hand and, on the other, take into account the democratic desires of the people for equality and participation.[4] And James O'Connor avers that bitter clashes between taxpayers and recipients of government largesse ultimately threaten the viability of the democratic capitalist order.[5]

Obviously, the resuscitation or establishment of an NEB would not solve the most serious social antagonisms and problems of the UK and US. But, as has been pointed out many, many times, if a moderate change within the existing order will make the life of the average citizen a bit more tolerable, one can argue that one should work for such a reform in the short run while simultaneously pushing for longer-run alterations to remove the flaws, whatever these be, that are embedded in the foundation of the current scheme of things. Thus, if an NEB is needed because the private sector is too cautious to assist certain firms that could employ significant numbers of people and/or make good products, one could reasonably come to its support even though it leaves capitalist contradictions intact.

More importantly, I feel today's democratic Marxists are guilty of imposing the label 'fundamental ('intrinsic', 'inherent', 'insoluble', 'insuperable') contradiction' upon certain conflicts in a democratic capitalist welfare state without clearly demonstrating that these conflicts deserve these adjectives. Historically, Marxism has declared that the grave tensions in non-socialist societies between the haves and the have-nots are 'intrinsic contradictions'. Modern democratic Marxists, as seen, spotlight as well, e.g., the feud in welfare state capitalist democracies between the taxpayers and the recipients of government assistance; and feel that this 'contradiction' too cannot be resolved as long as capitalism remains in place. But it is far from clear that it (or, for that matter any of the other wrangles in a democratic capitalist order) should be stamped as a 'fundamental', 'insuperable', etc. contradiction that thus cannot be satisfactorily resolved within the framework of the democratic capitalist *status quo*. It may be that, e.g., the conflicts between taxpayer and state, between those who furnish the cash needed for government endeavours (and who would like to keep this for themselves) and those who will get these funds from the state when it puts its programmes into effect, are simply disputes that can be reconciled by processes of negotiation and compromise between agents of the polity on the one hand and spokespersons for the taxpayers on the other. That is, it is conceivable that they are not huge chinks in the armour of democratic welfare capitalism that make this system basically unstable. And since the democratic Marxists cannot fully substantiate that the weaknesses they perceive in non-socialist states are invincible and deadly, it is wrong for them to oppose a body such as the NEB on the ground that it will not eliminate these weaknesses. (Of course, it is still open to a democratic Marxist to argue that the costs of an NEB would exceed its benefits.)

Moreover, conceding for the sake of argument that the deep divergences in existing democratic capitalist societies are 'contradictions' that threaten their stability, there is good reason to assume that a socialist society will also contain such contradictions. (For present purposes, I am defining a society as 'socialist' where the major part of the means of production and distribution is owned by the state or non-profit groups.) Above and beyond ethnic and regional antagonisms there, existing socialist nations show many deep splits that would be denominated 'fundamental contradictions' by Marxists were they to crop up in a capitalist order. The most obvious is the conflict in the Soviet Union between the bulk of its workers and peasants on the one hand and its military, political and economic leadership on the other. The former would like higher wages and more production of consumers goods; while many members of the latter would prefer investing resources in the arms and heavy industry sectors.[6] Also, the fistfights and shootouts during the Great Cultural Revolution in the People's Republic of China between groups all proclaiming their loyalty to Mao Tse Tung[7] make the disputes that have convulsed capitalist welfare states in recent years seem like veritable lovefests.

Since the splits in socialist societies are likely to be as great as those under welfare state capitalism, it follows that if one is going to condemn small-scale reforms in capitalist nations for not ending the 'fundamental' contradictions that underlie these polities, he/she ought logically to make the same attack on moderate reforms proposed for a socialist order. A less despairing and more sensible position to take is that both socialist and democratic welfare state capitalist societies do contain groups with sharply divergent interests; but that both types of regime can reconcile these interests using intelligence and the spirit of compromise. One who takes this attitude cannot automatically reject the call for modest reforms such as the establishment of an NEB in the UK and US on the ground that they will do nothing about the 'contradictions' that might be in the process of shattering the political systems of these lands.

NOTES

1. *Labour in power,* p. 128.

2. '"Industrial policy" - now the bad news', *Nation,* 4 June 1983, p. 687, 705.

3. *The deindustrialization of America,* pp. 246-47.

4. *The limits of legitimacy* (Free Press, New York, 1977), p. 7.

5. See his *The fiscal crisis of the state* (St. Martin's, New York, 1973), pp. 1-10.

6. See Frederic Barghoorn, *Politics in the USSR* (Little Brown, Boston, 1966), pp. 68-70, 245-49.

7. See William Hinton, *Shenfan* (Random House, New York, 1983), Ch. 72, 75, 76 for a description of these brawls.

20
The NEB: An Example of Co-operation

In the last two chapters, I have defended the proposal to create or resuscitate a National Enterprise Board from the conservative position that it will prevent the production of a subsidised good from being stopped where it is most socially efficient to do so, i.e. where price (social benefit) equals marginal (social) cost. We have also supported this proposal against left wing attacks that it will not redistribute power in society to working people and that it will not rid the *status quo* of fundamental contradictions. In doing so, we did have to grant that the call for an NEB is a proposal that Karl Popper would refer to as 'piecemeal engineering', a blueprint for a single, unpretentious institution.[1] Robert Dahl and Charles Lindblom would term the establishment or re-creation of the Board 'incrementalism', the adoption of a new policy that is 'closely related to existing reality...' since it makes 'relatively small adjustments in existing reality...'[2] As such, by the way, it should be accorded all the defences Popper and Dahl and Lindblom make on behalf of piecemeal social engineering and incrementalism. These include the greater predictability of the outcome of measured reforms; the relative ease in determining whether the new institution has produced the desired results; the relative facility with which mistakes due to small-scale changes can be corrected;[3] the great difficulty of judging the practicability of plans for major alterations in the current way of doing things; and the greater likelihood that democratic methods can be used to implement a limited as opposed to a grandiose change.[4] Moreover, an NEB would not require the revamping of human nature to dispense entirely with the profit motive. (If the UK or US government should opt for an NEB with tens of billions of pounds to spend that could, moreover, take a share in the leading enterprises of the country, its birth might be denominated by Dahl and Lindblom a 'calculated risk'. These two authors admit that such risks are sometimes necessary.[5])

Now that the theoretical strictures of conservative and radical have been attended to, it is time to cease humming a defensive tune about a call to create or revive an NEB to serve as a state venture capitalist. The strongest arguments supporting this summons are really those set forth in Chapters 16 and 17. These include the fact that the Board had some signal accomplishments when it wore this hat; that it carried out these achievements despite obstacles that would not have faced a private venture capitalist; and that the UK and US still have serious economic problems and some venture capital shortages and thus could use a state venture capitalist to bolster both their high tech and familiar industrial sectors.

In addition, there are arguments on behalf of the establishment of an NEB that have an ethical rather than an economic flavour. That is, an institution of this type would have the potential to better not only people's *standard* of living but also their *way* of living. What I would like to discuss in this concluding chapter is how this agency with very down-to-earth goals could heighten the quality of human lives and relationships. The points seem obvious when they are stated; but they may well be overlooked until they have been articulated.

First, a new or reborn NEB could swell the sum of personal creativity. It could, for example, make it possible for engineers to seek improvements in existing products. It could fund the development of new articles, as was done with the 2200 word processor. The moneys it gave the concerns in which it had a holding could be employed by them in basic research. And they could be used to encourage scientists, doctors and engineers to seek marketable applications for their laboratory triumphs.

Moreover, as seen, it would be desirable were a revived or new NEB to encourage some real degree of workers' control in its various enterprises. Among other benefits, this would make the workers themselves more creative human beings. Workers' control means that at least some rank-and-file employees will have to think about problems that are traditionally considered management prerogatives. (The list of these issues is endless, ranging from what the undertaking should produce and in what quantities to how much vacation time part-time typists should be allowed.) The attainment of adequate solutions to these difficulties could on occasion require almost as much insight and as much exercise of the skills of analysis and synthesis as does the perfecting of medical laser beams or computer software. There is no reason, furthermore, to assume that only persons in supervisory positions possess the talents needed to discover workable solutions to the puzzles presented by plant and personnel management.

A very important reason why the resuscitation of the NEB in the UK or the creation of a similar agency in the US is a very attractive ethical option is that agencies of this sort could facilitate *co-operation* among human beings, especially among some who previously have been wary of one another. The Board would, if the intentions of its founders were realised, get some individuals called business people to work together with some other human beings called government employees. As a man who has been a top-level civil servant and a banker reminds us, business and public institutions are composed of people, they 'consist of people, lay claims on people and offer benefits to people...'[6] Since they are made up of people, there is absolutely no reason why they cannot, and every good reason why they should, work together to further the common weal. After all, neither the state nor private firms exist by divine right. Both are set up by the citizenry -- in one case directly; in the other, using the polity as an intermediary -- to protect and foster the general welfare. (The corporation is treated as a legal person 'in order to regulate it for beneficial social and economic purposes'.[7]) If they continually squabble and work in opposition rather than in tandem, the welfare of the nation's residents that they are supposed to promote will be circumscribed rather than nurtured.

This point about the need for co-operation between the men and women who staff government and the men and women who staff private firms seems so self-evident that it is astonishing that one rarely hears about it in either the scholarly or the polemical social science literature. The blame for this lies with both the political right and the political left. Both have reified 'government' and 'private business' and assume that it is impossible or unlikely for the two to work together for the common good. The Marxist left on the whole feels, of course, that 'business' uses 'government' as a device to enable it to reach greater and greater heights of profitability. On the other hand, the conservatives see 'government' as a giant beast that preys on 'business'; and claim that 'business' is the only source of real wealth and that 'government' drains wealth away from its creators and gives it to unproductive parasites such as poor people and bureaucrats. Neither Thatcherite-Tory nor Marxist perceives that beneath the shells with which they have endowed the entities 'business' and 'government' are hundreds of millions of men and women who could, conceivably, join hands to seek the good of all.

Obviously, from the point of view of efficiency, co-operation is necessary 'as a means of overcoming the limitations restricting what individuals can do'.[8] But there are various reasons *not* apparent on the surface why co-operation among men and women is an ethical as well as an economic imperative. When you share a task with someone you assume, whatever the difference between you may be, that she/he is a human being (or, to use Kantian language, an end) whom you must respect for his/her humanity. And when you respect individuals for their humanity, you may to some extent use them to serve your own goals, but you will not deal with them ruthlessly or thoughtlessly.

More than this, co-operation among human beings takes place against an implicit background of recognising those with whom you join as *adults*. (Viewing them as adults will not only deter you from treating them meanly but will convince you to listen seriously to them and to let them, within very broad limits, lead their lives as they see best.) When I team with you to accomplish a particular task, I silently concede that you are an adult human being with something to contribute to our common needs. Thus if I join with you to teach a course in western political institutions and thought, I clearly am admitting that you are a mature person with a thorough knowledge of western political philosophy while you are quietly saying that I am a grown-up with a good grounding in the workings of western political institutions. Also, co-operation may even lead to the growth of trust in or emotional closeness with your co-workers.[9] In a world full of loneliness and paranoia, this effect of co-operation can only be a plus!

Of course, several caveats must be added to any paean to co-operation. Even as fervent an advocate of working together as Peter Kropotkin admits that fighting among individuals and groups has played some role in the evolution of the human race.[10] Second, there is the danger that an overemphasis on co-operation will be mistranslated into the doctrine that the group is everything and the individual is nothing, that the individual can have no rights against the larger unit. This does not refute the importance of combined, co-ordinated exertion as a means of achieving human goals; but merely warns its proponents that they must be on the alert to distinguish it from authoritarianism and totalitarianism. Third it is, naturally, possible that people will link arms for evil ends: obviously combined effort in and of itself will not insure the prevalence of justice and other human values.

Fourth, there is no guarantee that co-operation among individuals even for worthwhile goals will have desirable side-effects such as the growth of mutual credence and friendship. We have in our study of the NEB seen where working together did not overcome, or even where it fed, suspicion and dislike. We witnessed in our discussion of Nexos that after the delays in the delivery of the 2200 word processor, relations between Olga and Olga, Jr on the one hand and the Nexos Board on the other soon turned sour. 'Mutual trust soon gave way to mutual recrimination...'[11] The UK firms that were supposed to join in the Insac venture to develop software and market it abroad never overcame their distrust and began squabbling with the joint venture's first head. And let us recall, once again, the bad relationship between the NEB's Sir Leslie Murphy and Rolls Royce's Sir Kenneth Keith.

It must be confessed, fifth, that there are many reasons why partnership may not succeed. When parties are forced to co-operate against the will of one of them good relations between the two are unlikely to develop. This may be one of the causes for the hostility between Keith and Murphy: Rolls Royce was wary of NEB tutelage in the first place. Also there are occasions when no matter how beneficial it is for all that two or more individuals are working together, they dislike each other from the start and continue to do so -- the personal chemistry leads to repulsion rather than attraction. This also may have been a factor in the Keith-Murphy battling. Where, as in the Insac situation, the parties urged to link forces are all strong personalities each having a distinct point of view, fruitful joint venturing may be impossible.

However, we are not contending that collaboration will always have a happy ending; but simply that in addition to making it feasible for human beings to achieve specified goals, it might well tangentially produce, e.g., recognition of mutual adulthood, trust, and friendship. Organisations that can serve as a forum in which co-operation can take place thus ought to be encouraged (as long, of course, as they seek just ends). A new or reconstituted NEB would bring together persons now in business, men and women on temporary leave from their firms, and professional civil servants. It could create a feeling of unity not only between its staff and the entrepreneurs it aided, but also among all these people and the employees of whatever other institutions (public or private) it convinced to join it in bolstering this or that firm. The co-operation of all these human beings for common and certainly proper purposes not only might aid the economy but also might break down some of the barriers of suspicion that now separate many of them. (The NEB could be an especially potent solvent of business-government hostility because by making business people public employees for a limited period, it would educate both them and the civil service about the problems that both groups face in their daily working lives.) The NEB, as I have described it, is surely not a 'socialist' institution as most socialists would use that word. Yet one of its effects might be to further fellowship among formerly aloof or even sparring elements in the community; and fellowship is one of the basic goals of numerous socialist thinkers. In the words of the Guild Socialist G. D. H. Cole, '[M]y notion of democracy is that it involves a sense of comradeship, friendliness, brotherhood...I mean a warm sense - not a mere recognition, cold as a fish'.[12] It would be intriguing indeed were an agency upon which many socialists would look with suspicion to do its mite toward creating a society which they all would find more acceptable than a United Kingdom and a United States besotted with the 'enrich thyself' spirit that is the legacy of the administrations of Margaret Thatcher and Ronald Reagan.

NOTES

1. *The open society and its enemies* (Harper Torchbooks, New York, 1963), vol. 1, p. 159.

2. *Politics, economics and welfare* (Harper Torchbooks, New York, 1953), p. 82.

3. Ibid., pp. 82-3.

4. Popper, *The open society*, p. 159.

5. *Politics, economics and welfare*, pp. 85-6.

6. Lord Armstrong of Sanderstead, 'Government and industry relationships' at p. 77, 94-5 of Lethbridge, (ed.) *Government and industry relationships.*

7. Thomas Dunfee *et. al., Modern business law* (Random House, New York, 1984), p. 700.

8. Chester Barnard, *The functions of the executive* (Harvard U. Press, Cambridge, Mass., 1938), p. 23. See generally his Chapters I through V.

9. See, e.g., John Rawls, *A theory of justice* (Harvard U. Press, Cambridge, Mass., 1971), p. 470.

10. *Mutual aid* (McClure Phillips & Co., New York, 1902), p. 295.

11. Transcript of BBC-2 programme of 27 January 1985, 'The money programme', at p. 3.

12. *Essays in social theory,* paper ed. (Oldbourne, London, 1962), p. 98.

BIBLIOGRAPHY

Alun-Jones, J. D. (nd) 'My business experience at Burmah Oil and Ferranti: 1973-82', (mimeographed speech delivered by Ferranti's Managing Director).

Armstrong (Lord) of Sanderstead, 'Government and industry relationships' in Lethbridge, David (ed.) (1976) *Government and industry relationships*, Pergamon, Oxford.

Barghoorn, Frederic (1966) *Politics in the USSR*, Little Brown, Boston.

Barron, Iann *et. al.* (nd) *Transputer does 10 or more MIPS even when not used in parallel*, Inmos, Bristol.

Barnard, Chester (1938) *The functions of the executive*, Harvard U. Press, Cambridge, Mass.

Bluestone, Barry and Bennett Harrison (1982) *The deindustrialization of America*, Basic Books, New York.

Burton, John (1979) *The job support machine*, Centre for Policy Studies, London.

————(1983) *Picking losers*, Institute of Economic Affairs, London.

Coates, David (1980) *Labour in power*, Longmans, London.

Cole, G. D. H. (1962) *Essays in social theory*, paper edn, Oldbourne, London.

Committee to Review the Functioning of Financial Institutions (1977) *Evidence on the financing of industry and trade*, vol. 1, HMSO, London.

————(1978) *Evidence on the financing of industry and trade*, vol. 4, HMSO, London.

Coventry, Liverpool, Newcastle, N. Tyneside Trades Councils (1980) *State intervention in industry: a workers' inquiry*, Coventry, etc. Trades Councils, Newcastle upon Tyne.

Cripps, T., 'Economics of labour subsidies' in Whiting, Alan (ed.) (1976) *The economics of industrial subsidies*, HMSO, London.

Crosland, Anthony (1974) *Socialism now*, Jonathan Cape, London.

Curzon-Price, Victoria (1981) *Industrial policies in the European Community*, Macmillan, London.

Dahl, Robert and Charles Lindblom (1953) *Politics, economics and welfare*, Harper Torchbooks, New York.

Dizard, John (4 Oct. 1982) 'Do we have too many venture capitalists?', *Fortune*, p. 106.

Dunfee, Thomas *et. al.* (1984) *Modern business law*, Random House, New York.

Bibliography

Edwardes, Michael (1983) *Back from the brink*, Collins, London.

Equity Capital for Industry 1985 Annual Report, Equity Capital for Industry, London.

Ferranti 1983 Annual Report, Ferranti, London.

Field, G. M. and P. V. Hills, 'The administration of industrial subsidies' in Whiting, Alan (ed.) (1976) *The economics of industrial subsidies*, HMSO, London.

Finance for Industry plc 1981-82 Annual Report, Finance for Industry, London.

Foulds, Jon (1985) *We are searching for hidden entrepreneurs*, Investors in Industry Group, London.

Galbraith, John Kenneth (1984) *The affluent society*, 4th edn, North American Library, New York.

Ganz, Gabrielle (1977) *Government and industry*, Professional Books, Abingdon.

Gardner, N. K., 'Economics of launching aid' in Whiting, Alan (ed.) (1976) *The economics of industrial subsidies*, HMSO, London.

Greater London Council (1984) *Working for jobs in London*, Greater London Council, London.

Grylls, Michael and John Redwood (1980) *National Enterprise Board: a case for euthanasia*, Centre for Policy Studies, London.

Hague, Douglas and Geoffrey Wilkinson (1983) *The IRC, an experiment in industrial intervention*, Allen and Unwin, London.

Halloran, Michael (1983) *Venture capital and public offering negotiation*, Harcourt Brace Jovanovich, New York.

Hampton, John (1976) *Financial decision making: concepts, problems & cases*, Reston Publishing Co., Reston.

Hanson, A. H. and Walles, Malcolm (1970) *Governing Britain*, Fontana/Collins, London.

HC Committee of Public Accounts (1977) *Reports 1976-77, No. 8: Department of Energy, etc.*, HMSO, London.

————(1978) *Reports 1977-78, No. 8: Atomic Energy Authority, Department of Industry, National Enterprise Board*, HMSO, London.

————(1980) *Reports 1979-80, No. 6: Departments of Energy and Industry*, HMSO, London.

————(1980) *Reports 1979-80, No. 30: Department of Industry, National Enterprise Board, etc.*, HMSO, London.

————(1984) *Reports 1983-84, No. 15: DTI monitoring of British Technology Group*, HMSO, London.

————(1985) *Nexos: minutes of evidence*, HMSO, London.

Bibliography

Hinton, William (1983) *Shenfan,* Random House, New York.

Holland, Stuart (1975) *The socialist challenge,* Quartet Books, London.

Huntsman, Blaine and James Hoban (Summer, 1980) 'Investment in new enterprise: some empirical observations on risk return and market structure', *Financial Management,* p. 44.

Inmos 1978 and 1979 Annual Reports, Inmos, Bristol.

Inmos (nd) *Writing parallel programs in occam,* Inmos, Bristol.

Investors in Industry Group 1984 and 1985 Annual Reports, Investors in Industry Group, London.

Kropotkin, Peter (1902) *Mutual aid,* McClure Phillips & co., New York.

Magaziner, Ira and Robert Reich (1982) *Minding America's business,* Harcourt Brace Jovanovich, New York.

Makinson, W., 'The National Research Development Corporation' in Lethbridge, David (ed.) (1976) *Government and industry relationships,* Pergamon, Oxford.

Mansfield, Edwin (1975) *Micro-economics: theory and applications,* 2nd edn, W. W. Norton, New York.

Maunder, Peter, 'Government intervention in the economy of the United Kingdom' in Maunder, Peter (ed.) (1979) *Government intervention in the developed economy,* Praeger, New York.

Marx, Karl (1967) *Capital,* vol. 1, International Publishers, New York.

Mitchell, Philip (1982) *Directors' duties and insider dealing,* Butterworths, London.

National Enterprise Board, 1977 through 1986-87 Annual Reports, National Enterprise Board, London.

New York State Science and Technology Foundation (1985) *Corporation for innovation development program,* New York State Science and Technology Foundation, Albany.

O'Connor, James (1973) *The fiscal crisis of the state,* St. Martin's, New York.

Peacock, Alan (1980) *Structural economic policies in West Germany and the United Kingdom,* Anglo-German Foundation for the Study of Industrial Society, London.

Pearce Technology Limited (1985) *Corporate profile,* Pearce Technology, London.

Pollard, Andy and Rosalind Levačić, 'The British Leyland case study', Part six of Block five of the Open University Course (1983) *Decision making in Britain,* Open U. Press, Milton Keynes.

Bibliography

Popper, Karl (1963) *The open society and its enemies,* vol. l, Harper Torchbooks, New York.

Rawls, John (1971) *A theory of justice,* Harvard U. Press, Cambridge, Mass.

Redwood, John (1984) *Going for broke...,* Basil Blackwell, Oxford.

Rohatyn, Felix (18 Aug. 1983) 'Time for a change', *New York Rev. of Books,* p. 46.

Sainsbury, David (1981) *Government and industry: a new partnership,* Fabian Society, London.

Salvatore, Dominick (1986) *Microeconomics: theory and applications,* Macmillan, New York.

Schultze, Charles (Fall, 1983) 'Industrial policy: a dissent', *Brookings Rev.,* p. 3.

Scott, Bruce (Mar.-Ap. 1984) 'National strategy for stronger U.S. competitiveness', *Harvard Business Rev.,* p. 77.

Smith, Adam (1937) *Wealth of nations,* Modern Library, New York.

Smith, Trevor, 'Britain' in Hayward, Jack and Michael Watson (eds) (1975) *Planning, politics and public policy,* Cambridge U. Press, London.

Spray, C. (Aug. 1984) 'The capital adventure', *Management Today,* p. 72.

Stockman, David (1986) *The triumph of politics,* Harper and Row, New York.

Thorn-EMI 1987 Annual Report, Thorn-EMI, London.

Thurow, Lester (Fall, 1984) 'Revitalizing American industry', *California Management Rev.,* p. 9.

US Congress, Office of Technology Assessment (1983) *Technology, innovation and regional economic development,* US Congress, Office of Technology Assessment, Washington.

US General Accounting Office (1982) *Government-industry cooperation can enhance the venture capital process,* US General Accounting Office, Washington.

Vernon, Raymond, 'Enterprise and government in western Europe' in Vernon, Raymond (ed.) (1974) *Big business and the state,* Harvard U. Press, Cambridge, Mass.

Wade, H. W. R. (1982) *Administrative law,* 5th edn, Clarendon Press, Oxford.

Walkland, S. A., 'Economic planning and dysfunctional politics' in Gamble, A. M. and S. A. Walkland (1984) *The British party system and economic policy 1945 - 1983,* Clarendon Press, Oxford.

Wilson, J. Holton (1981) *Microeconomics: concepts and applications,* Harper and Row, New York.

Wilson, John (1985) *The new venturers,* Addison-Wesley, Reading, Mass.

Wiseman, J., 'An economic analysis of the Expenditure Committee reports on public money in the private sector' in Whiting, Alan (ed.) (1976) *The economics of industrial subsidies,* HMSO, London.

Wolfe, Alan (1977) *The limits of legitimacy,* Free Press, New York.

Young, Stephen and A. V. Lowe (1974) *Intervention in the mixed economy,* Croom Helm, London.

INDEX

'Able' Co., 81-2, 117, 119, 123, 125, 126, 225

'Ailsa' Co., 112-13, 124, 127

Alfred Herbert, 10, 31, 33, 35, 38, 45, 77, 78, Ch.11, 194, 206, 225

Alun Jones, J.D., 180, 181, 183n.14, n.17, n.18

American Telephone and Telegraph, 138, 149

Aregon, 147, 148, 149

Armstrong of Sanderstead, 243n.6

Arthur Andersen, 157

Automation and Technical Services, 36, 37

'Baker' Co., 82-4, 118, 119, 124, 126

Bank of England, 39

Barghoorn, Frederic, 236n.6

Barker, Colin, 23

Barnard, Chester, 243n.8

Barron, Iann, 130, 131, 135, 136, 144n.58

Barrow Hepburn, 60, 61

Benn, Anthony Wedgwood, 5, 7, 11, 14, 78, 172, 185

Bluestone, Barry, 219, 220, 233

Bowles, Samuel, 232

British Leyland (BL), 1, 3, 113, 194-96, 202, 225

    NEB and, 10, 11, 14, 15, 18, 20, 22, 29, 30, 31, 33, 35, 50, 51, 53, 54, 55, 65, 72, 77, 78, 79, 112, 113, 123, 124, 174, 175, 185, Ch.14, 206, 211, 212, 225, 232

British Shipbuilders, 3

British Tanners Products (BTP), 60, 61

British Technology Group, 23, 24, 105, 110

Britton Lee, 36, 37, 146, 151n.19

Brown-Boveri-Kent, 10, 38

'Bruce' Co., 113-15, 123, 124, 127, 207-08, 209

Buckley, John, 172, 174, 175

Burton, John, 230n.1, n.7, n.9, n.11, 231n.14

C.A. Parsons, 9

Callaghan, James, 52, 186, 190

Cambridge Instrument, 10, 38

Canadian Forest Products, 62n.17

'Carol' Co., 115-16, 117, 124, 127, 211

'Charlie' Co., 84-7, 125, 126, 127, 225

Chase Manhattan, 181

Chrysler, 3, 194

Civil Aviation Act (1949), 186

Coates, David, 25n.11, n.12, 26n.25, n.35, 203n.6, n.18, n.20, n.25, 232

Cole, G.D.H., 242

Colvin, Michael, 135

Committee of Public Accounts (House of Commons). See Public Accounts Committee (House of Commons)

Committee to Review the Functioning of Financial Institutions, 27n.53, n.65, 42 n.58, 43n.65, 74n.25, 217n.1, n.15.

communications management computer, 154, 159

Comptroller and Auditor General (C and AG), 68-70, 73, 76
Computer Analysts and Programmers (CAP Group), 36, 37
Computer and Systems Engineering (CASE), 36, 37
Confederation of British Industries, 6, 10, 21, 73
conservative critique of subsidies, Ch.18, 237
    critique of conservative critique, 226-30
Conservative Party, 2, 3, 8, 13, 18, 19, 20, 24, 25, 40, 44, 45, 46, 47, 49, 54-58, 59, 64, 65, 66, 70, 71, 72, 79, 91, 93, 118, 120, 124, 132, 133, 135, 146, 152, 157, 159, 172, 173, 178, 179, 186, 190, 200, 240
contradictions of capitalist countries, 233-36
contradictions of socialist countries, 235-36
conurbation enterprise boards, 214-15, 216
co-operation, 124, 239-42
Cotton Industry Act (1959), 2
Coventry, Liverpool, Newcastle, N. Tyneside Trades Councils, 27n.47, 28n.83, 175n.2, n.5, n.16, 176n.24, 183n.1, n.11, 192n.4, 203n.1, n.9, 204n.42
Cripps, T., 230n.13
Crawford, Douglas, 10
Crosland, Anthony, 6
Curzon-Price, Victoria, 230n.4

Dahl, Robert, 237
'Daisy' Co., 116, 117, 121
'David' Co., 86-8, 120, 121, 123, 127, 128, 208

Delphi, 154, 158, 159, 166
Department of Energy, 7, 89
Department of Industry (DOI), 3, 10, 20, 21, 22, 23, 24, 66, 67, 68, Ch.5, 86, 92, 94, 95, 108, 124, 157, 162-63, 165, 168, 172, 180, 185, 189, 190, 191, 200, 201, 202
    1985 Report on Nexos, 153, 160, 162, 163, 165
Department of Trade and Industry. *See* Department of Industry
Dizard, John, 34
Dobson, Richard, 197-98
duCann, Edward, 70
Dunfee, Thomas, 243n.7
Dunford and Elliot, 10, 38

Eastern Airlines, 192
Eaton, 47
Edwardes, Michael, 12, 80n.15, 175, 197, 198, 199, 200, 201, 203n.13, n.19, n.21, n.27, n.30, n.33, 204n.35, n.44, n.48
'Elspeth' Co., 88-9, 117, 123, 125, 127, 128, 208, 212
equity assistance, advantages of, 216-17, 232-33
Equity Capital for Industry, 40, 43n.67, 54, 94, 104, 110, 118, 214, 215, 217n.5
Exxon, 154

F.W. Elliot, 58-60
Fairchild, 137
Fairey Aerospace, 17, 23, 52, 57, 72, 124, 125, 127, 177-79, 183n.10, 206, 208, 209, 212, 226
Ferranti, 10, 23, 35, 38, 46, 53, 57, 61n.4, 72, 123, 179-82,

Ferranti *(cont.)*
183n.14, n.24, 194, 206, 207, 208, 209, 210n.1, 212, 226
Field, G., 25n.1, n.3, n.6
Finance Corporation for Industry, 39
Finance for Industry. *See* Investors in Industry
Focom Systems, 36, 37
Foot, Michael, 5
Ford, 3, 194
Foulds, Jon, 42n.63
Francis Shaw, 66
'Fred' Co., 89-90, 124, 125, 129n.3, 145, 207, 209, 213, 225

Galbraith, John Kenneth, 218
Ganz, Gabrielle, 11, 25n.10, 27n.50, 28n.86, 71, 192n.2, n.6, 193n.12, n.13, n.24
Gardner, Edward, 64
Gardner, N.K., 25n.5
Genentech, 34, 35
General Accounting Office (US), 35, 41n.26, 116n.1, 217n.7, 222n.2
general assistance to business, 2
General Electric, 9, 131, 137
General Motors, 194
Goodyear, 219
Gordon, David, 232
'Graham' Co., 90-1, 125, 225
Grant, George, 66
Greater London Enterprise Board 214-15, 216
Grosvenor Development Capital, 23, 94, 102
Grylls, Michael, 55, 56, 57, 61, 63n.37, n.43, n.49, 64, 65, 66, 67, 118, 132, 178, 192n.3, n.5, 193n.27, 230n.8

Guidelines for NEB. *See* NEB: Guidelines (1976) and (1980)

Hague, Douglas, 25n.9, 192n.1, 203n.4
Halloran, Michael, 34, 41n.24
Hampton, John, 40n.1
Hanson, A.H., 74n.26
'Harlan' Co., 91-2, 118, 120, 122, 123, 125, 128, 212, 215
Harrison, Bennett, 219, 220, 233
Hayward, Jack, 27n.62
Heath, Edward, 3, 19, 185, 186
Heffer, Eric, 5, 8
Herbert, Alfred. *See* Alfred Herbert
Heseltine, Michael, 8
Hills, P.V., 25n.1, n.3, n.6
Hinton, William, 236n.7
Hivent, 66
Hoban, James, 41n.32
Holland, Stuart, 4, 5, 15, 18
Hordern, Peter, 56-7
Huckfield, Les, 64, 65, 66, 71
Huntsman, Blaine, 41n.32
Hydraroll, 128

IBM, 140, 161, 216
incrementalism, 237
Industrial and Commercial Finance Corporation (ICFC), 39, 48, 54, 73, 81-2, 83, 93, 95, 101, 102, 108, 110, 115, 118, 124, 212, 215
industrial policy, 232
Industrial Reconstruction Institute (IRI), 4
Industrial Reorganisation Corporation (IRC), 3, 185, 195
Industry Act (1972), 3, 22, 76, 94, 172, 201

Industry Act (1979), 18, 19
Industry Act (1980), 22, 77
Industry Bill and Act (1975),
7-11, 13, 19, 22, 55, 75, 78
Inmos, 17, 23, 24, 31, 32, 51,
53-4, 56, 66, 67, 127, Ch.8, 207,
212
Insac, 17, 38, 73, 77, 89, 91,
125, Ch.9, 160, 213, 216-17, 241
Intel, 131, 140
intermediate assistance to busi-
ness, 2
International Computers Ltd
(ICL), 3
NEB and, 10, 23, 33, 35, 38,
72, 76, 160, 161, 194, 208
Investors in Industry (3i), 39,
42n.59, n.60, n.62, n.63, n.64,
82, 83, 95, 118, 214
ITT, 53-4
'Ivy' Co., 92-4, 117, 121, 122,
127, 225, 226

'Jane' Co., 93-4, 117, 120, 123
Joseph, Keith, 18, 19, 20, 21, 22,
44, 45, 56, 57, 66, 79, 80, 91,
132, 133, 137, 157, 158, 189,
192

Kaufman, Gerald, 64, 66, 71
Keith, Kenneth, 20, 49, 77, 175,
185, 186, 187, 188, 189, 190,
191, 192, 241
Kilroy-Silk, Robert, 65
King, John, 21, 22
Kleiner and Perkins, 34, 35, 37
Knight, Sir Arthur, 21, 22, 69,
79-80, 91, 133, 156, 200
Kropotkin, Peter, 241
'Krumpet' Co., 94-5, 123, 127,
208

Labour Party, 3, 4, 5, 6, 8, 12,
20, 25, 45, 51, 52, 55, 64, 65,
66, 70, 71, 78, 111, 112, 123,
135, 136, 152, 172, 180, 186,
190, 194, 199, 200, 210
Lamont, Norman, 55, 70, 74n.38
launching aid, 2, 186
Lethbridge, David 28n.88, 243n.6
Levačić, Rosalind, 203n.2, n.3,
n.5, n.7, n.10, n.14, n.22, n.25,
n.26, 204n.38, n.46, n.61, n.64
Lever, Harold, 6, 7
Lindblom, Charles, 237
Lockheed, 185, 188
Lowe, A.V., 25n.9
'Lulu' Co., 95-6, 117, 119, 123,
127

Macmillan, Harold, 2
Madden, Max, 66
Magaziner, Ira, 220
Makinson, W., 28n.88
management buyouts, NEB and,
47-8, 101, 108-09, 113-14, 127,
212
Mansfield, Edwin, 231n.16
Mao Tse Tung, 235
Marshall, Michael, 55, 132
Marx, Karl, 229, 231n.19
Marxists, 233, 234, 235, 240
Maunder, Peter, 25n.4
Medical Research Council, 91
Michigan state pension fund, 221
Mikardo, Ian, 5
Ministry of Defence (MOD),
114, 180, 190, 191, 206, 208,
209, 210, 213
Mitchell, Philip, 129n.2
Mitsubishi, 149
'Money programme' (BBC-2),
28n.98, 168n.2, n.21, n.25,

'Money programme' *(cont.)*
169n.27, n.36, n.38, n.42, n.57,
243n.11
Morris, Charles, 135, 136
Morris, Richard, 12, 20, 156
'Morton' Co., 97-8, 118, 119,
124, 211
Mostek, 130, 132
Motorola, 140
Muirhead Office Systems Ltd
(MOSL), 153, 159, 162, 165
Muirhead plc, 153, 158
Murphy, Leslie, 11, 12, 16, 17,
20, 21, 51, 61, 69, 77, 78, 79,
80, 104, 156, 173, 174, 178,
183n.10, 185, 188, 189, 192, 197,
198, 199, 200, 201, 217n.15, 241
Murray, Len, 7

National Coal Board Pension
Fund, 113, 124
National Economic Development
Office (NEDO), 16, 131
National Enterprise Board (NEB).
See also especially names of
NEB-aided companies (e.g.,
'Able', British Leyland) and
names of NEB officials (e.g.,
Murphy)
   attitude of big business to, 6,
   7-8, 72-3, 146, 213
   attitude of labour unions to,
   7, 86, 172, 173
   attitude of press to, 47-54,
   62n.17, 70, 72, 111, 131, 142,
   150, 178, 182, 186-87, 197,
   213
   boldness as venture capitalist, 118, 211-12, 226

NEB *(cont.)*
   catalyst for private venture
   capital, 211-12
   Corporate Plan, 16, 17, 65,
   66, 68
   defence efforts of investments, 113-14, 177, 179, 181,
   Ch.15, 213
   exporting activities of investments, 128, 179, 182,
   186, 212
   financial results, Ch.2, 44-7,
   150, 160, 212-13
   Guidelines (1976), 8, 13-16,
   18, 55, 78
   Guidelines (1980), 22, 44, 124
   improving management of investments, 120-21, 178-79,
   180-81, 201-02, 212, 226
   job creation by venture capital investments, 126-28, 139,
   149, 179, 212
   job-cutting by investments,
   attitude to, 123-24, 174, 179,
   198, 199
   need for in UK, Ch.16, 222,
   224, Ch.20
   need for in US, Ch.17, 224,
   Ch.20
   paperwork required by, 119,
   149, 174, 182, 188
   proactive strategy of, 125,
   177-78
   Regional Boards (Northern
   and Northwestern), 18, 24,
   52, 65, 66, 67, 95, 98,
   110-11, 115, 116
   secrecy, policy of, 58, Ch.4
   sells investments cheaply,
   44-7, 213
   speed in financing, 119-20

NEB *(cont.)*
  substantive management by, 121-22
  technological achievements of investments, 128, 141-42, 149, 160, 212
  venture capitalist, as, 33-40, Ch.6, Ch.7, Ch.8, Ch.9, Ch.10, 177-79, Ch.15, 211-14, 225, 226, 238
National Research Development Corporation, 23, 24, 105, 110, 114
NEC, 139
'Ned' Co., 98-9, 121, 127
Nelson, Anthony, 55
Nexos, 17, 23, 24, 31, 38, 77, 99, 125, Ch.10, 207, 208, 213, 241
New York Corporation for Innovation Development Program, 221
New York State Science and Technology Foundation, 223n.15
Northern Ireland, 2, 214

occam, 141
O'Connor, James, 233
Ohio Industrial Technology and Enterprise Board, 221
Oki Electric, 153
'Olga' Co., 45, 99-100, 118, 123, 125, 129n.3, 145, 153, 155, 156, 158, 159, 164, 167, 207, 209, 213, 225, 241
'Olga, Jr' Co., 153, 154, 155, 156, 157, 159, 160, 161, 163, 164, 165, 166, 167, 212, 241
Oppenheim, Phillip, 159

Palmer, Arthur, 136
Pan American Airways, 188-89

Parkinson, Cecil, 24
Peacock, Alan, 25n.7, 230n.6
'Pet' Co., 100-01, 117, 120, 123, 127, 209, 211, 226
Petritz, Richard, 130, 131, 132, 135
piecemeal social engineering, 237
Pigott, John, 48
planning agreements, 5, 7, 12
Pollard, Andy, 203n.2, n.3, n.5, n.7, n.10, n.14, n.22, n.25, n.26, 204n.38, n.46, n.61, n.64
Popper, Karl, 237, 243n.4
Powerdrive PSR, 47-9, 101-02, 117, 119, 127, 212
Prestcold, 78-9, 123, 200
Prudential Assurance, 40, 106, 124
Prutec, 40, 106, 124
Public Accounts Committee (House of Commons), 31, 41n.10, 59, 61, 63n.38, n.45, n.51, n.53, 68, 70, 71, 74n.27, n.37, n.39, 76, 80n.1, n.7, 163, 165, 168n.4, n.5, n.6, n.12, n.14, n.15, n.18, n.24, n.26, 169n.30, n.37, n.39, n.46, n.48, n.49, n.51, n.52, n.53, n.55, n.59, 170n.71, n.78, n.94, n.95, n.96, n.100, 183n.10, 191, 204n.56, n.58

'Quirk' Co., 102-03, 117, 119, 121

radical critique of subsidies, Ch.19, p.237
Rawls, John, 243n.9
Reagan, Ronald, 67, 220, 242
Redwood, John, 26n.30, 27n.48, 41n.23, 57, 61n.4, 63n.37, n.43,

Redwood *(cont.)*
  n.49, 118, 142n.1, n.4, n.21,
  143n.28, 167, 178, 180, 182,
  183n.14, n.20, n.24, 192n.3, n.5,
  193n.27, 203n.12, n.23, 204n.40,
  n.47, 230n.8
Reed and Smith, 36, 37
Reed International, 7, 50, 62n.17
Reich, Robert, 220
Renton, Timothy, 8, 56
'Richenda' Co., 103-04, 117, 118,
  120, 127
Ricoh, 153, 166
Ridley, Nicholas, 8, 65
Rodgers, John, 66
Rohatyn, Felix, 220
Rolls Royce (aerospace), 1,
  185-86, 190-91, 224
    NEB and, 1, 10, 14, 15, 18,
      20, 21, 22, 30, 31, 33, 35,
      49, 50, 55, 65, 72, 77, 174,
      175, Ch.13, 194, 199, 200,
      206, 209, 241
Rolls Royce (automobiles), 10,
  185
Ryder, Donald, 7, 9, 12, 13, 15,
  16, 49, 50, 51, 52, 53, 54, 58,
  59, 60, 62n.17, 78, 79, 80, 186,
  187, 196, 197
Ryder Report (Plan), 196, 198,
  199, 200

S. Pearson and Son, 179
Sainsbury, David, 129n.3, 175n.4,
  n.6, 180
Salvatore, Dominick, 231n.20
'Sam' Co., 105
Schroeder, Paul, 130, 131, 132,
  135
Schultze, Charles, 230n.10, n.12
Scotland, 2, 10, 46, 78, 79, 100,

Scotland *(cont.)*
  180, 181, 189, 200, 207, 214,216
Scott, Bruce, 223n.6
Scottish National Party, 10
Secretary of State for Industry,
  9, 10, 14, 64, 75, 76, 77, 162
selective assistance to business,
  2
shipbuilding industry, 2-3
Sinclair, Clive, 16
Sinclair Radionics, 16
Skinner, Dennis, 111
Smith, Adam, 229, 231n.19
Smith, Trevor, 27n.62
social benefit of last unit equals
  social cost of last unit theory,
  227-30, 237
Speke Plant (BL), 198, 202
Spray, C., 217n.2
state-local NEBs in US, 220-22,
  223n.15
Stockman, David, 223n.16
Supply and Marketing Agreement
  (Nexos-Olga, Jr), 155, 165-67
Systems Designers, 36, 37, 66
Systime, 53, 66

'Tamsin' Co., 105-06, 117, 123
Tandem Computers, 34, 35
Taylor, Robert, 61, 65
Texas Instruments, 140
Thatcher, Margaret, 18, 19, 20,
  24, 46, 56, 67, 71, 73, 87, 95,
  98, 132, 136, 191, 201, 215,
  223n.17, 240, 242
Thompson, Donald, 135
Thorn-EMI, 32, 138, 141, 143n.39
Thurow, Lester, 223n.6
Thwaites and Reed, 58-60, 178
Trades Union Congress, 7
Trafalgar House, 177, 178, 179

transputer, 140-42
Treasury Department, 10, 191
Tress, 178-79
Trident missiles, 222, 223n.17
2200 word processor, 153, 154-56, 157, 159, 160, 161, 163, 164, 165, 166, 167, 207, 212
Twinlock, 36, 37, 50

UDS, 153
unions, labour, 7, 12, 86, 96, 123-24, 172, 173, 175, 178-79, 195, 199
'Ulysses' Co., 106-07, 117, 124, 127, 128, 208
United Medical Enterprises, 36, 66, 67
US Congress, Office of Technology Assessment, 223n.14
US economy, problems of, 218-21

Varley, Eric, 7, 10, 14, 15, 55, 64, 66, 71, 77, 78, 79, 80, 189, 190, 197
'Velma' Co., 107-08, 118, 123, 129n.3, 145
venture capitalist, definition, 32-3
Vernon, Raymond, 25n.2

Wade, H.W.R., 26n.44
Waldegrave, William, 135
Wales, 10, 133, 134, 135, 136, 137, 214, 216
Walkland, S.A., 25n.11, n.12, 26n.19
Walles, Malcolm, 74n.26
Watson, Michael, 27n.62
Weisskopf, Thomas, 232

Whiting, Alan, 25n.1, n.4, n.5, 230n.13
Wilkinson, Geoffrey, 25n.9, 192n.1, 203n.4
'William' Co., 108, 122, 123, 125, 126, 145
Williams, Alan, 134, 135, 136
Willott, Brian, 157, 158
Wilson, Harold, 4, 5, 6, 7, 73, 172, 186, 190, 194
Wilson, J. Holton, 231n.17
Wilson, John, 41n.28, n.31, 42n.47, 222n.1
Wiseman, J., 25n.4
Wolfe, Alan, 233
Wood, Frederick, 22, 23, 24, 157, 158
workers' control of industry (industrial democracy), 9, 12, 233, 238-39

'Xerxes' Co., 108-10, 117, 118, 120, 123, 127, 208

'Yolanda' Co., 110-11, 117, 120, 121, 127, 208
Young, Stephen, 25n.9

'Zelda' Co., 46, 111-12, 121, 122, 124, 125, 128, 212